November 9-13, 2015
St. Petersburg, FL, USA

I0050874

**Association for
Computing Machinery**

Advancing Computing as a Science & Profession

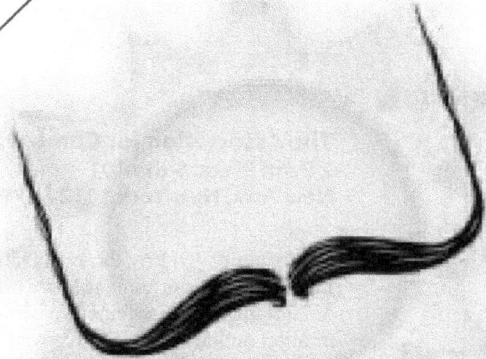

SIGUCCS'15

Proceedings of the 2015 ACM Annual Conference

Sponsored by:
ACM SIGUCCS

Association for
Computing Machinery

Advancing Computing as a Science & Profession

The Association for Computing Machinery
2 Penn Plaza, Suite 701
New York, New York 10121-0701

Notice to Past Authors of ACM-Published Articles
ACM intends to create a complete electronic archive of all articles and/or other material previously published by ACM. If you have written a work that has been previously published by ACM in any journal or conference proceedings prior to 1978, or any SIG Newsletter at any time, and you do NOT want this work to appear in the ACM Digital Library, please inform permissions@acm.org, stating the title of the work, the author(s), and where and when published.

ISBN: 978-1-4503-3610-9 (Digital)

ISBN: 978-1-4503-4107-3 (Print)

Additional copies may be ordered prepaid from:

ACM Order Department
PO Box 30777
New York, NY 10087-0777, USA

Phone: 1-800-342-6626 (USA and Canada)
+1-212-626-0500 (Global)
Fax: +1-212-944-1318
E-mail: acmhelp@acm.org
Hours of Operation: 8:30 am – 4:30 pm ET

Printed in the USA

2015 SIGUCCS Chairs' Welcome

Welcome to SIGUCCS 2015 in sunny St, Petersburg, Florida. With a theme of "Make Your Sun Shine," we hope this conference inspires you to learn, do your best, grow and shine for your institution.

We are excited about this year's lineup of engaging plenary speakers, technical as well as personal growth presentations by your peers, a poster session where successes and lessons are shared, opportunities to interact with vendors to learn more about their products as well as plenty of time to talk with colleagues about issues of the day and challenges of the future.

As you can well imagine, organizing the annual conference takes a village and we want to extend our appreciation and gratitude to the many people who have been a part of the planning and doing since back in August of 2014. Our core committee, Scott Saluga, Lucas Friedrichsen, Michael Cooper and Melissa Bauer were instrumental in making this conference a reality. From the efforts of the entire conference team, to the important contributions of the presenters and all the volunteers who make this conference possible, the level of enthusiasm and commitment to SIGUCCS is overwhelming and says something about the power of the organization.

The most rewarding aspect of SIGUCCS is that it provides an opportunity for us to meet our counterparts at other colleges and universities. We then can really appreciate that there are others who share and understand our unique concerns and problems. We learn new ideas and methods, and go home after the conference rejuvenated and excited about putting these new concepts into practice! For those of us who've attended the SIGUCCS Fall Conference in the past, we look for old friends and seek new ones. Newcomers are usually struck by the realization that they are not alone in their support endeavors! This camaraderie is what makes SIGUCCS special.

Combined, we have been attending SIGUCCS for many years. Leila's first conference was in 1989 and Kelly's was in 1993. SIGUCCS has contributed to the successes we have had in our careers and we know it will continue to do so. We hope you all enjoy the conference, learn something new, connect with colleagues new and old, and continue to find ways to "Make Your Sun Shine".

Kelly Wainwright
Lewis & Clark College
Co-Chair, SIGUCCS 2015

Leila Shahbender
Princeton University
Co-Chair, SIGUCCS 2015

Program Chair's Welcome

On behalf of the SIGUCCS 2015 program committee, we would like to thank you for attending SIGUCCS 2015!

SIGUCCS is an amazing environment to learn, grow, and build solid, life-long relationships with professional colleagues. Our goal for this year's conference was to provide and promote that environment for you as an attendee.

As program chairs, we were blessed to work with a large team of dedicated professionals who volunteered their time and worked hard to bring you a solid conference experience. That team includes the track chairs and readers who helped shape the programming of the conference. We could not have pulled together a program of this caliber without their efforts.

There are some exciting changes for the conference this year! First, the workshops have been combined and offered on Monday afternoon, before the Service and Support portion of the conference. Second, Service and Support and Management Symposium are running concurrently, Wednesday afternoon - Thursday morning. This was done to further encourage collaboration between the two portions of the conference. Third, the committee decided to utilize a new offering of scheduling software from Sched.org. In addition to many other features, this software allows you to build your own schedule from any device and see who is attending the same sessions you attend. Finally, Lightning Talks are formally part of the program this year. Experience multiple presentations during a single session!

This week will offer you a variety of opportunities. Experience a thoughtful half-day workshop to kick off your conference experience. Listen and engage with the plenary speakers, Patrick Rhone, David Rendall, and Becky Vasquez. Learn about the excellent work your colleagues are doing and discuss ideas in stimulating breakout sessions. Contemplate some exquisite art with your new and old friends at The Dali Museum during Wednesday nights Gala event. Take advantage of several opportunities to collaborate and network with peers from across the country and beyond. SIGUCCS will give you everything you need to grow, lead and adapt. We encourage you to look at the schedule and make a plan for what you want to attend so that you don't miss anything!

We encourage you to provide feedback for each session you attend and at the end of the conference. This helps your colleagues improve and provides information to help improve SIGUCCS overall and possible changes for the 2016 conference.

Finally, if you have the opportunity to give back and help this wonderful community, we encourage you to reach out to any volunteer or the program committee about volunteering!

This is just the beginning of your opportunity to "Make Your Sun Shine"!

Lucas Friedrichsen
Oregon State University
Management Symposium Program Chair

Scott J. Saluga
Oberlin College
Service and Support Program Chair

Table of Contents

SIGUCCS'15 Organization List ix

SIGUCCS'15 Sponsor & Supporters xi

Keynote Address

- **Care Enough to Change the World** 1
  Patrick O. Rhone *(Gladhill Rhone Consulting)*

Tuesday, November 10 - Morning Session

- **Lecture Butler – Teaching Reasonable Lectures from a Lecture Video Archive** 3
  Martin Malchow, Matthias Bauer, Christoph Meinel *(University of Potsdam)*

- **CAMMO (Creating Accessible Material in Microsoft Office): Developing an Atmosphere of Accessibility Through Training** 11
  Rob Morgan *(James Madison University)*,

- **Leadership Journey: Organization to Communication** 17
  Kenneth Janz, Robin Honken *(Winona State University)*

- **Windows to Go: Leveraging a Portable Operating System** 23
  Stephen G. Lewis *(Lehigh University)*

Tuesday, November 10 - Afternoon Session 1

- **Working in Higher Ed IT: Should I Stay or Should I Go?** 27
  Karen McRitchie *(University of Wisconsin, student)*

- **How We Deliver Our Desktop Support Services to Washington University in St. Louis the ITIL Way** 33
  Joshua Lawrence *(Washington University in St. Louis)*

- **Using FAQs to Help Users Help Themselves** 39
  John Fritz, Andrea Mocko *(University of Maryland, Baltimore County)*

- **Deploying and Managing State-of-the-Art Workstation Labs Like a Boss!** 43
  Muhammed Naazer Ashraf *(Lehigh University)*

Tuesday, November 10 - Afternoon Session 2

- **Faculty Development Through Special Initiatives at the University of San Diego** 49
  Shahra Meshkaty, Cyd Burrows *(University of San Diego)*

- **Be the Leader of Your Career: A Self-Centered Approach to Strategic Career Management** 55
  Randi R. McCray *(Union Institute and University)*, James L. Rawlins *(Pace University School of Business)*

- **Consistency and Convenience: Use of Canvas in Help Desk Staff Training** 59
  Jessica Morger *(University of Wyoming)*

- **Preparing for Your Software Asset Management Journey** 63
  Sean H. V. Mendoza *(Pima Community College)*

Tuesday, November 10 - Afternoon Session 3

- **A Real-time Application to Predict and Notify Students about the Present and Future Availability of Workspaces on a University Campus** 67
  Shamar Ward, Mechelle Gittens *(University Of The West-Indies Cave Hill Campus)*

- **Understanding Windows 10** 75
  Gale Fritsche *(Lehigh University)*
- **New York University Steinhardt Information Technology Group's New Methodologies for Developing Student Worker Skillsets** 79
  Lendyll Capitulo *(New York University)*

Wednesday, November 11 - Morning Session 1

- **Improving Communication and Building Communities with Google** 85
  Sean H. V. Mendoza *(Pima Community College)*
- **"TBD": A Flexible Technology Training Model for Smaller Campuses** 91
  Julio G. Appling *(Lewis & Clark College)*
- **Women in IT: The Endangered Gender** 95
  Vicki Leigh Noles Rogers *(University of Georgia/University of West Georgia)*
- **Who Says You Can't Go Home?** 99
  Jen Servedio, Jon Beers *(Colgate University)*

Wednesday, November 11 - Morning Session 2

- **Patch Management: The Importance of Implementing Central Patch Management and Our Experiences Doing So** 105
  Timothy Palumbo *(Lehigh University)*
- **Re-Inventing the Helpdesk. Again. in Five Weeks or Less.** 109
  R. Kevin Chapman *(Carleton College)*
- **Instructional Technology Communication and Outreach** 113
  Trevor M. Murphy *(Williams College)*, Randy Matusky *(Lyndon College)*
- **Signed, Sealed, Delivered: Improving Your Messages to the Community** 117
  Elizabeth Cornell *(Fordham University)*

Wednesday, November 11 - Poster Presentations

- **Implementation and Experience of Learning Support Application for Students in Classes** 121
  Naomi Fujimura, Kazuyuki Kusunoki *(Kyushu University)*, Shuhei Endo *(Big Ban System Corporation)*
- **Implementation and Experience of the Online Peer Grading System for Our Real Class** 125
  Shunsuke Noguchi, Naomi Fujimura *(Kyushu University)*
- **Open Source Platform for Teaching Administration of Unix-like Systems** 129
  Dmitri Danilov, Artjom Lind, Eero Vainikko *(University of Tartu)*
- **Student Driven Digital Signage** 133
  Raymond Scott Lawyer *(Siena College)*
- **Student Employee Attendance Point System** 137
  Carla Hoskins, Theresa Morgan, Anders Johansson *(Purdue University)*
- **Introduction of Unchanging Student User ID for Intra-Institutional Information Service** 141
  Yoshiaki Kasahara, Naomi Fujimura, Eisuke Ito, Masahiro Obana *(Kyushu University)*

Wednesday, November 11 - Lightning Talks

- **Five Things I Have Learned from My Travel Adventures That Have Made Me a Better Employee** 145
  R. Eddie Vinyaratn *(University of Southern California)*
- **Just Another Day at the Shop: From Small Business to College IT** 147
  Travis Freudenberg *(Carleton College)*

- **A Wearable LED Matrix Sign System Which Shows a Tweet of Twitter and Its Application to Campus Guiding and Emergency Evacuation** 149
  Takashi Yamanoue *(Fukuyama University)*,
  Keiichiro Yoshimura, Kentaro Oda, Koichi Shimozono *(Kagoshima University)*

- **Are You Prepared for Tomorrow? Developing and Offering Technology Repair Services** 151
  Brandon Lindley, Andrew Turner *(Columbus State University)*

Author Index 155

2015 SIGUCCS - ST. PETERSBURG, FL

Conference Chairs: Leila Shahbender *(Princeton University)*
Kelly Wainright *(Lewis & Clark College)*

Management Symposium Program Chair: Lucas Friedrichsen *(Oregon State University)*

Service and Support Program Chair: Scott J. Saluga *(Oberlin College)*

Treasurer: Michael Cooper *(West Virginia University, Ret.)*

Board Liaison: Melissa Bauer *(Baldwin Wallace University)*

Publications: Jacquelynn Hongosh *(Oberlin College)*

Artwork and Digital Graphics: Jared DiMartine *(Princeton University)*

Communications Awards: Lisa Brown *(University of Rochester)*

Webmaster: Jim Yucha *(Virginia Commonwealth University)*

Exhibitor Chair: Allan Chen *(Muhlenberg College)*

Registrar: Mariann Miller *(Princeton University)*

Social Networking Chair: Chris King *(North Carolina State University)*

Publicity Chair: Debbie Fisher *(The Citadel)*

Session Chair/Volunteer Coordinator: Miranda Carney-Morris *(Lewis & Clark College)*

Evaluations Chair: Melissa Bauer *(Baldwin Wallace University)*

Lightning Talk Coordinator: Mo Nishiyama *(Oregon Health & Sciences University)*

Photography Coordinators: Terry Wolff *(University of Southern California)*
Karl Owens *(University of Oregon)*

Poster Session Chair: Lisa Barnett *(New York University)*

Awards Committee Chair: Greg Hanek *(Indiana University)*

Conference App (Sched.org) Coordinator: Becky Klein *(Valparaiso University)*

Conference Coordinators: John Lateulere *(IMS Solutions)*
Joanne Lateulere *(IMS Solutions)*

Program Committee-Track Chairs: Kristen Dietiker *(Menlo College)*
Jean Tagliamonte *(Vassar College)*
Jean Ross *(Vassar College)*
Kathy Fletcher *(West Virginia University)*
Dan Herrick *(University of Colorado)*
Trevor Murphy *(Williams College)*
Miranda Carney-Morris *(Lewis & Clark College)*

Additional Readers: Robert Haring-Smith *(West Virginia University)*
Gail Rankin *(Salem State University)*
Kelly Andolina *(Union College)*
Lisa Barnett *(New York University)*
Laurie Fox *(State University of New York, Geneseo)*
Skip McFarlane *(University of Oregon)*
Mo Nishiyama *(Oregon Health and Science University)*
Allan Chen *(Muhlenberg College)*
Cate Lyon *(Whitman College)*

SIGUCCS 2015 Sponsor & Supporters

Sponsor:

Exhibitors:

CCI

KI
Furnishing Knowledge®

wēpa
print away

journeyEd
.com

LabTech®

Care Enough to Change the World

Patrick Rhone
Gladhill Rhone Consulting
patrick@gladhillrhone.com

Abstract

What do you need first to solve a problem? We like to think the first step in solving a problem is having the right tools or having the know-how. Perhaps, we think we need permission or to be given the responsibility. I argue it is none of these. The first step to solving any problem, big or small, is to care. The interesting thing about caring is that it scales. Caring about even the smallest things, and letting that charge fuel your action and commitment, has the potential to change the world.

Bio

Patrick Rhone is a Writer, Commentator, and Technology Consultant for the past 20 years. He is a partner in Gladhill Rhone, LLC – a firm that assists individuals, micro-businesses, and small non-profits get the most out of business and technology. Through his written work, he explores the intersections of technology and life, and attempts to deliver it in ways that are both practical and rational. He is also author of several books including *enough* and *This Could Help*. His work can be found at patrickrhone.com. Patrick is based in Saint Paul, MN

SIGUCCS '15, November 09-13, 2015, St. Petersburg, FL, USA
ACM 978-1-4503-3610-9/15/11.
http://dx.doi.org/10.1145/2815546.2815548

Lecture Butler - Teaching Reasonable Lectures from a Lecture Video Archive

Martin Malchow, Matthias Bauer, Christoph Meinel
Hasso Plattner Institute (HPI)
University of Potsdam
Prof.-Dr.-Helmert-Straße 2-3
Potsdam, Germany
{martin.malchow, matthias.bauer, christoph.meinel}@hpi.de

ABSTRACT

Lecture video archives offer a large variety of lecture recordings in different topics. Naturally, topics are described superficially, easily or detailed in different lectures. Users interested in certain topics have problems finding lectures describing a topic chronology from basic lectures to more detailed difficult lectures. The Lecture Butler is going to automatically offer e-learning students lectures for the topics of interest in chronological playlists. The approach is finding lecture information using title, description, OCR and ASR data. This data is indexed and searched by an in-memory database to fulfill the speed requirements for playlist creation. In the search results lectures are going to be ordered by lecture occurrence in the university semester time schedule or by given lecture level of difficulty. As a result students can automatically create playlists for their topic of interest in sequence of the lecture level. Hence, students are not overstrained by lectures when they start with basic lectures first. Basic lectures provide information to understand more complex lectures. The research shows that an automatic approach by adding the level of difficulty or university semester time table is going to show reasonable playlists to find topics of interest. This solves the main problem students encounter when they try to learn a topic step-by-step using recorded lectures. The approach will support and motivate students using e-learning opportunities.

Categories and Subject Descriptors

K.3.1 [**Computer Uses in Education**]: Distance learning; H.3.3 [**Information Storage and Retrieval**]: Information Search and Retrieval—*Information filtering, Relevance feedback*

General Terms

Human Factors, Reliability, Documentation, Experimentation

Keywords

Teleteaching; Tele-Lecturing; Distance Learning; E-Learning; OCR Search; Semantic Web; In-Memory Database; Lecture Video Archive

1. INTRODUCTION

Lecture archives have grown up for more than ten years in general. One of the first approaches was the tele-TASK lecture archive mentioned in 2002 [8]. During this time more than 5500 lectures in different areas were recorded. The idea of the Lecture Butler is to find the most appropriate lectures for a student's field of interest. Furthermore, the student should have the possibility to find lectures which are close to their field of interest so that they can understand connections and context of a topic more deeply. Finally, the level of difficulty should also be considered. When taking into account that the lectures are held from the first Bachelor semester up to the Master program it is obvious that the lectures have different levels of difficulty. The idea is to take this level of difficulty into account to show lectures in the order of their level of difficulty in order to let people understand the topic of interest from scratch and motivate them to go on learning. When starting with a lecture which is too hard to understand students would become demotivated quickly and would stop learning [4].

This paper is separated into 5 parts. In the following section, related work in context of this topic will be described to show other research approaches and to highlight ideas used for the Lecture Butler's realization. This section is followed by the Lecture Butler approach. In the Lecture Butler approach the topics "Level of Difficulty for Lectures", "Setting a Predecessor of Series and Courses", "Network of Connected Words", "Synonym Structure", "Search for Custom Lecture Collection", "Playback Lecture Results", and "Self Tests" are discussed to illustrate their feature and the implementation details. In the evaluation in Section 4 a student survey will be discussed. In this survey we asked 43 students who are familiar with the lecture archive to evaluate the Lecture Butler features. As a result it shows which features are most important for students and should be implemented in lecture archives. Furthermore, it also shows which Lecture Butler feature does not enjoy great student popularity. Finally, the paper ends with a conclusion of the whole Lecture Butler topic and exhibits impressions for future work which can improve the learning experience of students using lecture video archives.

2. RELATED WORK

Interesting related work for the Lecture Butler approach was a lecture archive search algorithm using OCR detection and in-memory database technologies [7]. This approach is able to find most reasonable lectures by analyzing the lecture slide content. This slide content of all lectures will be considered when a lecture search is performed. Furthermore, this approach can handle the full text lecture search in a reasonable time of around 300ms per request. Due to the fast response time and the full text analysis of the lectures this search approach is suitable for the Lecture Butler implementation.

Another interesting research result is the automated keyword extraction from OCR data [9]. This approach finds OCR keywords of the slides. The keyword ranking method for multi-modal information resources algorithm is based on a "term frequency-inverse document frequency" (tf-idf). This research result is used for the Lecture Butler approach to extract keywords for the creation of the network of connected words. This network will be used in the Lecture Butler to find keywords connected to the main field of interest. Due to the described precalculation of the network this approach uses the precalculated keywords for the OCR detection result. There are also other methods like the keyword extraction on topic-level for learning objects [3]. This keyword extraction is suitable for learning objects in a special area. Nevertheless, in the first evaluation of the Lecture Butler approach the first keyword extraction method [9] created more appropriate results. One reason is that it is focusing on OCR data and the topic variety of the lectures has a wide range, which makes it more difficult for a topic-level keyword extraction. Especially, due to the fact that the topics have to be selected for every lecture or series manually in the worst case.

Furthermore, the semantic of the extracted keywords has to be analyzed. This is necessary to create the dependencies of terms to other connected topics. As base the DBpedia network will be used to get structured data [2]. DBpedia offers the Wikipedia knowledge as structured data in RDF format. These semantic connections can be used for own semantic analyses. In the Lecture Butler use case the found keywords will be analyzed with the DBpedia data and links to other Wikipedia topics within the Wikipedia topic page of the keyword. Finally, topic related terms can be used for the Lecture Butler search.

Another approach to use semantic technologies in video lecture archives is the semantic extraction of meta data used on lecture slides [1]. This work will find links in lecture slides and make them directly accessible for the user with a simple click. This avoids having to type links from the lecture slide manually. Additionally, links are checked for errors and unreachable or unavailable pages. This is necessary due to the fact that not all links are recognized correctly by the OCR detection. Furthermore, RFC numbers, ISBN book numbers, and Digital Object Identifiers (DOIs) are automatically detected and processed so that users can access the full mentioned resources in a lecture with one click.

Finally, a lecture archive system should be mentioned here. tele-TASK is a product portfolio starting from recording the lecture as dual stream, using the post production tool to edit lectures to publish the videos in the tele-TASK lecture archive portal [5]. The dual stream contains one video with the lecturer and another video with the lecture slide or desktop content of the lecturer's computer. This video is recorded simultaneously and will be played back synchronously in the lecture archive with the dual stream video player.

3. APPROACH

The idea of the Lecture Butler approach is to find parts or full lectures for a student's field of interest. Therefore different tasks have to be performed in advance. These tasks are to set up the level of difficulty for lectures, create a network of topic connected words, and create a structure of synonyms. To realize the final search of the Lecture Butler four different search options are available "Lectures only", 'Sections of lectures', "Dive into the topic", and "Dive deep into the topic".

3.1 Level of Difficulty for Lectures

The level of difficulty of a course or lecture series has to be determined. Therefore, two options are discussed in this work. One approach is to set the level of difficulty by values between 1 (easy) and 10 (hard). Another approach with the same evaluation method is the idea to set the difficulty level by the semester the course is planned in the university schedule. For example, courses planed in the fifth Bachelor semester get a number five and courses planed in the second Master semester get a number eight. Due to different durations of Bachelor and Master studies at different universities these values have to be adjusted according to the common durations of the Bachelor and Master programs.

A major challenge is the requirement to manually edit every course and add the semester information. As a solution predecessor courses are introduced. For every course a predecessor can be set up and when accessing the information for a semester the chain of predecessors will be gone through and only the oldest lecture needs to have the actual semester information. This information can, in addition, be used in the course overview. It enables the users to see all previous courses easily.

3.2 Setting a Predecessor of Series and Courses

When searching for lectures in different courses we should put lectures in an order according to their occurrence and difficulty. To realize this ordering semester information or the level of difficulty is necessary for a lecture. Due to the properties of a lecture, lectures will be repeated every year as a complete course. This characteristic can be used to reduce the effort of setting up a semester for every lecture or every course. Only the first course needs information about the level of difficulty or the semester it will be taught. All following courses in the following years get the lecture information from a previous year or semester as a predecessor is set up already. When calculating the index for the Lecture Butler search the semester or level of difficulty can be saved for every lecture by gathering course information and finding the semester in the dependencies of the courses. Furthermore, this information can be used for browsing through the courses from different semesters in the regular lecture archive portal.

3.3 Network of Connected Words

For automatic creation of the network of connected words DBpedia is the selected information resource in this approach. To read DBpedia information SPARQL requests are used as customized SQL language for RDF Processing. For searching terms we use the DBpedia property "wikiPageWikiLink". This property is shows resources which are mentioned in the Wikipedia page of the requested resource.

However, DBpedia does not offer the "wikiPageWikiLink" information at the SPARQL online endpoint to avoid performance issues for the online version of DBpedia. Therefore, the DBpedia files can be downloaded[1]. In our case using DBpedia version 3.9 in English and German is sufficient. The two most important DBpedia packages for the creation of the network of connected words are named "page_links_en" and "page_links_de". They contain all connections from one Wikipedia document to another. With this additional information the connected words can be recognized automatically. To run the DBpedia SPARQL Service locally Virtuoso[2] has to be downloaded and installed with the already mentioned DBpedia files. After setting up the server, a SPARQL request can be generated to create the network of connected words. An example of a small part of the network for "WWW" is shown in Figure 1.

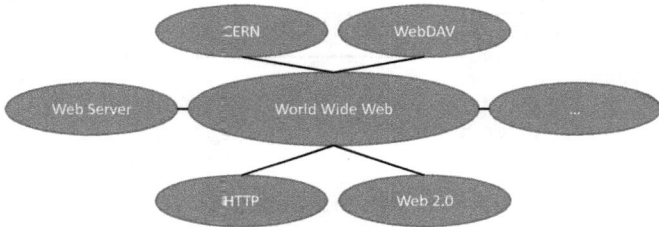

Figure 1: Network of Connected Words for the term World Wide Web

After finding all connected words in DBpedia, this information has to be stored for the Lecture Butler. Due to, the long execution time of SPARQL DBpedia requests the network of connected words are precalculated. The precalculated index will be stored in a database with the following two-table structure as network. One table stores all terms with a unique ID and a flag if it is a found keyword in a lecture or a keyword which was found with the help of DBpedia. The other table stores the connection between terms of the first table with the direction and a weight. Normally, the weight is just one as DBpedia does not store the number of connections to other Wikipedia topics. Nevertheless, the network is staff-editable and is just created automatically when a new lecture keyword [9] is indexed. Due to this behavior also the weight of a link can be edited by staff users to make some connections stronger than others. To persist staff-edited network settings there will be no re-indexing with DBpedia when a term is already in the term database and has the "found keyword in a lecture" flag. To handle issues with synonyms the approach uses an additional synonym structure described in the following Section 3.4.

3.4 Synonym Structure

In addition to the network of connected words described in Section 3.3 a synonym structure is necessary to build smaller networks to define what search terms have the same meaning. This is also necessary if different lectures use a different terminology for the same terms. For the realization a synonyms service like synonyms.net[3] is used to automatically create a network of synonyms. This network is saved in a database like the network of connected words. There is one database table with all words and marked basic words which are used in the network of connected words called "Synonym". Another database table is used for connecting the basic words with other words to mark synonyms called "Synonym_Relation". With the help these two tables synonym information is stored. This information can be visualized like it is shown in Figure 2 for "World Wide Web". The automated processed described with synonyms API is only used for the first creation of a synonym network. If the word already exists, no additional actions will be done automatically. Due to this implemented behavior users should be able to edit the network in the administration area without destroying this information in the database. Manual editing is reasonable because not all synonyms can be recognized correctly and completely by a computer in the process of automatic detection.

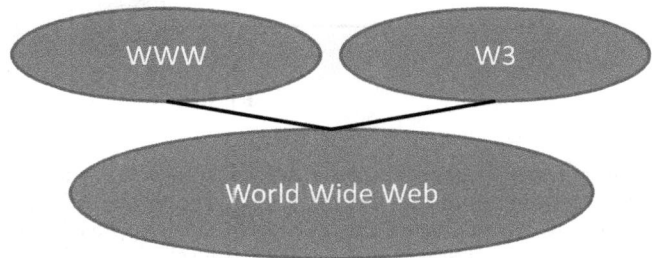

Figure 2: Synonym Network for World Wide Web

3.5 Search for Custom Lecture Collection

The most complex part of this work is the search of all data customized to users knowledge. The work flow to find suitable lectures is shown in Figure 3.

In the first step the user has to specify a search term, which is the topic of interest. Furthermore, the user can decide how deep this search is going to be performed. There are 4 search options available "Lectures only", 'Sections of lectures", "Dive into the topic", and "Dive deep into the topic".

Using the "Lectures only" option a full text search is performed using the OCR slide search approach [7]. The results are limited to 10 when the in-memory database query is executed. Finally, the ten most appropriate lectures will be found and ordered by the semester as described in Section 3.1. The complete customized SQL query from [7] is shown in Listing 1. This query will select the ten most appropriate lectures and the semester if the semester information is available. The result of the ten most appropriate lectures has to be ordered by the semester information after getting the information from the database. To visualize the results

---

[1] http://downloads.dbpedia.org/3.9/

[2] http://sourceforge.net/projects/virtuoso/

[3] http://www.synonyms.net/

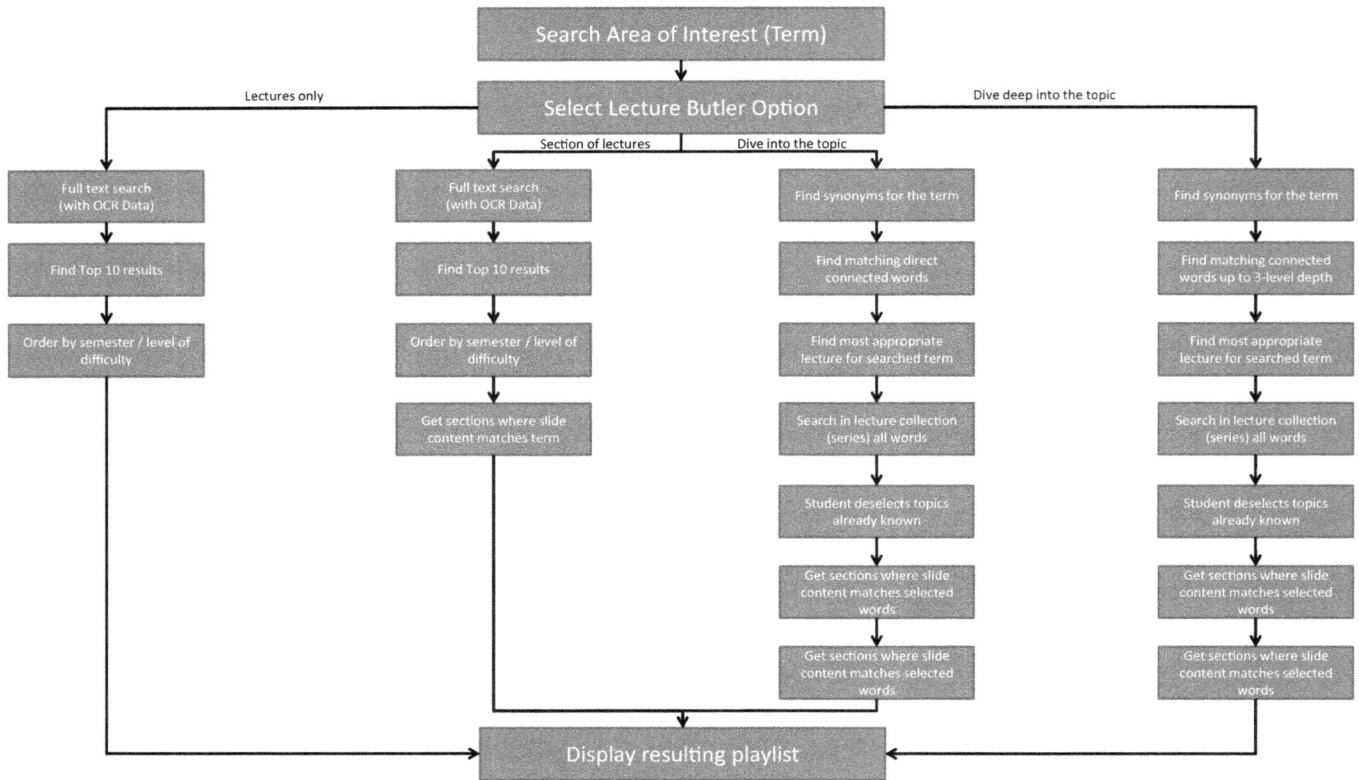

Figure 3: Workflow for Lecture Butler Search

the semester is shown in a progress bar to show how difficult it is to understand this lecture. Figure 4 shows an example of a search result using this approach. This approach also works if the semester is replaced with a level of difficulty for a lecture.

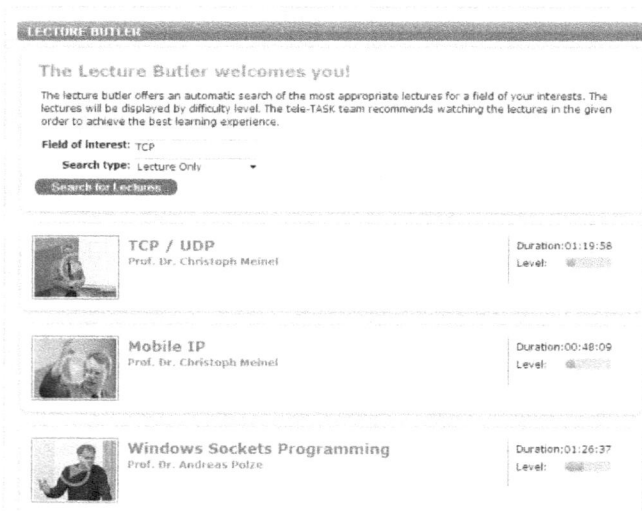

Figure 4: Lecture Butler search result for first option

Listing 1: HANA SQL statement to perform a lecture search selecting the newest lecture ordered by semester

```
SELECT SCORE() AS SCORE, T1."NAME",
T1."LECTURE_ID", T1."SEMESTER"

FROM "LECTURES" AS T1 INNER JOIN
  (SELECT "NAME", MAX("LECTURE_ID")
   AS "LECTURE_ID" FROM
    "LECTURES"
   GROUP BY ("NAME")
  ) AS T2

ON  T1."LECTURE_ID" = T2."LECTURE_ID"
WHERE CONTAINS
((T1."NAME", "OCR_TEXT"),
'searchterm', FUZZY(0.8)) AND "SEMESTER" != 0
ORDER BY SCORE DESC LIMIT 10
```

To perform a search for the option "Sections of lectures" the search goes more into the lectures by analyzing the OCR data of the slides for every section of a lecture. During the first step the search is performed like it is described for the option "Lectures only". In the following step all OCR data for the sections of the ten most appropriate lectures is analyzed. As a result the ten most appropriate lectures are found with highlighting the parts of interest by sections. This improvement avoids watching sections which are not necessary for understanding the topic of interest. Furthermore, students are more motivated to watch the parts because it is not so time-consuming and the educational objective can be reached faster.

The third Lecture Butler option "Dive into the topic" enables students to learn a topic with contextually close topics. This means that students will get a broader overview of a topic to understand the connections with other relevant fields. To realize this Lecture Butler option the most appropriate lecture for a topic has to be found first. Additionally, information for the series of the lecture is loaded. In this context a series of a lecture is the pool of all lectures of a course. At this point, the network of connected words described in Section 3.3 will be used. This network of words can find topics which are connected to the field of interest. Now the topic of interest and all found terms in the first depth of one level in the network of connected words will be searched in all lectures of the series. Furthermore, the synonym structure described in Section 3.4 will also be searched for synonyms within the field of interest and connected terms. These additional synonym results are also considered for the search in the series. This leads to the next interaction step for the user. All connected words to the topic of interest which are also found in the preselected series will be shown on an overview page. At this point, the student can deselect terms he or she is already familiar with and which should not be shown in the final Lecture Butler result. Finally, the Lecture Butler shows all relevant lectures and the relevant sections with a description which field of interest topics and topics out of the network of connected words is discussed in this part. These results are ordered in the occurrence of lectures in the corresponding series. Figure 5 shows an example result page for this approach.

Figure 5: Lecture Butler "Dive into the topic" lecture result

Another option in this Lecture Butler paper is the use of the option "Dive deep into the topic". The idea is similar to the one described in the option "Dive into the topic". The main difference is the used depth in the network of connected words. Using this option neighbor topics in the depth of three will be discovered and not only the depth of one, like described in the previous option. This will lead to more results and enables the user to understand a topic more deeply with numerous of background information.

3.6 Playback Lecture Results

Typically the lecture results calculated like described in Section 3.5 can be played back in the standard player of the platform. In case of tele-TASK there are an HTML5 and a Flash Player. To handle jumps to special sections the URL time attribute can be used to start at the special sections part. Nevertheless, this basic idea has several drawbacks. When jumping to a special section and starting the video there is no possibility to stop the video after the section is finished. In case the search result offers sections two and four of a lecture as parts of interest the student will also watch section three and all following parts after section four.

Furthermore, when different lectures are in the result set of the search the student will watch a part and then has to go back to the result list and watch the next lecture result. This leads to a lot of manual effort for the students which could demotivate them using our Lecture Butler approach.

To avoid demotivated students the idea is to play the results one after the other automatically. For the realization HTML 5 video technologies will be used. The user can decide to play results completely. Now all found lectures and sections of lectures will be gathered in the right order. The video will start with the first lecture part in the given time frame. When this part is done there will be a split screen showing the lecture title, section name, and corresponding topics of the following lecture part. This will continue until all relevant lecture video parts are played back. As an extension of the player self tests can be added to enable students to check if the lecture content is memorized. This approach is described more detailed in the following Section 3.7.

3.7 Self Tests

Self tests give users the opportunity to check their knowledge after or while watching a lecture. An implementation idea and exchange format with a MOOC platform is used like described in [6].

In our environment we can import self tests from our MOOC platform and reuse them for the lecture archive or create own self tests. This self test will be shown after a lecture is finished in the normal player. When playing it in the HTML5 Lecture Butler mode after a lecture is showing information and the question is familiar with the topic of interest the question will be shown at the end before the following video will start like it is shown in Figure 6.

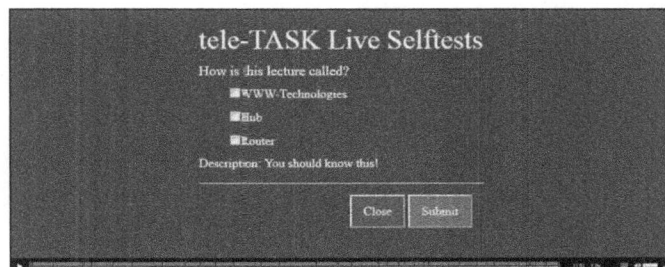

Figure 6: Lecture Self Tests in HTML5 Player

4. EVALUATION

For the approach evaluation 43 students who are familiar with the lecture archive answered several questions about the Lecture Butler. In the first step the students should search for a topic of interest. They then rated the value of the Lecture Butler search results. The results are visualized in Figure 7.

Like it is visible most students were satisfied or at least partly satisfied with in conclusion 93 percent. Only 7 percent of the students were dissatisfied with the results. When analyzing the search terms of users who are unsatisfied we noticed that they mostly searched for recordings they know which were not categorized as lectures. These recordings are categorized as colloquia. The Lecture Butler only searches for recordings categorized as lectures. Especially, to set the level of difficulty for the lectures according to the univer-

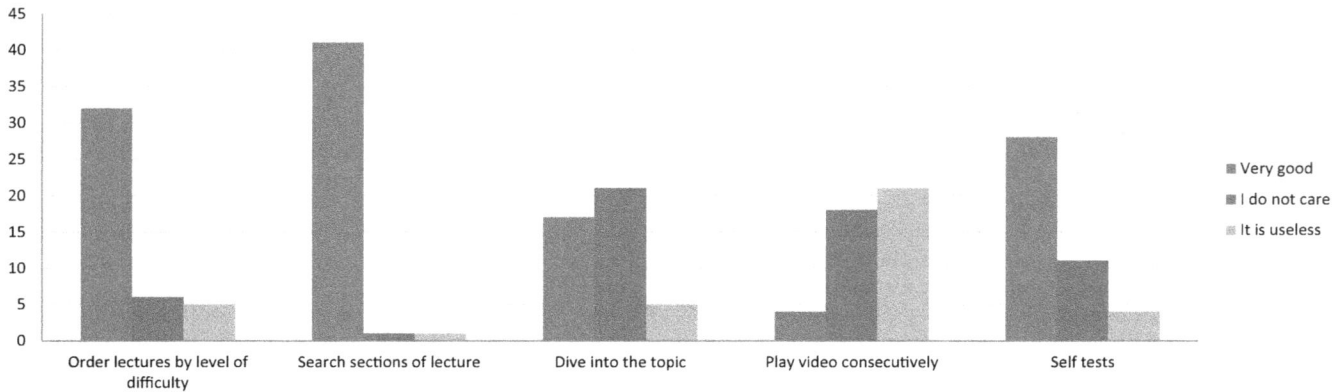

Figure 8: Student Evaluation of Lecture Butler Approaches

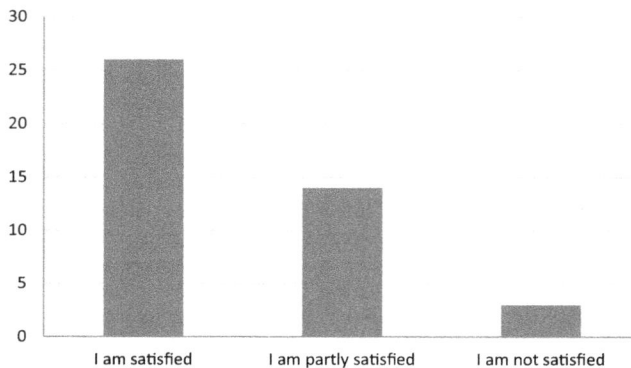

Figure 7: Student Search Result Satisfaction

sity schedule. Therefore, the results of the approach of the Lecture Butler are very good.

In the following the extensions of the Lecture Butler will be discussed. The evaluation results regarding the acceptance of the Lecture Butler's additional features are visible in Figure 8. To avoid to overwhelm students with complex questions the evaluation uses a simple structure. It analysis if a student likes a feature ("Very Good"), they think the feature is not necessary but other students might need it ("I do not care") or the feature is not necessary at all ("It is useless").

The first feature the students were asked to evaluate was the ordering of the lectures by level of difficulty. 32 of the 43 students thought it is very useful to have an ordering by difficulty. Six students said it was not necessary and five students thought there was no reason to order lectures by level of difficulty. Some of the students said that they did not understand which rules this ordering is based on and thought it could be a subjective ordering by teachers. Therefore, the method for ordering lectures by level of difficulty should be described in the description of the Lecture Butler. When adding this information students understand how this ordering was done and trust the level of difficulty more if the ordering method is reasonable for students. In conclusion, ordering by level of difficulty seems to be an use-

ful approach, since most students attending the evaluation liked this Lecture Butler feature.

The following approach is "search sections of lectures". Students also evaluated this feature. Students decided clearly that searching for sections of lectures is very reasonable functionality. 41 students liked this feature, one student thought it was not necessary and one student found this feature completely useless. As a clear result it is obviously helpful to use this Lecture Butler feature in lecture archives as students can find needed information fast.

"Dive into the topic" is the next considered feature of the evaluation. The majority (21) of students did not care about this feature. Only 17 students liked it and five students decided that it was useless. Due to a positive statement from over one third of the students an implementation of this feature seems useful. Nevertheless, there should not be too much time invested in implementing this feature so more popular features shown in Figure 8 can be implemented with a higher priority. Furthermore, these results show that the option "Dive deep into the topic" is not necessary as students did not like the "Dive into the topic" very much. Furthermore, "Dive deep into the topic" will produce a enormous result with a lot videos and video parts. This might be very time consuming to watch.

The Lecture Butler feature to play videos consecutively in one player was not of interest to students. The students like to click on a video and play the clicked video back which is the result of the user evaluation. 21 of the students thought that this feature was useless, and 18 students did not care about a feature like this. Only four students thought it was a good idea to show all videos and video parts which mention the terms of the field of interest directly after one another.

The final student evaluation was performed in the self test context. 28 students decided that the self test approach was very useful while watching lectures. 11 students did not care about the self tests and 4 students thought that self tests were useless for their learning experience on lecture archive platforms. This result shows that it makes sense to implement this feature in the video player. Nevertheless, the player should have an option to disable self tests for students who want to focus on watching and not on answering questions.

The evaluation shows that most of the students were satisfied with the approaches and ideas of this paper. Except when it comes to the consecutive video playback. Furthermore, not all features seem to be useful for all students using a lecture archive platform. To satisfy most of the users the features of the Lecture Butler should be optional. So students can enable or disable functionality.

5. RESULTS AND FUTURE WORK

This paper describes the approach to find reasonable lectures for a topic with the Lecture Butler. The Lecture Butler consists of several parts to realize a satisfying search experience for students. The first steps involve analyzing the lectures and must be done before the user executes the first search. These steps are to define the level of difficulty, setting the predecessor of series and courses, create the network of connected words, and create the synonym structure. When this process is finished the search can use the indexed data to perform the Lecture Butler search. The Lecture Butler search is separated into four options "Lectures only", 'Sections of lectures", "Dive into the topic", and "Dive deep into the topic". Like the evaluation shows these options are necessary to fulfill the different requirements of students to give complete flexibility to search lectures with different strategies. Finally, the Lecture Butler offers different options for playing back the lectures out of the search result. The obvious playback possibility is directly using the player of the lecture archive. A more complex approach is to use a HTML5 player to show all relevant video parts in a sequence. Furthermore, a customized player can show self tests to remind students of important topics and help them think about the ideas of the lecture.

Even thought the Lecture Butler is already very powerful future work has to be done. The evaluation result shows that especially students need a variety of options due to different learning behavior. The HTML5 player showing all video parts in a sequence should be optional and links to the normal lecture or lecture parts should be provided additionally. Furthermore, self tests should be disabled in the video player. This gives students the flexibility to decide freely about the learning experience. Finally, the basic search can be optimized by analyzing additional data like "Automatic Speech Recognition" (ASR) or by optimizing the search algorithm. Optimization can be done especially by indexing lecture information in the HANA. Currently, the bottleneck is gathering of lecture information from the MySQL database. Finally, a user analysis service should be added to the Lecture Butler to evaluate which options are mostly used and which topics are in the focus of students' interest. With this additional information the Lecture Butler can be optimized for students' needs and improve support and motivation.

6. REFERENCES

[1] M. Bauer, M. Malchow, and C. Meinel. Enhance teleteaching videos with semantic technologies. In V. L. Uskov, R. J. Howlett, and L. C. Jain, editors, *Smart Education and Smart e-Learning*, volume 41 of *Smart Innovation, Systems and Technologies*, pages 105–115. Springer International Publishing, 2015.

[2] C. Bizer, J. Lehmann, G. Kobilarov, S. Auer, C. Becker, R. Cyganiak, and S. Hellmann. Dbpedia - a crystallization point for the web of data. *Web Semantics: Science, Services and Agents on the World Wide Web*, 7(3), 2009.

[3] K. H. Coursey, R. Mihalcea, and W. E. Moen. Automatic keyword extraction for learning object repositories. *Proceedings of the American Society for Information Science and Technology*, 45(1):1–10, 2008.

[4] J. Falout, J. Elwood, and M. Hood. Demotivation: Affective states and learning outcomes. *System*, 37(3):403 – 417, 2009.

[5] F. Grünewald, H. Yang, E. Mazandarani, M. Bauer, and C. Meinel. Next generation tele-teaching: Latest recording technology, user engagement and automatic metadata retrieval. In A. Holzinger, M. Ziefle, M. Hitz, and M. Debevc, editors, *Human Factors in Computing and Informatics*, volume 7946 of *Lecture Notes in Computer Science*, pages 391–408. Springer Berlin Heidelberg, 2013.

[6] M. Malchow, M. Bauer, and C. Meinel. The future of teleteaching in mooc times. In *Computational Science and Engineering (CSE), 2014 IEEE 17th International Conference on*, pages 438–443, Dec 2014.

[7] M. Malchow, M. Bauer, and C. Meinel. Enhance lecture archive search with ocr slide detection and in-memory database technology. *Computational Science and Engineering (CSE), 2015 IEEE 18th International Conference on*, Oct 2015. to appear.

[8] V. Schillings and C. Meinel. tele-task: teleteaching anywhere solution kit. In *Proceedings of the 30th annual ACM SIGUCCS conference on User services*, pages 130–133. ACM, 2002.

[9] H. Yang and C. Meinel. Content based lecture video retrieval using speech and video text information. *Learning Technologies, IEEE Transactions on*, 7(2):142–154, April 2014.

CAMMO (Creating Accessible Material in Microsoft Office):
Developing an Atmosphere of Accessibility Through Training

Rob Morgan
James Madison University
Computing Support, IT Training
1015 Harrison Street
MSC 5804
Harrisonburg, VA 22807
540-568-6258
morganrm@jmu.edu

ABSTRACT
In this paper, we describe the creation of a universal design training class for faculty and staff at James Madison University. The paper will discuss the process by which the class was created, the theories that guide the learning process, the guidance of what was chosen to be included in the class, and how the class was rolled out to the campus. The paper may also be used as a guide for other colleges and universities that are interested in implementing an accessibility initiative.

Categories and Subject Descriptors
K.4.2 [**Social Issues**]: Assistive technologies for persons with disabilities

K.6.1 [**Project and People Management**]: Training

K.8.1 [**Application Packages**]: Spreadsheets, Word processing

General Terms
Human Factors, Design, Documentation

Keywords
Universal Design, Accessibility, Microsoft Office 2013, Training

1. INTRODUCTION
"Universities may not, under federal law—as the Department of Education again made clear with its May guidance on accessible instructional materials and related technology—acquire, offer, or recommend technology that is inaccessible to those with print disabilities," summarized Daniel Goldstein in an email [4]. A simple search online for "Higher Education Accessibility Lawsuits" will return numerous examples as to why this topic is important in today's colleges and universities. The proliferation of technology in education has outpaced accessibility initiatives,

SIGUCCS '15, November 09 - 13, 2015, St. Petersburg, FL, USA
Copyright is held by the owner/author(s). Publication rights licensed to ACM.
ACM 978-1-4503-3610-9/15/11...$15.00
DOI: http://dx.doi.org/10.1145/2815546.2815566

leaving many students at a disadvantage, and many schools at risk for sanctions. By implementing a few simple techniques, content creators can radically alter the delivery of course material to support a wide range of learner differences. Whether you are a professor, a trainer, a communicator, or anyone who produces material in Microsoft Office or Google Documents, the material presented in this paper will assist you in ensuring that your content is accessible.

2. CLASS BEGINNINGS
In 2013, the Virginia Department for the Blind and Vision Impaired provided a demonstration of a screen reader at James Madison University. This was the author's first experience with a screen reader and it is not at all what he was expecting. While the author was expecting something like a tablet that attached to the computer that the learner intended to use, a screen reader is actually "software programs that allow blind or visually impaired users to read the text that is displayed on the computer screen" [1].

As a result of this training, it was decided that the IT Training team at James Madison University and the Office of Disability Services at James Madison University would collaborate to create a training course for faculty and staff at the university. The training would center on how to create accessible content at the university. The 90-minute class would be hands-on and provide participants with tangible information that could be used immediately to begin creating accessible content.

2.1 Naming the Class
As the preliminary research was being done for the new class, it was discovered that many of the disabilities that are prevalent in classrooms today are invisible to the naked eye. A professor, by simply looking at his room full of students, may not be able to tell that there is anyone in attendance who needs accessible content provided. These hidden disabilities were the stimulus for the name of the new training class offered by the IT Training team at James Madison University. The class was named CAMMO and the cover of the book uses a camouflage background to tie in with the idea of hidden disabilities. The class Creating Accessible Material in Microsoft Office (CAMMO) would offer content creators an opportunity to expand their understanding of universal design in content creation and discover some of the tools available to them in Microsoft Office 2013.

2.2 Background

2.2.1 IT Training

The IT Training team at James Madison University exists as an extension of the Computing Support department that is an integral part of Information Technology at James Madison University. The mission statement for Information Technology is to "Deliver a technology environment and services that enable the university community to learn, innovate, collaborate, and provide excellent service" [2].

The IT Training team exists to enhance performance and improve effectiveness, while encouraging employees to develop the technical skills and competencies to perform their job duties efficiently. The ability to train content creators on how to successfully create accessible material aligns with the goals of the team.

2.2.2 Office of Disability Services (ODS)

The vision of the Office of Disability Services is "To be the strategic campus partner for removing barriers and building capacity to ensure inclusion and equity for people with disabilities" [3]. At James Madison University, this office is the primary resource for students with disabilities and assists content creators with creating accessible material or updating inaccessible material so that it can be accessed by students with a disability. The ODS department served as the subject matter experts (SMEs) for the CAMMO project.

2.2.3 Why is Accessibility Important?

Apart from the laws and school policies that require that content be made accessible, what are the reasons to promote accessible content in higher education? A 2008 study by the Government Accountability Office showed that over 10% of higher education students have some form of disability and this number appears to be increasing [6]. By creating content that is universally designed, the content creators not only ensure that their content is compliant but they save themselves additional work in the future were a person with a disability to become a constituent and require access to their content in an accessible format.

2.3 Creating the Class

The initial idea for training content creators on how to make their content accessible was to conduct a training class in one of the training labs at the IT Training Center (ITTC). The labs would allow the trainers to apply social learning theory by modeling the expected procedures that should be followed when creating accessible material. The training lab also allows for a safe controlled environment where the trainers could have the students easily and quickly access training content that had been stored on the lab computers.

2.3.1 What to Train On?

It was decided that the class would focus primarily on creating accessible material in Microsoft Office 2010 while also including some helpful features outside of Microsoft Office such as closed captioning and YouTube videos.

When the training was initially created in 2013, James Madison University had not yet pushed managed computers to Office 2013. The training labs were still running Office 2010 and the training classes (Excel, PowerPoint, Word, Outlook, SharePoint) were using Office 2010. It was decided that since Office was the primary tool that was being used to create content on campus it would therefore be the most effective tool to train on. While creating the content for the CAMMO class, it was discovered that much of what worked in Office 2010 would work in other content creation software as well.

The trainer focused the CAMMO class on Microsoft Word, Excel, PowerPoint and Outlook, as these were programs that were already being trained on at James Madison University.

In 2014, the training labs at IT Training were upgraded to Office 2013 and in the Fall of 2013, there was a push across campus to upgrade all managed computers to Office 2013 and to encourage departmental computers that were not managed to upgrade as well if possible. The CAMMO class was upgraded to utilize Office 2013 in early 2014 to make it consistent with what content creators would be using in their offices.

2.3.2 Focus on Visual Impairment

Much of the training in the CAMMO class is referenced and/or focused on creating content for visually impaired students. While studies shows that the most common disability that will be seen in the classroom is a "mental, emotional, or psychiatric condition/depression" [6], the research that was conducted during the preparation for the CAMMO class showed that content created with a visually impaired student in mind provided a best case scenario for creating content that was universally designed.

2.3.3 Training on Background Information

The training classes that are offered by the IT Training team typically include a course material packet that contains a class training manual. For the CAMMO class the trainer created a 26-page handout that the learners could follow during class and reference when they returned to their departments.

The class begins with an introduction to federal mandates and University policy that provides the learner with a background for why they are required to create accessible material. This is followed by an appeal to the ethics of the learners by providing them with reasons to be intrinsically motivated to create content that is accessible. The class then discusses universal design and why, if created correctly, they do not need to create a subset of content for learners who have a special need but simply create their content initially with a goal of making it accessible for the greatest audience possible.

The trainer uses both a cartoon and a narrative story to express what universal design is and why content created or used at the university should adhere to universal design principles. An emphasis is placed on the resolving the false assumption that content creators need to design custom content for a specific group of people. In contrast, the class teaches that if content is initially created with universal design principles in mind, there is not a need to change much in regards to your content, regardless of your audience.

3. TRAINING MATERIAL

All participants received a copy of the training course material previously mentioned in addition to a bookmark with the *10 Keys to Accessibility*. In a class for occupational therapist graduate students, the learners were also given a USB drive provided by the Office of Disability services that included a letter from the ODS director and some general information on working with students with a disability.

The training material was all created in-house by the James Madison University IT Training team. The labs in the IT Training Center, where the classes were held, included practice documents that the learners worked on during the class. Providing the learners with content that they could work on in class allowed for a hands-on experience in creating content that was accessible.

3.1 Training on Universal Office 2013 Features

After setting the stage for the reasons why accessible material was needed and what universal design was, the training class began to focus on tools that were available in all, or most, Microsoft Office 2013 programs. After explaining what a screen reader is and showing a demonstration of a screen reader online via http://webaim.org/simulations/screenreader-sim.htm, the trainer demonstrated Microsoft's Text-to-Speech feature which allows users the ability to have content read back to them in Microsoft Word, Outlook, OneNote, and PowerPoint. While not necessarily a screen reader, this feature can allow many students with varying needs the ability to have content read back to them. In the CAMMO class, it is pointed out that this feature can be helpful to learners with a visual impairment but also to a host of other learners such as those whose native language is not English, learners who suffer from dyslexia, and learners with a cognitive disability. The learners are shown how to add the Text-to-Speech feature to the quick access toolbar and how to use it.

The next topic that is covered in CAMMO, which transcends a multitude of applications, is the importance of the use of color in creating content. Participants are instructed to veer away from using color as a primary tool to communicate their message. Color should be an enhancement to the content and not the only vehicle for transfer of information. The course material provides the participants with information on multiple types of color blindness in addition to some facts and statistics surrounding color blindness. The class also discusses color contrast and what online tools are available for free to check the contrast of foreground and background colors prior to publishing the content.

Laser pens, which are frequently used in training/educational settings, are discussed at this point in the training as well. It is pointed out that the two most common colors for laser pens (green, red) are also the two colors that are most associated with difficulty viewing for individuals who suffer from color blindness. Participants are given instruction and insight on how a laser pen may appear to a learner who is color blind.

3.2 Training on Word 2013

As Microsoft Word is one of the most common tools used when creating content, it is the first program that is discussed in CAMMO. The participants are trained on three primary topics in Word: (1) Styles/Outline Format, (2) Page Breaks, (3) Alternate Text.

In 1956, George Miller of Harvard University introduced learning theorists to the magic of the number seven. He argued that a learner's working memory had the ability to remember seven items plus or minus two, at any one time [5]. This research paved the way for chunking our content in learning—a strategy that most educators, trainers, and instructional designers are familiar with. Content creators will often chunk their content

without being formally trained in the benefits by creating content with an outline mindset and separating sections with the use of font formatting. A self-trained user of Word will frequently change the size or color of a section heading and perhaps make it bold or italicized. This formatting is not wasted on the sighted learner who can mentally chunk the content based on the different appearance of the section headings. However, to a learner using a screen reader to consume the content, the text is not differentiated. In the CAMMO class, this is demonstrated by showing a document that is twenty pages long. We provide the learners with a fictional scenario where the professor has told his class that they really only need to focus on *Topic X*. As sighted learners, the class is quickly able to scroll through the document glancing at the section headers until they locate the section that was assigned. This would take the students a matter of seconds to complete. To simulate a vision impaired experience for the class participants, the projector is blacked out and the trainer turns on the text-to-speech feature. The participants have to listen through three-pages of text that takes approximately five minutes to complete before discovering the section that has been assigned.

If the content creators use Word's built-in style headings, a learner on a screen reader can request that the screen reader read just the headings to the learner rather than the learner having to listen through multiple pages irrelevant content. This only works if the content creator used Word's style headings. For content creators at a school that utilizes Google's suite of tools as opposed to Microsoft, this feature works the same way when using the built-in heading styles in Google Docs.

One of the most impactful items discussed in the CAMMO class is how universal design is beneficial to both the learner with a disability and the other learners as well. The analogy that is given in class is an electric sliding door that is helpful to the individual in a wheelchair but also to the delivery driver pushing a dolly, the employee carrying boxes out of the building, and the mother pushing a stroller. This point is demonstrated in CAMMO by showing the participants how to they can easily create a table of contents with one click if they have used style headings.

3.3 Training on Excel 2013

Excel introduces some special obstacles for learners with a disability. In the CAMMO class the learners are taught how to add alternate text to tables, charts, and SmartArt. They are also trained on how to create column headings and advised against creating tables with blank rows. The participants work in provided training workbooks to add names to worksheets which is helpful for all learners. It is common for a self-taught user of Excel to leave the default worksheet names (Sheet1, Sheet2, etc.) However, it can be helpful for both a sighted and a visually impaired learner to have the worksheets named with appropriate titles. In the CAMMO class the participants open an Excel workbook and they apply our provided worksheet names to each of the worksheets.

3.4 Training on PowerPoint 2013

Much of what is trained on in Word and Excel is transferrable to PowerPoint as well. However, there are some situations in PowerPoint that are unique in terms of accessibility. The participants are encouraged to add titles to all of their slides and are trained on how to hide the titles from sighted learners if they prefer. Considerable time is also spent training the participants on how to place the content of their slides in logical order so that it is read back correctly via a screen reader.

A feature that can be very helpful for individuals with a disability is the inclusion of audio recorded over the slides. The CAMMO class instructs the participants on how they can record audio for their slideshows.

3.5 Training on Outlook 2013

The training lab at the IT Training center does not have an Outlook profile added to the desktop image, which takes a considerable amount of time. So, this is the only program that is presented in the CAMMO class without the participant getting hands on practice. A PowerPoint presentation is used to convey the important accessibility features to consider when working in Outlook. These topics include font selection and colors, plain text vs HTML, alt text for images/links, and signatures in emails.

3.6 Portable Document Format Files (PDFs)

PDF files play an important role in many of the classes at James Madison University. Unfortunately, if not created correctly, these files can prove to be inaccessible for learners with disabilities. A portion of the CAMMO class focuses on training participants on how to create accessible PDF files.

Participants are encouraged, if they have the opportunity, to always create PDFs from their electronic files. A PDF that is created by exporting in Microsoft Word 2013 is accessible by default. However, if an electronic copy of the content is not available, the CAMMO class teaches the participants about the difference between text-based PDFs and scanned images. There is also instruction on optical character recognition copiers and a guide to where these machines are located throughout campus.

3.7 Accessibility Checker

The most influential resource that the participants acquire in the CAMMO class is instruction regarding Microsoft's Accessibility Checker. Similar to the spell checker and grammar checker, the accessibility checker can quickly scan a document and provide the content creator with a list of items that may be problematic. The checker categorizes issues in three ways: (1) Errors, (2) Warnings, (3) Tips. In addition to making the creator aware of the issues, the checker also provides justification to the creator as to why the particular issues may be problematic and instructions on how to remedy each situation. The class participants are told that if they only learn one thing from the training, the knowledge and understanding of the Microsoft Accessibility Checker should be that takeaway.

3.8 Training on YouTube captioning

The CAMMO training class finishes with a short discussion about the importance of closed captioning on videos. The trainer discusses the YouTube automatic caption feature, both its benefits and shortcomings. The suggestion is given that the content creators use the automatic caption tool as a starting point and then manually make corrections if they do not have a time stamped script to upload.

A humorous video is played in the final minutes of class that shows YouTube artists singing Taylor Swift songs and then letting YouTube auto caption the songs that they then sing back with the new lyrics [7]. This final activity allows for the class to close on a high note and provides a good example of why it is important that the content creators check the auto caption tool.

4. MARKETING AND RESULTS

One of the initial hurdles that needed to be overcome was how to get participants to attend the CAMMO training class. IT Training collaborated with Office of Disability Services to offer the class during their Disability Awareness Week (DAW) event. The class was promoted on the DAW website and on posters placed throughout campus. Both IT Training and ODS promoted the event on their Facebook pages as well. An email list of individuals at James Madison University who had an interest in accessibility initiatives had recently been created and that group was emailed a promotional video that was created using PowToons.

4.1 Disability Awareness Week 2014

It was decided that the initial class would be offered twice during Disability Awareness Week. The IT Training lab has a maximum capacity of eighteen learners. Out of thirty-six possible participants, the class had an enrollment of thirty-two learners. The marketing department of James Madison University sent out a reporter/photographer to cover the class and published their story on the James Madison University website.

4.2 Occupational Therapy Students

The IT Training team received multiple requests from professors asking that the content be made available for their students. While resources limited what they were able to assist with, they did agree to collaborate with the Office of Disability Services to offer training for graduate students in the Occupational Therapy program. The class of roughly thirty students was split into two groups and rotated between the CAMMO class and a tour of the new location for the Office of Disability Services.

4.3 CIT TLT Conference 2014

In the Fall of 2014, IT Training presented a condensed version of the CAMMO session to faculty at James Madison University as part of the Center for Instructional Technologies (CIT) department's Teaching and Learning with Technology (TLT) conference. This was the first time that the class was offered specifically for faculty at the University.

4.4 CAMMO for Faculty

Following the CIT conference, the IT Training team received multiple requests to offer the CAMMO class for faculty. It was decided that a special faculty class would be offered in the Fall of 2014. Eleven faculty attended the training at the IT Training center.

4.5 Brainstorm Conference 2015

In the Spring of 2015, IT Training presented a condensed version of the CAMMO material at the Virginia Society for Technology in Education (VSTE) Brainstorm conference at James Madison University. The conference is designed to provide K-12 teachers resources regarding using technology in their classrooms. There were fifteen middle and high school teachers who attended the CAMMO workshop at this conference.

4.6 Disability Awareness Week 2015

In the Spring of 2015, IT Training and ODS partnered once again to offer two session of the CAMMO class for faculty and staff at James Madison University during Disability Awareness Week. Sixteen participants completed the training during this event.

4.7 Numbers Trained

Since beginning the CAMMO class in 2013, the IT Training department has offered it eight times. Six of those classes have been for James Madison University faculty and/or staff. One class was for graduate students and one class was for K-12 teachers in the community. There have been a total of 122 learners who have completed the course.

5. LESSONS LEARNED

The initial response to the CAMMO class was favorable and we saw good numbers and positive feedback from the University community. We did not expect or prepare for the number of colleges and faculty who would want us to provide private sessions of the content to their constituents. Being that the primary audience for IT Training is faculty and staff, we were not able to provide for and meet the demands of all these requests. The most important take away that we were told the CAMMO class provided was the Accessibility Checker. As a result, the IT Training staff has begun incorporating that feature into all of their trainings on Office 2013 applications. We also published a post on our Facebook page explaining what the Microsoft Accessibility Checker is and how to use it.

5.1 Moving Forward

Recent training numbers for the CAMMO class show that, while there was initial high-level interest from certain employees at the University, that group has now been trained and the number of additional employees wishing to be trained has declined. The current rationale is that those who had an interest in accessibility came through the training initially and now that they have been trained, there needs to be additional marketing and education to get others in the University involved. One possibility that has been discussed is creating an asynchronous online version of that class that will be available on demand. There have also been some discussions of providing new faculty with a CAMMO introduction during their onboarding so that they come onto campus knowing that accessibility is something that is taken seriously and that a class is offered to provide them with the tools and resources to make their content accessible.

As James Madison University and other higher education institutions continue to focus on accessible material both inside and outside of the classroom, the intentional development of universally designed content will be integral to success. The experiences at James Madison University with the CAMMO class can provide a blueprint for developing an accessibility initiative at other universities as well.

6. REFERENCES

[1] American Foundation for the Blind. 2015. *Screen Readers*. April 23. https://www.afb.org/ProdBrowseCatResults.asp?CatID=49.

[2] Information Technology. 2014. Missions Statement. Harrisonburg, VA: James Madison University Information Technology.

[3] JMU Office of Disability Services. 2015. *About Us*. April 26. https://www.jmu.edu/ods/contact/index.shtml.

[4] Joly, Karine. 2011. Web Accessibility: Required, Not Optional. *University Business*.

[5] Miller, George A. 1956. The Magical Number Seven, Plus or Minus Two: Some Limits for Our Capacity for Processing Information. *The Psychological Review* 81-97.

[6] United States Government Accountability Office. 2009. HIGHER EDUCATION AND DISABILITY: Education Needs a Coordinated Approach to Improve Its Assistance to Schools in Supporting Students. *GAO-10-33* 2.

[7] https://www.youtube.com/watch?v=7MuDgfX9C2w

Leadership Journey: Organization to Communication

Kenneth Janz
Winona State University
Somsen Hall 207
Winona, MN 55987
1-507-457-2299
kjanz@winona.edu

Robin Honken
Winona State University
Somsen Hall
Winona, MN 55987
1-507-457-2215
rhonken@winona.com

ABSTRACT
Leadership development has been a high priority for the Information Technology Services (ITS) unit at Winona State University. Each year the Chief Information Officer (CIO) works with the leadership team collaboratively on yearly themes in which the members of the ITS leadership team conducted a deep dive into an issue and work to enhance the employees' impact on the University. Over the years the following themes have been selected:

- 2008 – 2009 Organization of ITS - Educational Lean
- 2009 – 2010 Project Management - Long Range Planning
- 2010 – 2011 Building a Culture of Assessment
- 2011 – 2012 Professional Development Planning and Core Competencies
- 2012 – 2013 Connecting the Strategic with the Tactical
- 2013 – 2014 Workplace Civility (Code of Conduct)
- 2014 – 2015 Communications (Internal and External)

This paper highlights lessons learned on the leadership journey. Some themes have had more impact than others over the years but in many ways the ITS leadership team is continuing to build on a solid foundation. Each theme builds on work of a prior theme.

Categories and Subject Descriptors
K.6.1 [**Project and People Management**]: Management

General Terms
Management, Measurement, Documentation, Performance, Design, Economics, Human Factors, Standardization, Theory

Keywords
Leadership; Management; Communication; Organization; Workplace Civility; Code of Conduct; Educational Lean; Strategic Planning; Long Range Planning; Project Management; Project Intake; Professional Development Planning; Metrics; Mission; Vision; Values; Goals; Assessment; Organizational Performance; Culture; Listening; Outreach

SIGUCCS'15, November 9–13, 2015, St. Petersburg, FL, USA.
© 2015 ACM. ISBN 978-1-4503-3610-9/15/11...$15.00.
DOI: http://dx.doi.org/10.1145/2815546.2815555

1. INTRODUCTION
1.1 Institutional Context
Winona State University is a public university with 9,000 students and about 450 faculty members. Since 1997 with its *e-Warrior: Digital Life and Learning Program* every student has received a laptop computer, and in 2013 the program evolved to also include a tablet [3]. There are just over 50 information technology staff members at Winona State University.

1.2 Journey Begins
An organization's culture has a funny way of trumping logic and sometimes a manager's best intentions. Leaders or managers trying to "fix" an organization from a structural perspective are dismayed when they assess the product or output of the work and nothing has really changed. On the other hand, leaders or managers, who believe that being a highly effective organization is a journey not a destination, know there are no quick fixes and real change occurs over time.

Having been a team at Winona State University for the last seven years, the authors are using this paper as a way of reflecting on the journey. The authors are working to continuously improve and support a highly effective organization, of which all the members of the Winona State University ITS leadership team can be proud.

The process documented in this paper started seven years ago with the arrival of a new CIO at Winona State University. One of the top priorities with new leadership at the institution was the development of the ITS leadership team. Each year the CIO would work with the leadership team collaboratively on yearly themes in which the members of the ITS leadership team conducted a deep dive into an issue and worked to enhance the employees' impact on the University. Over the years the following themes have been selected:

- 2008 – 2009 (FY09) Organization of ITS - Educational Lean
- 2009 – 2010 (FY10) Project Management - Long Range Planning
- 2010 – 2011 (FY11) Building a Culture of Assessment
- 2011 – 2012 (FY12) Professional Development Planning and Core Competencies
- 2012 – 2013 (FY13) Connecting the Strategic with the Tactical
- 2013 – 2014 (FY14) Workplace Civility (Code of Conduct)
- 2014 – 2015 (FY15) Communications (Internal and External)

2. FY09 - Organization of ITS and Educational Lean

The fall of 2008 saw the development of the Mission, Vision, and Values of ITS at Winona State University. Visitors to Winona State will still see the work product several years later in the posters around ITS conference rooms, open areas, and front matter of several ITS documents. This early work still drives long range planning and prioritization of incoming projects. Below are the items developed in the fall of 2008:

Mission

Information Technology Services (ITS) provides the technology-based foundation to support and empower the Winona State University (WSU) community to meet and exceed their educational and business needs.

Vision

Information Technology Services endeavors to position the University as a national leader in the innovative and effective use of technology to support the academic enterprise.

Values

People, Performance, and Innovation

As stated earlier the ITS mission, vision, and values still drive much of the decision making that goes on within the unit. Routinely the ITS Leadership team will ask themselves, will this project truly provide the technology-based foundation to support and empower the WSU community to meet and exceed their educational and business needs. The statement does guide our actions and a lens to look at institutional issues and challenges.

During the summer 2008, the ITS organization was structured into seven units with one of these units actually reporting outside of the CIO office. The units that made up ITS were as follows: communications, media services, e-learning, operations, laptop program, development, and systems. By the spring of 2009 ITS had reorganized into the four units that exist today: teaching and learning technology services, user services, infrastructure services, and development and web support services. Two additions have taken place since that time: a one-person IT security office and a one-person project management office.

During the summer of 2009, work had begun to embrace educational lean. The ITS leadership team participated in five days of training over the main constructs behind educational lean. During the training participants learned the principles and practices of educational lean including: identifying symptoms of non-value, developing current state value stream maps, and future state implementation plans, conducting effective root cause analyses, and facilitating Kaizen events. The training provided an occasion for team building within the ITS leadership team and it also provided an opportunity to build connections across campus. Since the lean training several members of the ITS leadership team have been asked to facilitate a number of non-ITS lean events across campus. While not always referred to by name, principals of lean are still in use today in ITS.

3. FY10 Project Management - Long Range Planning

During the fall of 2009, several members of the ITS team attended a three-day project management workshop presented by Fissure. This training focused on team building, soft skills, project plans, resource planning, status reports, and control charts. This training provided the attendees a common vocabulary to discuss project management. With this training, the leadership team determined that the most important part of the project management process was the initial evaluation of the request, discussing how the request supports the university mission, and conversation about the best way to develop a solution for the WSU community. [1]

The team also recognized work was needed in these areas at Winona State and decided to capitalize on the previous year's educational lean focus by organizing a lean event to evaluate and improve the IT project intake process. This event led to a successful project intake process which is still in place and used today. The process aligns with the following flowchart (see Figure 1):

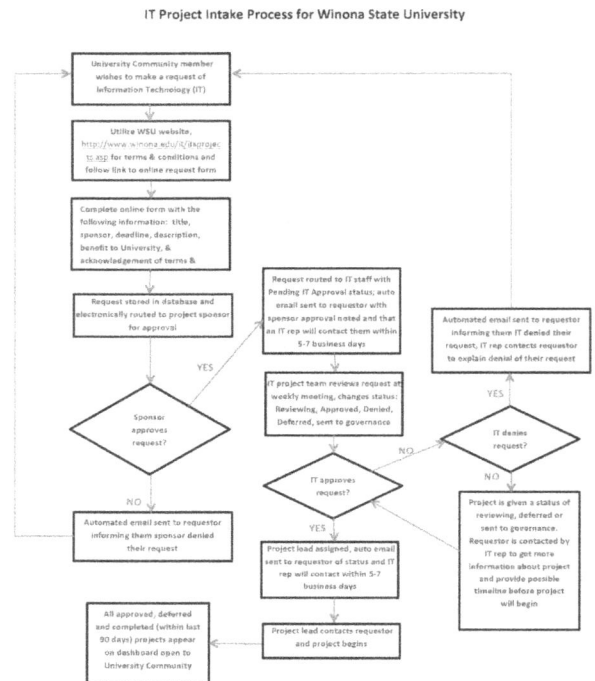

Figure 1. Project Intake Process

The Project intake process highlighted the need for long range planning in information technology at the University. Also during the fall of 2009, the process to create a long-range plan that ended up taking the form of what is now known today as the "Technology Master Plan" began. With the All University Technology Committee (AUTC) developing buckets and listening sessions to taking the plan through the university's governance process and getting final approval by cabinet took most of the academic year.

4. FY11 Building a Culture of Assessment

With the creation of a Technology Master Plan and a more formal approach to project intake it was important for the IT organization to measure its impact on the University. This need for high quality performance data (metrics) for information technology was driven by program and institutional accreditation as well a request from the Minnesota State College and University (MnSCU) Board of Trustees in regards to Winona State

University's *e-Warrior: Digital Life and Learning Program.*
However, to meet these requests gaps in information technology assessment strategy emerged requiring a more comprehensive approach. Working with students and faculty, a plan was developed and implemented. The plan has already resulted in improvements to many facets of information technology support. [2] Figure 2 below shows the many pieces to the assessment process.

One side benefit of creating a culture of assessment and using national instruments is that Winona State has compared very favorably to other institutions of higher education. In addition, the success of this work can be seen in the growth and respect the MnSCU IT community has shown in the work done by Winona State IT staff. Each year MnSCU awards three IT units within the system "Outstanding Achievement Awards" (First place and two runner ups). In 2011 and 2012, Winona State received the runner up for the Outstanding Achievement Award. This success was improved with the 2013, 2014, and 2015, 1st place Outstanding Achievement Award.

5. FY12 Professional Development Planning and Core Competencies

After collecting data around the outcomes related to IT measures it became evident that there were gaps in the development of the professional IT staff. Starting in the spring of 2012, ITS started to tie the use of travel and professional development funds to a new process created by the ITS leadership team. Directors worked with employees during the evaluation process to determine collaboratively what skills were needed in the unit and what professional growth was of interest to individual employees. This process created a document called the Professional Development Plan or now referred to as the PDP for all ITS employees. These plans are now directly linked to requests for training, travel, and professional development.

In addition, development and web support services began the processes to integrate core competencies into the review process. Position descriptions were enhanced to include language around employees: acting as an effective IT partner, growing collaborative relationships, self-awareness, productive team

member, ability to multi-task, adaptive to change, and drives for results.

6. FY13 - Connecting the Strategic with the Tactical

Prior to the fall of 2012, it had become evident that some units within ITS were having trouble connecting the activities in the technology master plan to day-to-day work of the unit. To assist that process the ITS leadership developed the ITS Work Plan. The work plan broke down the technology master plan into measureable goals or tasks that could be completed by a unit each year. Each tangible goal in the work plan was directly aligned to the umbrella technology master plan document. So the working of the work plan was also working the master plan. Plan the work; work the plan (see Figure 3).

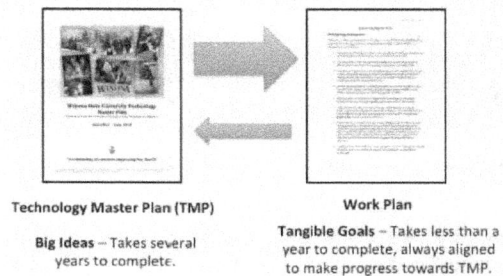

Connecting the Strategic with the Tactical

Technology Master Plan (TMP)

Big Ideas – Takes several years to complete.

Work Plan

Tangible Goals – Takes less than a year to complete, always aligned to make progress towards TMP.

Figure 3. Connecting the Strategic with the Tactical

7. FY14 Workplace Civility (Code of Conduct)

During the 2013-2014 academic year, ITS leadership team selected civility as its theme to build a common framework for team building and conflict resolution. This grew out of the request from ITS leadership team members to begin work on soft skills of the professional staff. The entire ITS staff participated in a two-day Thera Risings workshop called "Self-Defeating Habits

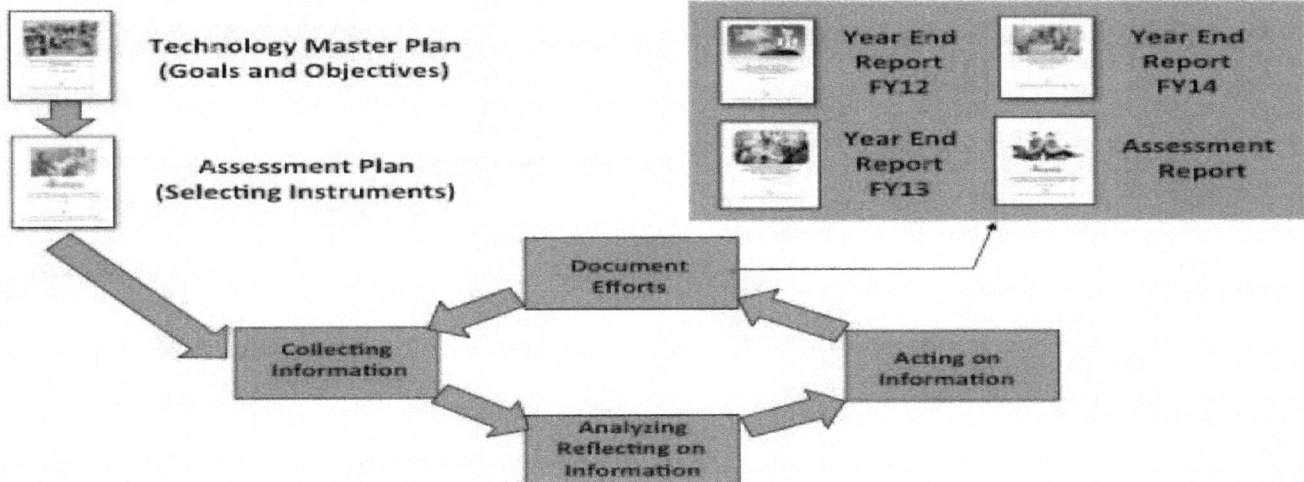

Figure 2. Assessment Process

of Otherwise Brilliant People". The group later spent half a day creating a Code of Conduct. A group of ITS volunteers pulled out common themes and found four areas of concentration for the code of conduct. Smaller groups detailed out each of four areas. A finalized version of the Code of Conduct was ready in early October and shared with the entire ITS staff. The next graphic is the finalized Code of Conduct for ITS (see Figure 4).

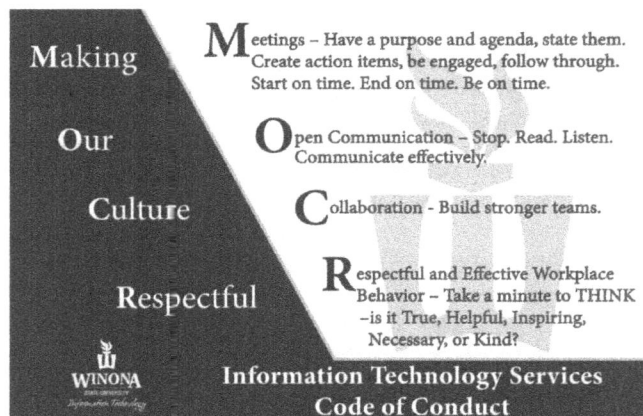

Figure 4. Winona State ITS Code of Conduct

Small groups of ITS staff then created a strategy and plan on how to communicate the new Code of Conduct with the entire ITS community. This work was completed in December of 2013. The spring of 2014 a presentation to unveil newly created ITS Code of Conduct was done to at an all ITS staff meeting. Several tools were used to communicate the new Code of Conduct to ITS staff including pens, posters, and handout to communicate key details of the code of conduct. Out of this process it was clear the ITS leadership team wanted the following year's theme to focus on internal/external communication.

8. FY15 Communications (Internal and External)

When developing the Code of Conduct, it became evident that we needed to take a more strategic look at our communication processes within ITS. In the fall of 2014, the ITS leadership team engaged a consulting firm to assist ITS in the development of a communications and marketing plan. After four months of work, the plan was delivered to us, and we are currently in the process of moving forward with implementing the strategies outlined in the plan.

The plan objectives were to enhance understanding of the ITS Department and the array of technologies and support available to enhance learning, improve morale within the ITS group as a whole, and increase effectiveness of internal and external communication. The strategies presented in the plan were based on qualitative and quantitative research examining current attitudes, beliefs, and behaviors. Surveys were given to internal IT staff and others within the WSU Community. ITS Leadership and staff were interviewed, and focus groups were formed to provide feedback.

The strategies and tactics for external audiences were as follows:

- **View and treat faculty, staff, and students as clients.**
  To do this, it was suggested that we change our language, including the name of our unit from User

Services to Client Services. The term client infers that we perceive them as customers and we are here to meet their needs.

- **Keep clients informed.** Once they create a work order or project request, we should develop communication to let them know we've received their request and an approximate time they can expect action.

- **Revamp the ITS website and other online resources.** Through the research done, it became evident that our clients had difficulty navigating the website. It was suggested that we create a project team to get this done, work with WSU Marketing and Communications to develop a new navigation system, and finally test with our clients as we develop the new site and make changes based on client feedback. The scope would include the external website, internal eHome page and Technology Knowledgebase Wiki.

- **Stick to email.** Although internal and external audiences acknowledge they get too much email, it still remains the preferred method by the majority of those responding to the survey or interviewed. It should not remain our only method of communication, as face-to-face and social media are preferred by some audiences.

- **Coordinate mass communications.** We should develop a template for all message sent, as well as a coordinated schedule. We should use uniform language, a consistent voice and terminology understood by a non-technical audience.

- **Communicate face-to-face with clients.** It was suggested we hold a client forum annually where we receive feedback from our clients, as well as inform them of technology enhancements for the upcoming year.

- **Work towards branding our technology support.** With AskWSU being the brand for student support services, it was suggested that IT follow that lead and create AskTech. We could start with creating an email account (AskTech@winona.edu) for clients to send technology requests. We can move towards creating AskTech FAQ for easy access to technology questions that can be rolled out with the revamped website.

- **Clarify email channels.** Create an email account that can be used to send mass messages, such as campus-wide technology notices. This email account should be used only to send and limited to only a few in ITS. Lastly this account should not allow clients to "reply to," and signature should include how to notify ITS if there are questions about the notice being sent.

The strategies and tactics internal to ITS were as follows:

- **Re-examine the definition of a project.** To ensure staff are on the same page and following consistent methods of documenting projects, we need to ensure we all follow the same definition.

- **Adapt and use same project management system throughout the department.** Establish and enforce protocols related to documentation of projects consistently throughout all units in ITS.

- **Re-examine protocols for handling all incoming requests.** Ensure that all work is classified as a project or a work order consistently and those that are not clear are discussed amongst the project team. It was suggested that we review the project team meetings and make changes to them to ensure we maximize communication about current and upcoming projects.

- **Establish a protocol for handling planned and unplanned outages.** Create a criteria to determine who should receive the communication and how. We should also designate a department representative to coordinate the communication, so that the technical folks dealing with the issue are not the same individuals expected to do the communication.
- **Share reports from leadership meetings.** It was suggested we have one individual take minutes that will be proofed by the leadership team. Once approved, they will be shared out with the department, so all receive same message.

The final part of the plan suggested that we hire a dedicated communications professional within ITS. This individual should have marketing and communication experience, report directly to the CIO, and participate in all high level meetings. This individual would be responsible for leading the effort to implement the majority of the initiatives listed above.

The leadership team has taken the communication plan seriously, and we have recently done some restructuring in ITS to help support the implementation of this plan. We have hired a communication professional on a part-time, temporary basis to help jump-start some of the initiatives above. She is currently working on developing an inventory of all the communication we do in ITS and how we deliver the communication plan with the goal of developing a mass communication strategy for ITS. This individual is highly experienced in the world of marketing and communication and the hope is she will provide guidance on how we should move forward permanently with this position when her temp position is over.

In addition, we have created a Project Management Office (PMO). We have tasked our lead developer to develop the PMO office for Winona State. This individual is PMO certified and can now focus on parts of the plan related to project management.

9. Conclusion

When you reflect on a journey you gain insights into the operation of an organization. The authors believe some themes have had more impact than others over the years but in many ways the ITS leadership team is continuing to build on a solid foundation. Each theme builds on work of a prior theme. The authors can say confidently, over time, this work is making a positive impact at Winona State University.

10. REFERENCES

[1] Honken, R. and Janz, K. 2011. Utilizing educational lean to enhance the information technology project intake process. In *Proceedings of the 39th annual ACM SIGUCCS conference on User services* (SIGUCCS '11). ACM, New York, NY, USA, 189-194. DOI=10.1145/2070364.2070413 http://doi.acm.org/10.1145/2070364.2070413

[2] Janz, K. and Feller, D. 2011. Leveraging both quantitative and qualitative data sources to improve IT help desk support services. In *Proceedings of the 39th annual ACM SIGUCCS conference on User services* (SIGUCCS '11). ACM, New York, NY, USA, 35-42. DOI=10.1145/2070364.2070375 http://doi.acm.org/10.1145/2070364.2070375

[3] Janz, K. and Graetz, K. 2009. Status of a digital life and learning program. *In Proceedings of the 37th annual ACM SIGUCCS fall conference: communication and collaboration* (SIGUCCS '09), ACM, New York, NY, USA, 33-40. DOI=10.1145/1629501.1629510 http://doi.acm.org/10.1145/1629501.1629510

Windows to Go:
Leveraging a Portable Operating System

Stephen G. Lewis
Lehigh University
EWFM Computing Center
8B East Packer Avenue
Bethlehem, PA 18015 USA
+1 610 758 3000
sgl3@lehigh.edu

ABSTRACT

Windows To Go (WTG) is an oft-overlooked feature first included with Windows 8 Enterprise Edition. WTG allows for the effortless creation of portable USB-based Windows 8 (and later) operating system instances.

WTG is not a stripped-down version of Windows; it is a full Windows operating system, indistinguishable from a conventional installation. Unlike traditional portable operating systems such as Windows PE, WTG offers a fully-functional yet persistent environment. WTG instances can be joined to an Active Directory domain, be managed using Group Policy, accommodate the installation of most software, and retain individual user profiles.

The use of WTG has value for both PC support technicians and end-users. WTG provides these capabilities, and more, with USB 3.0 support, UEFI boot compatibility, and BitLocker disk encryption.

This paper recounts the events that led up to Lehigh University embracing WTG, and also describes how WTG increases the efficiency and effectiveness of PC support technicians.

Categories and Subject Descriptors

C.5.3 [Computer System Implementation]: Microcomputers – *personal computers, portable devices.*

General Terms

Design, Management, Security, Standardization

Keywords

BitLocker, Bring Your Own Device (BYOD), Ghost, Imaging, USB, Universal Imaging Utility (UIU), WIM, Windows 8.1 Enterprise, Windows To Go

SIGUCCS'15, November 9-13, 2015, St. Petersburg, FL, USA
Copyright is held by the author. Publication rights licensed to ACM.
ACM 978-1-4503-3610-9/15/11 $15.00
DOI: http://dx.doi.org/10.1145/2815546.2815554

1. INTRODUCTION

1.1 Lehigh University Overview

Lehigh University is located in Bethlehem, Pennsylvania, USA and boasts an enrollment of over 5,000 undergraduates and 1,500 graduate students. Students are supported by nearly 500 faculty members and 1,100 staff. Both library and computer services are combined in one integrated organizational unit known as Library & Technology Services (LTS). LTS owns and maintains over 500 classroom and lab PCs while also supporting nearly 2,300 departmental PCs.

2. PC IMAGING & SERVICE AIDS

2.1 2004 and Earlier – Minimal Imaging Used

Through 2004, Lehigh University used two distinct methods for deploying new Windows PCs. Computer lab environments, consisting of homogenous hardware configurations, were imaged using Symantec Ghost from a single master image.

Conversely, faculty and staff PCs represent a heterogeneous hardware environment. These PCs consist of multiple models from multiple manufacturers. Using a single master image was not feasible due to different hardware abstraction layers, processor architectures, and other technical barriers. LTS also found it impractical to create a separate image for each type of faculty/staff PC. Instead, technicians would utilize the OEM-preinstalled operating system, install additional software titles from CD, and configure per customer requirements. This manual, hands-on approach often required several hours of technician time, especially in cases where the operating system required reinstallation due to virus infection or hard drive failure.

2.2 2005 – Universal Imaging Begins

In 2005, Lehigh University began using the Universal Imaging Utility (UIU), a product of Big Bang LLC, to create a single hardware-independent disk image. This allowed support personnel to deploy the same Symantec Ghost image to nearly any business-grade computer, regardless of model. The UIU product includes an extensive driver database and a collection of utilities that strip down the operating system files, hardware driver files, and registry settings of a computer to a very basic level. [1]

Many colleges and universities load PC images via their network. Circumstances made this approach impractical at Lehigh University. The universal image for faculty/staff computers includes a variety of commonly used software applications. The image size is approximately 30 GB which is a challenge to transfer via the local area network (LAN). The campus LAN was installed in the early 1990s. While the core and distribution network infrastructure has been kept up-to-date, antiquated wiring has limited many end-users to 10 Mb or 100 Mb connection speeds. As of September 2015, 51% of LAN connections run at speeds of 100Mb or less. The image transfer speed over 10/100 Mb Ethernet is 450 minutes and 45 minutes respectively. Such slow transfer speeds are not acceptable and LTS technicians instead use external USB storage to both backup local user data and load the universal image.

LTS has used a variety of USB storage devices since 2005. Technicians first used 40 GB Pocketec DataStor USB 2.0 drives, later followed by LaCie 100 GB Mobile Hard Drives equipped with USB 2.0 and FireWire 1394. Handling the drives on a daily basis caused some hardware failures. By 2009, LTS had upgraded to the LaCie Rugged portable USB drive. This model incorporated internal anti-shock rubber bumpers and a shock-resistant disk. The rugged USB drive indeed proved more reliable than its predecessors.

2.3 2010 – Heightened Data Security Concerns
As time went on, technicians became increasingly concerned about the security of client data stored on their USB hard drives. Many had chosen to use TrueCrypt encrypted containers on their USB drives for storing client data during PC transfers or re-imaging. In the event a USB drive was lost or stolen, the data was password-protected. Although the TrueCrypt solution was functional, it was not a guarantee of data security; it was still possible for a technician to accidently store client data in the non-encrypted portion of the drive.

In 2010, LTS replaced the fleet of technician USB hard drives with the 500 GB Apricorn Aegis Padlock Pro. This drive utilized 256-bit AES encryption and a built-in PIN keypad to provide hardware encryption. Such a design eliminated any possibility of data being stored in a non-encrypted format.

The Apricorn Aegis Padlock Pro USB drives performed well and were bootable on nearly all hardware platforms. LTS did experience a few drive failures from the constant travel and daily handling, but this was a small price to pay for the enhanced security and functionality.

2.4 2013 – Solid State Drives & USB 3.0
As solid state drives and USB 3.0 became prevalent, it seemed prudent to test new products that incorporated these features. Staff hoped to upgrade their secure USB drives with updated versions that performed faster and were less susceptible to damage from shock and vibration.

Beginning in 2013, a variety of hardware-encrypted SSD / USB 3.0 drives were evaluated. A thorough testing process was undertaken in order to choose the next generation of technician portable drives. The first drive tested was the Apricorn Aegis Padlock USB 3.0 SSD drive. Data throughput was speedy, but many computers were unable to reliably boot from this drive. Next tested was the Datalocker DL3 drive. The DL3 included a unique utility that allowed an ISO image to be mounted to a separate partition within the drive. Test computers could reliably boot from the DL3, but it was unsatisfactorily slow. The final drive tested was a Kingston-branded Windows To Go (WTG) drive. These drives, certified by Microsoft, provide a portable Windows 8.1 operating system. BitLocker full-volume encryption is also used to maintain high data security. Testing revealed that most modern (manufactured after 2010) PCs could boot from these drives without issue and they performed exceptionally well.

The Windows To Go drive was ultimately selected as the preferred replacement technician drive.

3. WINDOWS TO GO
3.1 Description & Overview
WTG is not a stripped-down version of Windows; it is a full Windows operating system indistinguishable from a conventional installation. Unlike traditional portable operating systems such as Windows PE, WTG offers a fully-functional and persistent environment. WTG instances can be joined to an Active Directory domain, be managed using Group Policy, accommodate the installation of most software, and retain individual user profiles. WTG can run on most PCs capable of booting from USB 2.0 or USB 3.0.

3.2 Applications of WTG for End-Users
At the Microsoft Build Developer Conference in 2011, Microsoft presented three common use-case scenarios that demonstrate the benefits for end-users using WTG: (1) An employee working from home on a personal PC can use a WTG drive that contains a corporate-managed Windows environment isolated from the employee's personal hard drive. (2) Individuals bringing their own device (BYOD) into an organization can use a common operating system image. (3) Employees using PCs that are shared by multiple people can maintain a consistent experience when roaming from PC to PC, even in the absence of network connectivity. [2]

Lehigh University has yet to supply end-users with WTG devices, but expects this would be useful for disaster recovery and business continuity purposes. LTS will soon reach out to the campus community in order to identify WTG pilot project opportunities. At present, LTS PC technicians are the primary users of WTG.

3.3 Applications of WTG for PC Technicians
WTG provides technicians with a powerful tool for servicing PCs. Traditional portable operating systems, such as Windows PE, are cumbersome to create, modify, and keep up-to-date. This is especially true considering that BIOS and UEFI system architectures require different Windows PE builds. Technicians need no special skills to manage and personalize their WTG environment. They can install additional programs, Microsoft Updates, and customize preferences just as they would in a conventional Windows environment.

The WTG environment allows for technicians to perform common tasks, including data backup/recovery, image loading or capture, virus scanning, and hardware testing. Technicians are also free to install their own preferred utility programs to aid in their duties.

Technician efficiency increases when using WTG. LTS technicians appreciate the network connectivity built into WTG, as it allows them to simultaneously service and image PCs while also responding to customer emails, updating work orders, and researching support issues.

Table 1. Some Utilities Included in the LTS WTG Image

Utility Name	Function
CPU-Z	Identifies CPU specifications and capabilities
DISM	Capture/deploy WIM disk images
FastCopy	Facilitates bulk copying files with integrity verification
Ghost	Capture/deploy GHO disk images
Kill Disk	Erases disk drives
Malwarebytes	Detects and removes malware
Notepad++	Feature-rich text file editor
SSH Secure Shell	Allows for secure transfer of data

3.4 Creating a WTG Environment

The procedure for creating a WTG environment is quite simple. First, install and configure Windows 8 or later on a master PC. Second, use Sysprep with an appropriate XML answer file and generalize the master PC. The configuration should include a mechanism to activate Windows upon deployment. This could be accomplished using Active Directory-Based Activation (ADBA) or via Key Management Service (KMS) specified using FirstLogonCommands in the answer file. Do not use Multiple Activation Keys (MAKs) as a key will be consumed every time the host PC hardware changes. Third, capture a WIM image of that PC using the Deployment Imaging Servicing & Management (DISM) tool. Finally, use the Windows To Go creation wizard to create individual WTG drives based on the WIM image.

3.5 Use of WTG-Certified Hardware

Microsoft has a certification program for WTG USB devices. Microsoft's graphical wizard to create WTG drives will only function with certified USB devices. Currently, Microsoft has certified devices from Kingston, Imation, Spyrus, Super Talent, and Western Digital. [3]

Microsoft uses the certification program to ensure hardware has the required performance characteristics to support WTG. The complete list of certification requirements is published in the Windows Hardware Certification Kit. Some of these requirements include being reported as a "Fixed Disk" as opposed to "Removable Drive", having high random read/write speeds, being durable enough to have at least a two-year manufacturer warranty, and capable of BIOS and UEFI boot on all hardware certified for Windows 7 and later.

3.6 Use of Non-Certified Hardware

Certified Windows To Go drives are quite costly compared to their non-certified counterparts. For example, a non-certified 64 GB SanDisk Extreme USB 3.0 drive can be purchased for less than $35 while a certified 64 GB Kingston DataTraveler Workspace USB 3.0 drive costs approximately $130.

USB devices that identify themselves as "Removable" via the Removable Media Bit in STORAGE DEVICE DESCRIPTOR cannot be used for Windows 8.1 To Go. According to the popular blog RMPrepUSB.com, one can manually create a Windows 8.0 WTG drive in this situation with the caveat that some Microsoft Updates will be unable to install. [4]

Since Microsoft's graphical WTG creation wizard will not function with non-certified drives, manual steps must be taken to prepare a non-certified USB drive for WTG. First, the drive must be formatted using the NTFS file system. Second, a Windows WIM image must be applied to the drive using DISM. Third, BCDboot must be used to create a Boot Configuration Data (BCD) store on the drive so that it becomes bootable. Finally, optional BitLocker encryption is enabled.

There are several disadvantages to using a non-certified USB drive. Not all drives are fully compatible with WTG. Lehigh University tested several non-certified USB drives and experienced various degrees of dysfunctionality. For example, some non-certified drives failed to properly boot WTG, yet others booted successfully, despite the fact that each drive was created using the same procedure.

The most significant difference between certified and non-certified drives is their performance. Typical USB drives are designed with the goal of fast sequential reads/writes. This correlates to the typical use-case of copying large files to/from the drive. Random read/write performance is most important for WTG. Few USB drive users elect to run an operating system from their drive, thus making random read/write performance a low manufacturer design priority for ordinary USB drives. Performance test data highlights this divergence.

Table 2. Speed Test Results of Various Devices (Tested with AS SSD Benchmark Utility)

USB 3.0 Drive Name	Avg. Rand. R/W Speed	Avg. Seq. R/W Speed
Super Talent Express RC4 (certified)	R: 19 MB/s W: 24 MB/s	R: 278 MB/s W: 191 MB/s
Kingston DataTraveler Workspace (certified)	R: 14 MB/s W: 25 MB/s	R: 230 MB/s W: 113 MB/s
Imation IronKey Workspace W300 (certified)	R: 8 MB/s W: 8 MB/s	R: 360 MB/s W: 219 MB/s
SanDisk Extreme (non-certified)	R: 8 MB/s W: 4 MB/s	R: 250 MB/s W: 52 MB/s

3.7 Complications & Disadvantages

The most obvious disadvantage of WTG is the cost of Microsoft-certified hardware. Those unfamiliar with WTG and its hardware demands may find it difficult to accept the fact that appropriate USB storage devices are often more than triple the cost of their non-certified counterparts. Proper education of users, technicians, and management is required in order to address this issue and communicate the value of high-performance hardware.

Lehigh University's experience reveals that WTG devices are extremely sensitive to unsafe and/or surprise removal. For instance, removing a WTG drive while a computer is running and then attempting to boot it on a different PC will often corrupt the WTG drive, requiring reimaging; this is the equivalent of unplugging the internal hard drive of a running PC. To help mitigate this practice, WTG includes a safety feature where, upon removal of the drive while a PC is still running WTG, the operating system pauses all activity and warns the user against doing so again. The PC will power off if the drive is not reinserted within 60 seconds.

Similarly, WTG drives do not react well to surprise removal when they are mounted in other operating systems. A technician may elect to use his WTG drive to backup data from a user's PC. The technician risks corrupting the WTG drive unless he remembers to use the "Safely Remove Hardware and Eject Media" feature. The WTG image used by Lehigh University includes reminder warning messages on the desktop wallpaper emphasizing these sensitivities and encouraging careful use.

4. TRANSITION TO WIM IMAGING
Lehigh University has been using Symantec Ghost for over 10 years to image PCs. Shortly after support technicians began using WTG, LTS also transitioned from Symantec Ghost to the Windows Imaging Format (WIM).

4.1 Sector vs. File-Based Imaging
Ghost is a sector-based imaging tool that can clone an entire physical disk, including boot configuration data. The WIM file format is a file-based imaging tool. WIM images do not contain information about partition tables or boot data; WIM images contain file data only. WIM deployment typically leverages two other Microsoft tools: Diskpart and BCDboot. Diskpart is used to create and manage hard disk partitions. BCDboot is used to create boot files on a system partition.

4.2 Universal Imaging Utility (UIU) Still Used
Before transitioning to WIM imaging, LTS used UIU (version 4) to transform a base PC image into a hardware-independent image. UIU accomplished this by using innovative code and copying a large driver database into the base image. The process is different in the WIM environment; instead of putting all drivers into the base image, the UIU (version ≥5) now runs at deployment time. A hardware scan of the system is run which allows UIU to identify

system components. UIU then obtains the identified drivers, from either a network share or locally-hosted repository, and stages them on the target PC for enumeration by the OS. This new approach increases efficiency as adding and updating drivers no longer requires modification of the base image.

Lehigh University's investment in UIU continues to be very worthwhile, especially considering the diverse hardware LTS must support. Using UIU relieves Lehigh University from having to locate, test, organize, and package device drivers. UIU support personnel also provide valuable technical assistance with any imaging-related issues, sometimes even beyond the scope of support they are required to offer.

5. CONCLUSION
Windows To Go has proven itself to be a useful tool for increasing PC technician productivity.

6. ACKNOWLEDGEMENTS
The author acknowledges and thanks the following individuals for their contributions concerning Windows To Go at Lehigh University: Bruce A. Eisenhard, Keith B. Erekson, and Timothy J. Foley of Lehigh University; Gene Ashley of Learning Tree International; and Adam Murphy & Jason Stewart of Big Bang LLC.

7. REFERENCES
[1] Brazille, Jeremy C., and Adam C. Murphy. Universal Imaging Utility Program. Adam C. Murphy, assignee. Patent 7512833. 9 May 2005.

[2] Silverberg, Steve. "Running Windows from an External USB Drive with Windows To Go." YouTube. Proc. of Microsoft Build Developer Conference, Anaheim Convention Center, Anaheim, California, USA. Google, 9 Oct. 2012. Web. 11 Apr. 2015. <http://www.youtube.com/watch?v=IYZaw38EGOw>.

[3] "Windows To Go: Feature Overview." Microsoft TechNet, 30 June 2014. Web. 17 Apr. 2015. <https://technet.microsoft.com/en-us/library/hh831833.aspx>.

[4] "Windows 8/8.1 To Go (boot Windows 8 from a USB Drive!)." RMPrepUSB.com. N.p., n.d. Web. 8 May 2015. <http://www.rmprepusb.com/tutorials/win8togo>.

Working in Higher Ed IT: Should I Stay or Should I Go?

Karen McRitchie
Student
402 P Street
South Amana, IA 52334
1 (319) 660-0605
karen.mcritchie@gmail.com

ABSTRACT

Work culture has changed over the past 50 years. In the 1960s, men went to work, women stayed home or had gender-specific jobs like secretaries and teachers until they had children of their own. The cliché, gold watch, was known as a retirement gift for those men who had served the same business until retirement. Managers were trained to find holes in a person's work history and stay away from those jumping from job to job every few years.

Today's work culture has had a paradigm shift as younger generations have different values and ideas about their work culture. Employees of today have different expectations for their time spent working, and they stay in a job as long as they are providing something of value and learning. Once they have mastered the skills and knowledge from a job, they move on to another job that will teach them new skills and knowledge.

A higher education job with an information technology services (ITS) team can be very challenging and very rewarding, but how long does an employee stay? What are the signs that they need to try something new or different? As employees, we put an emotional investment into our jobs, and the thoughts of leaving a job usually bring fear. If the time has come when employees are not engaging in their work, then it may be time to be brave, tune up the resume, and take a different road—amazing things could happen!

Categories and Subject Descriptors

K.6.1 [Management of Computing and Information Systems]: Project and People Management – *Staffing*.

General Terms

Management, Performance.

Keywords

Career plan, employment,

1. INTRODUCTION

In 1981, the English punk rock group, the Clash recorded a song that had these lyrics:

SIGUCCS'15, November 09-13, 2015, St. Petersburg, FL, USA
© 2015 ACM. ISBN 978-1-4503-3610-9/15/11…$15.00
DOI: http://dx.doi.org/10.1145/2815546.2815564

"If you say that you are mine
I'll be here 'til the end of time
So you got to let me know
Should I stay or should I go?" [3]

Whether to stay or to go is a dilemma in all relationships, especially at work. Many people have an emotional attachment to their work and their employer—but should the emotions create a relationship that lasts "'til the end of time." There are signs that it is time to change careers or employers. There are signs that your employer is going to make the change for you. Regardless of whose decision it is to go, there are some tasks that should be completed to make the transition a positive experience.

2. THE GOLD WATCH

The tradition of giving gold watches at retirement originated back to the 1940s and The PepsiCo Company. "The concept of 'you gave us your time, now we are giving you ours,' made sense when people stayed with a company for three or four decades"[4]. Parents and grandparents often worked at the same business until they were old enough to retire. There was a bond and often a pension that connected the two.

The 21st-century employee is much different in the way they see this employer-employee connection. Remaining at the same job and retiring from it, are no longer expectations.

3. PARADIGM SHIFT

The Generation X and Millennial employees have different expectations than the baby boomer and older generations. They have seen parents and grandparents work entire lives at the same job, sometimes losing their retirement benefits because their company files bankruptcy. Where the values and expectations of the older generations were to be able to provide for their families and have that house with the white picket fence, today's employees value their lives outside of work, their global contributions, and lifelong learning. They are taking responsibility for their retirement plans and may only remain at a job for 3-5 years before moving on to a new challenge or learning experience. In the past, potential employers would find a person who had moved from job to job, an unsatisfactory hire. Today an employee may be questioned as to why they stayed more than five years at the same job.

4. THE BREAK-UP

There are several reasons why a relationship needs to end. It is much better to have some control over the break-up, especially being able to find a new job. However, sometimes, the break-up can be a surprise and wreak havoc. I experienced the havoc-wreaking type.

In 2013, I lost my mom, my job, and turned 50 all within six months. (The last was not so bad, but it makes a better story.) So…

Once upon a liberal arts college, a consultant was hired to come in and break the information technology services department. Of course, that was not the initial intention, but sadly, the outcome. He didn't understand higher education and especially, the college's culture. The VP said to the IT staff, "No one will lose their jobs." The first to go was the Director. The consultant took on the role of the Director as well as the consultant. Over the next few months, there were three different organizational models proposed. Team members were assigned new roles, often without their knowledge. The helpdesk was closed, as the consultant wanted the support staff to handle all customer service, and he did not support having students working in the department. It became a department of fear and bullying rather than of teams and support.

By the third rendition of the organizational chart, I was demoted out of the senior staff meetings, which were held every Wednesday for 3 hours. After one meeting, which was supposed to be secretive, I found out that there was a plan to reorganize some staff right out of their jobs. I suspected that I would be one of them.

Finally, a "mandatory" meeting was scheduled on a Monday at 4pm for the department. "No one was excused" it stated in the Outlook meeting invitation. Then I received a second meeting request at 2pm with the consultant. It had a blank agenda and a generic title, so I accepted and it went into my Outlook calendar. Next, being an astute technical person, I did a free/busy search on the rest of the department staff. There were three others with a meeting like mine: 2:30, 3:00, and 3:30pm. That is when I knew. I confided in the others that I thought we were all losing our jobs Monday. At least we had the weekend to clean out our offices and have some time to get emotions under control.

I dressed up very nice on Monday for my firing. They attempted to say what an excellent employee I had been for 15 years, and I interrupted with, "Let's just get on with it." The absurdity of the situation was growing. The human resources director even asked if I wanted a going away party, "as many on campus would like to be able to say goodbye." I looked at her and said, "I am being fired, not the best time for a party."

There are other less dramatic reasons to look for a new position. You could be looking for an opportunity to be more involved in management, but your current employer has a flat organization with few opportunities to advance. It could be that you find one part of your position that greatly excites and energizes you has been reorganized out of your position description.

There are also opportunities that come with your growing experience. The types of positions that are available as you begin your career expands greatly once you have five years experience in higher education IT. It makes sense that one would reassess the opportunities available after working for some years and gaining valuable knowledge about other positions in IT. One could transition from a help desk position to an instructional design position, for example.

5. HINDSIGHT

EVERY experience is a learning opportunity. Sometimes a person does not see it at the time, but later, can reflect on the learning experience. If I had followed the signs, and left my job sooner, I could have avoided the physical and mental health issues of working in a toxic environment. .

5.1 Staying Even When It Gets Bad

Employees remain in a toxic environment for financial and emotional reasons. They often make decisions based on fear—fear of leaving, fear of going somewhere worse, fear of change. I think that even if our comfort zone is toxic, it still feels safer than to face an unknown environment.

When working in higher education, we become part of the campus community. We establish friendships with others who work for the college. We contribute to the success of the students, and it feels good. It is usually much more than a job to punch in and out. Our work is a significant part of our identity and to lose that identity is stressful.

The audacity of hope is another reason that some stay in a job. At first the consultant brought us hope for positive change—who would not want that to happen? There is hope that things will get better next week, next month when the new budget is available, or this or that—always some hope that we cling to as humans usually do. Employees often spend much time hoping things will improve.

5.2 Stress

A person's job situation is often a catalyst for their stress, and often the degree of the stress is not comprehended until that catalyst is removed. Weekly migraines, sleep issues, depression, and some physical health symptoms were all my effects of stress. After the shock of losing a job passed, I started to recognize that I had not had a migraine yet this week, then it went to a month, then six months. I started sleeping better and not waking up so much during the night. I stopped having feelings of nausea before I went to work—since I was not going to work. It was unbelievable how much the stress had been killing me emotionally and physically. We do not realize how difficult it is to go to a job where you have a daily fear of being fired or to dread attending a meeting because people get publicly berated. At one point, we had to account for every minute of time worked because there was no trust. Employees can get so caught up in the stress that we become blind to its effects. I kept noticing my team not wanting to participate in things or even share ideas like we used to do at meetings. Then it is gone. There is an immediate change. The next morning, I felt fantastic.

5.3 Disengagement

According to Gallup's 2013 State of the American Workplace report, 70% of US workers are either "not engaged" or "actively disengaged" at work. The projected cost in lost productivity is estimated to be as much as $550 billion annually. [1] A disengaged employee is an unfulfilled employee. This is someone going through the routine every day and doing what is expected, but not enjoying the work and gaining any intrinsic value from their efforts. We know when we disengage from our work. The exact time and date may not be decipherable, but one-day thoughts about other opportunities start becoming more common and maybe it is harder to get out of bed and get to work. A person may vent more to their partner or colleagues. I disengaged around 2008—that is when I should have found another job. I did not have the courage at the time and kept hoping things would improve. I did put more effort into my student staff program, which was highly successful and gave me that feeling of doing something of value. Too many employees stay in a job that is unfulfilling or stressful—if the work is no longer providing a reward, then it may be time to start looking for something new.

5.4 Being "released" was not a bad thing

Most people were devastated when I was "released." At the time, I was the only one on campus providing accommodations for our students with disabilities, and they released me one week before final exams. There was much backlash from various students and faculty that made me feel good. I was lucky as I received some severance pay and didn't need to get another job right away, so I took the summer off.

Since I have worked in higher education, people have always assumed that I have the summers off, and for once, I did. I did nothing all summer except be with my dogs, sit out on the deck and watch birds at the feeders, cry a little, and work on my e-portfolio. It was a much-needed reprieve from the stress. Even in spite of being ok with losing my job, it was very scary because, since the age of 15, I have always had a job. Who knows how long I might have stayed if they had not fired me? The department only worsened after I left, and since then, my entire team has quit. If not for being "released" I would have had to suffer through more months of the chaos and stress.

There are also several signs that your employer may be considering your "release", according to an article by Gwen Morgan for Fast Company. She states a change in the interactions with the boss, goals not being met, increase in colleague's workloads, having to train someone, request for an accounting of time worked, and a change in leadership. [5] Looking back, I had a change in boss interactions, accounting of time, and change in leadership—all signs of an impending breakup.

5.5 Opportunities exist

For the open minded, there are other employers and other jobs available and open to the skills and knowledge base of a higher education IT professional. If you aspire to another position or another job, then being proactive and working toward that next transition is the reasonable response.

6. ANALYZE YOUR GOALS

Whether you have a job or are released from your job, it is time to figure out some goals. One of Steven Covey's seven habits is: *begin with the end in mind.* [2] Get out some index cards or sticky notes and write down things that describe the job you want including skills needed. It is very helpful to take a look at job advertisements on www.highered.com or www.herc.com to see what things interest you. If you see a job that seems interesting, use the requirements to help you make your notes. There may be many things that you have not thought of or encountered in your current job.

Maybe what you do now is ok and you just need to do it in a more supportive environment. Not everyone wants to move up the ladder, some are happy with their current job or may seek a lateral move. If staying in your position is your preference, determine if there is an opportunity to work on other projects or in another area.

Find a large table or use a blank wall to sort your notes. Look at each one and determine if this is 1) necessary 2) somewhat important, or 3) could live without it. Group the cards in rows or piles—do whatever works! Other things to consider:

- Would I relocate for a new job? If so, how far?

- Would I take a change in pay for a new job? If so, how much? Would I accept other benefits with lower pay?

- Do I have finances to cover a transition to a new job? If not, would I be able to plan for this change?

When you are looking at your cards, mark any that need additional skills or knowledge so you know some of the things you may need to learn or experience to move to a different position. For example, if you want to move to management, what are some things you might be able to do in your present position to gain some management experience? Are you able to work with a mentor? Do you need to participate in workshops or take some classes?

As you move things around on the table and the wall, you will start to see patterns, and you will decide that some of the notes are not that important and can be left out. You should end up with some ideas for where you want to go with your career.

Twenty years ago, I loved managing my desktop support team, working with faculty on technology projects, and project managing new software roll-outs or building projects. After years of working with our students with disabilities, I found that to be uplifting and energizing. I loved helping faculty create a classroom or course that is more accessible. It felt wonderful to help students succeed—I no longer felt that same intrinsic reward for managing a new IT project. I knew that I needed to do work that seemed valuable and rewarding, and I love technology. I wanted to continue to work with assistive technology and that brought me to a decision to work with students with disabilities and technology as a full-time job.

7. NEEDS ASSESSMENT

When you start putting the job ideas together and determine where you want to go with your career, you will need to assess the skills and experience that you need to achieve that new role. Do you need more education? Do you need training? Do you need a mentor? Write it down as these will become part of your plan.

It is also important to talk to some objective colleagues and friends about your plans. Ask them to tell you what types of skills or experience that they feel will help advance your goals. Use last year's performance review for guidance if appropriate. You may feel like you can manage a team, yet maybe don't realize a communication difficulty—trusted friends and colleagues would honestly provide feedback.

In my case, I had an excellent background in management, technology, and many other related areas, but what I was lacking was a formal study in special education. Therefore, I had to go back to school. Not everyone will need additional education to move forward and maybe only need to do some reading—it is important to make this assessment and apply for those jobs for which you qualify.

8. THE PLAN

At some point, reality does set in, and you have to face the facts and get moving. Every day I did something that related to my job search, even if it was just a phone call or sending an email. This is the time to create the career plan—it is a beginning.

The first thing to do is analyze your goals and figure out those things that have meaning. List all of your skills and accomplishments—which makes you happiest? Figure out what type of job would be engaging and bring out creativity and innovation. Then decide if you need any other skills or education to work in this job.

Analyze the finances and figure out what is necessary to live on during this time? If you are not working, apply for unemployment benefits and start researching jobs on higher education websites.

Since I needed some special education background, I decided to go back to school full time. I researched the top 20 online programs and ended up at the University of Wisconsin.

9. CAREER PLANNING

Whether you have planned a career change or it finds you unexpectedly, there are some important things to accomplish.

9.1 An ePortfolio

People always recommend having an up-to-date resume, but when you are in a job that is satisfactory, it is not a task that is high on the priority list. I also wanted to create a web presence so before compiling the necessary information for a resume; I created an ePortfolio using Google Sites.

Google sites is simply a template site for creating a website. There are many companies out there who provide this service and tools to create the site. I like Google because it connects to my Gmail, Google Calendar and also doesn't have advertising. Some of the other free sites are free because they throw their own or other third party advertising in with your site.

This was a big project. It took me about a month of full-time work to get this site together. It is worth the effort! Not only does it function as an online comprehensive resume, but it also serves as a complete reference to my work history and accomplishments. Creating this site forced me to look up dates that I attended seminars, pull together samples of my work and even serve as a record of projects.

I used a journal to start recording all of the items I could remember, separating items by categories. For example, I have management data, leadership data, and project management data. There was volunteer experience such as serving on the Board of Directors for Girl Scouts of Greater Iowa and my work for SIGUCCS. I led the technology portion of the science building renovation/addition on campus. I have attended Educause training programs. These were all important pieces of my dossier. As I compiled information for my site, I found things I had not remembered, so I tried to include everything pertinent to my career history and future.

Do not forget to make sure to utilize design concepts and rules, or use a template, so that your site is easy to navigate and is pleasant to visit. My site includes many photographs. In the section about setting up a helpdesk and student staff, I include pictures of the helpdesk and students. I have photos of the science building renovation and computer labs. If a person wants to know about a particular item in my resume, all they need to do is go to the site and click on the details.

Another important part of creating this site is to include samples of work. I have a section for all of the SIGUCCS papers that I have published/presented with links to the documents. I have samples of all of my graphic design and technical writing projects—maybe even just a page to show the design and content. The idea is to have the content available in case you want to reference it. It also becomes a nice repository for personal use. For example, if I want a copy of an article I had published, I can go there for the link.

Once the initial site is set up, and most of the content organized, it is easy to maintain. For every project or accomplishment, it is easy to add to the site. I keep a running list on my iPad of things I want to include so that I can always have the site up-to-date.

9.2 The Resume

I use my ePortfolio site to create my resume. From it, I pull the info that I feel is most important for the resume and my resume also has the link to the full portfolio also. I believe that this not only shows that I am organized and proficient at my job, but also that I have the technical ability to create a well-designed website.

Those of us who have been through the resume reading process know that not much of a resume is read in the initial phase of hiring. Usually just 2/3 of the first page. I create a resume for the particular job I am applying, modifying the key highlights to go with the job, then the regular stuff like work experience and education is on the back page.

A link to my site is also on first page—I am trying to impress. When the cover letter is written, make sure you look carefully at the job advertisement and connect with their key points. If your resume is being automatically reviewed, the algorithms look for keywords to forward your resume on for review.

9.3 Talk to People Who Have Your Job

Find people who work in the field or specifically, in the position that you are trying to find. They can give you advice on those things that are necessary for the job that you want. There may be an additional certification or other things to know/do that will be helpful.

Find out what organizations are recommended for the field and join them if you have the resources. Utilize their websites, professional development, and conferences to make contacts and learn more about the field.

9.4 References

Determine whom you want to have for references and contact them about performing this service. In my case, I created a list of six references, each one being able to provide a unique perspective of my work. For example, I want to work with students who have disabilities in higher education, my references are:

- o My previous supervisor in accessibility
- o A student with a disability whom I worked with for four years while they attended courses
- o A parent of a student that I had worked with during their daughter's tenure at the college
- o A faculty member whom I worked on disability/accessibility issues as well as universal design for the classroom
- o An IT colleague
- o An upper administrator in Academic advising whom I worked with assisting students with accommodations.

My idea was to give a prospective employer a choice of perspectives from which they could select those they were most interested.

9.5 Utilize a Dropbox service

Set up a cloud service like Dropbox to store all of your job search information and resume contents and create a folder for each prospective employer. As you make modifications to your resume and cover letter, store them in the corresponding folder for later reference. In this folder, include a PDF of the initial advertisement and if you get an interview, any research for that employer.

10. CONCLUSION

I cannot tell you if my plan has worked as I will not officially be looking for a job until I have completed my courses. I have applied for two positions this past year and received the response "we had so many applicants…blah, blah, blah" which is disheartening. As much as my experience being "released" turned out to be a positive one, it is difficult not having a job. I spend most of my time on homework, and I miss the daily contact with students and colleagues—not the work or the employer. I am excellent at what I do, and I hope to get the opportunity to let someone know. I think it will be easier once I am in the position to move to another state, and I cannot do that until school is over.

As devastating as it was to lose a job, I have learned so many things. I have learned not only about changing careers, but also about setting limits at work so that a toxic environment is never again the cause of so much stress and depression. Hindsight allows us to look back and see the signs that were shouting that it was time to go—next time I will pay attention.

Where ever you plan to go next, planning ahead will help you land in that next meaningful position you envisioned for yourself.

11. REFERENCES

[1] Celestine, Marques. "Which Is the Real Problem: Employee Disengagement Or the Way We View It?" The Huffington Post. TheHuffingtonPost.com, 11 Sept. 2011. Web. 22 May 2015. <http://www.huffingtonpost.com/marques-celestine/which-is-the-real-problem_1_b_3908007.html>.

[2] Covey, S. R. (1986). Seven habits of highly effective people. Provo, UT: Steven R. Covey & Associates.

[3] Jones, Mick. Should I Stay or Should I Go? The Clash. The Clash, 1981. CD

[4] Laura, Robert. "Saying Goodbye to Retirement Traditions." Forbes. Forbes Magazine, 26 Jan. 2013. Web. 11 May 2015. <http://www.forbes.com/sites/robertlaura/2013/01/26/saying-goodbye-to-retirement-traditions/>.

[5] Moran, G. (2015, June 04). Signs You Might Be About To Be Fired (And What You Can Do About It). Retrieved from http://www.fastcompany.com/3046980/know-it-all/signs-you-might-be-about-to-be-fired-and-you-can-do-about-it.

How We Deliver Our Desktop Support Services to Washington University in St. Louis the ITIL Way

Josh Lawrence
Washington University in St. Louis
One Brookings Drive
St. Louis, MO 63130
(314) 935-5000
jlawrence@wustl.edu

ABSTRACT

The Solutions Center service desk at Washington University in St. Louis provides desktop and server application support for the administrative departments and two schools. As part of a Shared Services initiative, we are rebalancing the IT resources across the university. This will provide opportunities to leverage existing areas of innovation. In particular, our team has undergone ITIL-based organization and service design strategy efforts.

This paper will review how we use ITIL's Service Design framework to strategically structure our desktop computer service. I will describe how the processes, people, partners, and products combine to create a highly functioning support desk that provides call center and desk side support to over 2500 staff, faculty, and students across campus

Categories and Subject Descriptors

C.5.3 [**Computer System Implementation**]: Personal computers

General Terms

Management; Measurement; Theory

Keywords

Desktop Support; Desk Side Support; ITIL; Service Delivery; Service Desk.

1. INTRODUCTION

1.1 Washington University in St. Louis

Washington University in St. Louis is a medium-sized, world leading university in teaching, research, patient care, and service to society. The student body is made up of 12,202 undergraduates and 14,163 graduate and professional students. We receive over $550 million in research funding each year. There are 3,376 instructional faculty. Of those, there are 1,256 full-time faculty at the School of Medicine representing more than 75 specialties providing clinical care to more than 430,000 adults and children at 49 clinical sites through Washington University Physicians, one of the five largest academic clinical practices in the nation, in fiscal year 2013 [3].

SIGUCCS'15, November 9–13, 2015, Seattle, Washington, USA.
© 2015 ACM. ISBN 978-1-4503-3610-9/15/11...$15.00.
DOI: http://dx.doi.org/10.1145/2815546.2815567

1.2 ITIL©

In our environment, we target a ratio of one technician to 150 customers. With over 2,200 customers, we use ITIL organizational structure, processes, and metrics to provide great service to those customers. Using the ITIL framework, our approach can be represented by the processes, products, people and partners that we use to deliver our service [1].

1. **People**: Staff with an understanding of their role in the organization, staff rotations, training, coaching, customers

2. **Processes**: Client profile sheets, onboarding, scheduled hardware refresh, software licensing purchase and renewal, desktop engineering, operating and application lifecycle management, security, dynamic call center, inventory, and checklists

3. **Products** (tools): Ticketing system, transactional surveys, remote desktop tools, asset database, desktop automation, deployment tools, profile capture/load, , knowledge base

4. **Partners**: Customers, hardware and software vendors, internal application development teams, external staffing companies, other university help desks

The organizational structure and the implementation of ITIL-based methodologies including Service Design, Service Transition, and Service Delivery has given us the ability to provide a robust, customer-focused service that can scale up and down to increase capacity and execute additional projects. This paper describes the ITIL process relating to delivery. This is how we deliver our Desktop Support service.

2. DELIVERING DESKTOP SUPPORT SERVICES

2.1 Organizational Structure

Desktop support services are delivered using the following teams: Solutions Center, Personal Computer Support Services (PCSS – Field Technicians), Senior Engineering, and Account Management.

In order to provide high quality desktop support services, we use the following resources:

2.2 Solutions Center Service Desk

The Solutions Center Service Desk is composed of five full time staff and five to seven students. Customers initiate an incident ticket via a phone call, email or submitting a ticket using the web site. Most customers use the phone method because this is the quickest, most responsive way to engage our service. We target no more than a 5% abandon rate. This means customers' calls will be answered on the first call 95% of the time. Depending on call volume, the Solutions Center will conduct level 1 to level 2 diagnostics. They will work to assess the priority of the issue (emergency, high, medium and low), the severity and complexity of the problem. They will work for up to 20 minutes to resolve the issue, longer if call volume is low and the customer is willing; however, they are mindful of the customer's time, and so they may continue to work, but will not keep the customer on the phone. If they cannot resolve the issue, they will escalate the ticket to the level 2 Field Technicians for further troubleshooting. If it is an emergency or high priority ticket, they will contact the Field Technician directly. In this case, the Field Technician will respond within 20 minutes. This translates to a total of no more than 40 minutes or less for a Desktop Technician to be at your desk in the case of an emergency or high priority issue.

The Solutions Center answers 1,600 calls and creates 1,200 tickets per month. They resolve 85% of the issues at the Solutions Center and escalate 15% to the Field Technicians. 95% of all calls are answered on the customer's first attempt and the customer waits no more than 12 seconds in the queue before the call is answered.

2.3 Field Technicians or Desk Side Support

The Field Technicians team is made up of one supervisor, eight full time technicians, and several students. They are responsible for level 2 support and 15% of their time is allotted for project work. The Field Technicians are strategically assigned to a specific group of departments or school. We group departments by technology, role, or geography to help ensure collaboration points are well understood. For example, the same technicians support Parking and Transportation and the Police Department because they often share the same systems and frequently collaborate.

The Field Technicians are responsible for 15% of ticket volume, with the Solutions Center closing 85% of issues at the Solutions Center. They keep all tickets updated, with frequent communications to the customer. No tickets go more than three days without an update. Field Technicians focus on departmental unique applications, level 2 issues that can't be resolved at the Solutions Center, and issues that require a desk side visit. Additionally, they conduct computer deployments, which includes hardware refreshes and re-images resulting from virus infections or related issues.

Field Technicians are held accountable to enabling the Solutions Center to close 85% of tickets, so they are motivated to provide the information needed to close tickets that are unique to their departments. The primary ways Field Technicians make unique knowledge available is through the Client Profile Sheet, ticket resolution and problem identification.

The Client Profile Sheet is a template that is maintained by the Field Technician assigned to each department or school. This is basically a "cheat sheet" for the department. It includes department-specific information that would enable any desktop technician to support most issues in the department. The Client Profile Sheet includes, but is not limited to, the following key data points:

- Contact information, departmental acronyms

- File share locations

- Printer information (IP address, common problems, locations, primary uses)

- Domain architecture, including unique group policies and the justifications for the policies as appropriate

- Administrative passwords

- Statement of their IT needs and business critical applications

- Most common problems and most problematic users

- VIP users

- Quick tips for the department

The Client Profile Sheet is kept updated by the Field Technicians. They are highly motivated to keep the information current and accurate so that as many tickets as possible can be closed by the Solutions Center.

The other mechanism that drives closing 85% of the ticket at the Solutions Center is adding resolutions to tickets. Field Technicians are required to document the resolution to the ticket when it is closed. This gives the Solutions Center staff an opportunity to search, find, and apply a fix before it ever gets to the Field Technician. Over time, the ticketing system becomes a searchable repository of resolutions that is searchable by anyone working tickets.

In addition to closing tickets and being responsible for their resolution, the Field Technicians are responsible for server application support, vendor management (issue escalation and resolution), computer imaging and deployments.

2.4 Senior Engineering

The Senior Engineering team is composed of two engineers and one engineering supervisor. They are responsible for level 3 support, new technology testing and integration, application lifecycle sunrise/sunset, desktop automation, application packaging, and application server upgrades. In addition, they spend up to 20% of their time resolving level 3 issues. The level 1 and level 2 technicians are responsible for identifying "problem" tickets. If an issue happens multiple times, it becomes a problem. Problem tickets are assigned to the level 3 staff for resolution as needed.

This team manages new technology integration. Projects that they have been working on this year include: desktop encryption, power management, upgrades to anti-virus software, remote access, imaging, and the capture/load tool.

This team leads the efforts to manage application and operating system lifecycles. They track the release dates of new products and schedule evaluation and testing to determine the timeline for when products should be implemented. Based on these timelines, we develop plans to upgrade or transition to the new products.

Desktop automation and application packaging is developed and executed by this team. This effort reduces the work needed to be done by the level 1 and level 2 technicians by enabling packages to be deployed across the entire population.

2.5 Account Management

The fourth component of our organization is account management. The account management team is composed of six managers and directors from various teams. They are responsible for building relationships with liaisons from each department and school. They meet with their liaison periodically to review these top three things:

1. Quality of Service – how are we doing?
   a. Is the staff friendly when they answer?
   b. Are issues being escalated when needed?
   c. Are issues being followed up appropriately?
   d. Is our follow-up timely?
2. Projects – projects that are coming or are underway, system changes or upgrades.
3. Hardware orders – provide recommendations for equipment refresh, timing of the deployment schedule.

The deployment schedule is an annual calendar that was put in place to address the problem that occurs when many departments order their equipment at the same time, and the team not having the capacity to deploy at that volume. The Account Managers met with each department to negotiate a time in the calendar year that worked best for their deployments. The various departments have different times of the year that they are busy or slow, so we were able to configure a calendar in which the work is spread across the calendar smoothly. This took several meetings, and a year of going through the cycle to establish this pattern, but it has resulted in understanding, compliance and consistent and expeditious deployments.

The Account Manager's role is to ensure customer satisfaction by acting as the customer's advocate for all IT services. We focus on Desktop Support, but the project component of the conversation includes working with other IT organizations to ensure projects are progressing appropriately. This has been an effective role because the Account Managers have more insight into the IT organization and ability to engage them more so than our customers.

3. STRATEGIES EMPLOYED TO MEET OUR METRICS

We use a dynamic call center approach, student workers, staff rotations, and staff supplementation to meet the demands of our customers during periods of high activity and requests for projects that are beyond our capacity.

3.1 Dynamic Call Center Strategy

Depending on call volume, the Solutions Center will adjust their response approach to efficiently address high volume times and make better use of low volume times. During exceptionally busy times, they will move to "triage mode." In this mode, they assign the majority of technicians to answer the phones and limit the call duration to no more than five minutes. They are to quickly assess the priority of the issue, and if it is an emergency or high priority, they will assign it to the designated long call technician, who will immediately work on the ticket. If it is not an emergency or high priority, they will spend no more than five minutes assessing the problem and either schedule it for resolution during an anticipated downtime, such as a Wednesday or Thursday afternoon, or will route the ticket to the appropriate support team.

During normal call volumes times, they will conduct level 1 and level 2 diagnostics as appropriate, but will spend no more than 20 minutes on the line with the customer. If it cannot be resolved in 20 minutes or requires a desk side visit, the ticket is routed to the Field Technician for additional diagnostics and resolution.

During low call volume times, they will extend their call duration as appropriate to conduct level 2 diagnostics, but will avoid keeping the customer on the phone. In addition, we use low call volume times, which are highly predictable, to do projects and other work. Projects and tasks from this year include:

- Implement a loaner laptop program
- Conduct process maintenance (on-boarding/off-boarding, computer ordering, response to email requests, deployment checklists, asset entry)
- Develop a student worker program
- Conduct new technology training for Service Center staff (Windows 10, Office 365, Box, OneDrive, and new mobile devices)

This dynamic strategy enables us to react to changing needs and to meet our metrics. It also allows us to use downtime to complete tasks, work on projects, or conduct online training.

3.2 Staff Rotations

The Solutions Center and Field Technician staff are rotated regularly in order to ensure knowledge transfer takes place, to develop and maintain strong bench depth, and to be able to have resources that can be assigned to any department as needed. They have the same skillsets (desktop support experience, customer service, good oral and written communications, professional appearance and demeanor.) This enables us to move them between the different roles for the following benefits:

1. Gain familiarity with the other role's challenges and opportunities:

   Field Technicians get an understanding of what it feels like to answer the phones and why a ticket may be escalated quickly.

   Service Desk staff get an opportunity to be in the field, working face-to-face with customers.
2. Gain exposure to departments and customers with whom they don't typically interact.
3. Build redundancy in our team. This enables us to provide coverage for when people are on vacation, in training, or out sick.

3.3 Student Workers

The Solutions Center manages students to provide additional resources that can be used to supplement the teams where needed. We recruit students with an interest in IT. The students go through an individualized training program that exposes them to each aspect of the organization for two weeks at a time. A manager then interviews them after each engagement to determine where they have the best fit and where their interests lie. This has the following benefits:

1. It gives them insight into to each part of the organization, which gives them the opportunity to see how each part of the team works to contribute to the whole.
2. It gives them the opportunity to discover what they like and what matches to their career goals and interests.

3. It gives us the opportunity to get feedback from them about their experiences, which helps us guide them to the teams and work that can benefit both of us the most.

After the orientation period, the students are placed on the team that fits their interests yet also fills a need on the team. The goal is to provide a meaningful experience that contributes to their professional development. We start by focusing them in one area in order to build expertise, but we also rotate them between teams as needed to address business needs.

Currently, students close 11% of the tickets from the Solutions Center. We have had days where they close as many as 25% of the tickets.

3.4 Supplemental Staffing

We frequently employ external contractors to provide supplemental staffing during periods of turnover or projects.

We maintain partnerships with several contracting companies in our area to ensure they understand our business culture and needs in order to quickly provide consultants as needed. We occasionally have a need to quickly hire consultants to fill in during staff transitions, long term illness or to provide supplementary staff for projects. We also use consultants to backfill for positions to allow full time staff to work on projects. The duration of their contract can be from 30 days to one year or more.

The value this brings is that we have several options when the need arises, and these consulting companies can quickly provide staff that are a good fit for our organization. They have fast turnaround when we request a resource. And if the consultant is a great fit, we have the option to hire them on as full time staff.

This is particularly helpful during times of transition because we can hire staff to supplement existing staff in order to maintain service levels. This also gives us an opportunity to observe their productivity and fit before considering them for permanent positions.

4. AREAS FOR IMPROVEMENT

We have identified several areas that we can develop as we move forward. The areas in which we see opportunities are:

- Knowledge base and knowledge transfer
- Asset management
- Customer Communications
- Test labs for testing changes to the desktop
- Reporting analytics

4.1 Knowledge Base and Knowledge Transfer

It is widely known that any Service Desk can benefit from a knowledge base to ensure quicker incident and problem resolution, knowledge retention, and improved processes. Our teams generally experience high turnover resulting from career advancement within the university and opportunities in corporate environments. This requires significant knowledge transfer in order to minimize the time it takes someone to get up to speed and be effective. We currently use staff shadowing and Client Profile Sheets for knowledge transfer. A good knowledge base that has the following features would dramatically improve our ability to rotate staff and to handle transitions:

1. Include information that enables a technician to quickly get an understanding of the technical and political layout of a department, including: specifying the unique tools, configurations, common issues, answers to common requests for that department, and identifying the key VIPs and problem customers, or "canaries."

2. Accessible from any mobile device, including phones and tablets.

3. Easy to create new articles, update and comment

4. Organized with well-formatted templates

5. Easy to search with obvious keywords

6. Roles and responsibilities well-defined: assign senior staff to regularly approve articles and perform scheduled periodic maintenance

In addition, a knowledge base should accommodate different audiences:

1. Internal (technical staff)
   a. Ticket resolutions for common issues
   b. One-off issues and their solutions
   c. Departmental and organizational configuration and issue resolutions

2. External (customers)
   a. Customer-facing FAQs
   b. Self-help documents
   c. How to request services (new hires, request for hardware or software)

A good knowledge base that includes all of these components and is frequently maintained with effective, periodic reviews would enable us to bring new staff, contractors, and students up to speed quickly. In addition, it would facilitate faster incident and problem resolution, knowledge retention and improved processes.

4.1.1 Knowledge Base Design

Knowledge base design should follow social media's successful model, which is to rely on the community's contributions. The entire organization should be allowed to contribute. You can build credibility in the knowledge base by attributing articles to their authors and enable users to rank and comment. These rankings are indicators of trust. As users learn to trust authors, the knowledge base becomes more useful. This builds trust into the system because users learn to trust authors of articles that have helped them. Allowing users to comment gives opportunities to improve articles. Articles with the most comments and highest rankings should populate a leaderboard. The most used and commented articles should float to the top. This enables a dynamic knowledge base that thrives on contributions from all users [3].

4.2 Customer Communications

Our customer communications consist of email, meetings and daily interactions. We email important communications, such as service outages, system updates, changes, and planned maintenance; however, email communications are often overlooked, unread, or misunderstood. We need to consider social media technology and use multiple approaches to communications. Newsletters, websites, Twitter and instant messaging are all opportunities to reach and interact with our customers, but spending resources developing and maintaining these can be costly and difficult to justify. Without convincing justification supported by metrics, and without resources, good planning and leadership support, efforts to build beyond an experiment often fail.

4.3 Ticket Analytics

We currently use data for measuring performance, history, workloads, and work allocation, but we do not partner with customers to use analytics to measure success.

Ticket analytics are currently employed for reporting purposes to track workload and performance. Using our ticket system and call center data, we track the following metrics:

- Monitor and track the number of open, updated, and closed tickets across date spans and current state.

- Compare ticket counts and call volume between workers to track performance.

- Watch for tickets that are not updated to ensure tickets are resolved or updates provided to the customers.

- Identify how time is used across different types of requests; e.g., email, software or hardware and how time is spent across different groups and departments.

- Track the volume of tickets across the following categories: how-to, break/fix, provisioning.

We are not partnering with customers to determine what metrics meet their business needs. Partnering with customers and agreeing on the response times, number of calls, amount of desk side visits, and the number of after-hours calls is essential to avoid a misunderstanding of the costs and an inability to meet unarticulated expectations. Setting expectations and agreeing to them beforehand gives customers the opportunity to understand what they can expect to get from what they are spending.

We create reports and analyze the data for our consumption, but we have not taken the extra step to share that data with our customers in order to openly discuss and set expectations.

5. REFERENCES

[1] Ballmer, R., Scarborough, M., Lora, K., & Baer, B. (2008). Basic Concepts of Service Design. ITIL Foundation. Cary, North Carolina: Global Knowledge Training LLC.

[2] Fitzgerald, Mark P. 2014. Making Sense Out of Information Chaos. In *Proceedings of the 42nd annual ACM SIGUCCS conference on User services* (SIGUCCS '14). ACM, New York, NY, USA, 33-36. DOI=10.1145/2661172.2661173 http://doi.acm.org/10.1145/2661172.2661173.

[3] Washington University in St. Louis. About WUSTL University Facts. Washington University in St. Louis. Washington University in St. Louis, 1 May 2015. Web. 01 May 2015.

Using FAQs to Help Users Help Themselves

John Fritz
University of Maryland, Baltimore County (UMBC)
1000 Hilltop Circle
Baltimore, MD 21250 USA
+1 410-455-6596
fritz@umbc.edu

Andrea Mocko
University of Maryland, Baltimore County (UMBC)
1000 Hilltop Circle
Baltimore, MD 21250 USA
+1 410-455-3234
andrea.mocko@umbc.edu

ABSTRACT

Four years ago, UMBC's "tier 1" Technology Support Center [1] (formerly Help Desk) moved from the obscure basement of our main Division of Information Technology (DoIT) building to the bright, open first floor of our new Information Commons in the Library. Since then, the TSC has virtually reinvented itself by also focusing on helping users help themselves. We completely revamped our campus knowledgebase [2] that has grown from 3k annual page views to more than 400k. As a result, support phone calls have been reduced 30% and ticket volume has decreased 3% (since FY10) or remained flat while all other campus support requests have skyrocketed through widespread adoption [3] of our RT (Request Tracker) ticketing system.

Guided by an excellent orientation manual with a novel, but simple ticket-grading rubric [4] encouraging support staff to recommend relevant FAQ articles as an acceptable *initial* resolution to user support requests, student consultants now resolve half of all the TSC's tickets each week; previously they were not allowed to do so for fear they would make mistakes. With just two FT staff and 12-15 student consultants resolving 8k of DoIT's overall 25k tickets annually, the TSC has become a model of efficiency and effectiveness. Overall, DoIT enjoys a 90% "excellent" customer satisfaction rating on an optional survey every customer receives following a resolved ticket.

Categories and Subject Descriptors

K.4.3 [**Computers and Society**]: Organizational Impacts – *Computer-supported collaborative work*

K 6.1 [**Management of Computing and Information Systems**]: Project and People Management – *Strategic information systems planning*

General Terms

Documentation.

Keywords

Knowledgebase, Support.

1. INTRODUCTION

Located on 500 acres 8 miles south of Baltimore and 34 miles north of Washington DC, the University of Maryland, Baltimore County (UMBC) is a mid-sized, public research university with 13,979 students (11,379 undergraduate, 2,600 graduate), 769 faculty and 1,248 staff as of Fall 2013 [5]. UMBC is one of the 11 campuses comprising the University System of Maryland, and the Carnegie Foundation ranks UMBC as a "Research University – High Activity" institution, with $71.2M in FY13 research expenditures [6]. In addition, UMBC's Division of Information Technology (DoIT) consists of 75 full-time staff (30+ who are alums) and 105 part-time students [7] that, if converted to full-time equivalent (FTE) status, would account for just over 40 additional FT staff (115 total), assuming all students work an average of 15 hours per week.

2. PROBLEM

Each year, DoIT resolves about 25k support requests or "tickets" through our Request Tracker (RT) ticketing system. This now represents about a quarter of the campus's overall RT ticket volume as shown in Figure 1, notable in its own right, as few campuses have any enterprise ticketing system to track all support service requests, let alone multiple offices and domains that use it.

While UMBC's overall adoption of RT has helped standardize service tracking across campus, what does it mean to manage 25k requests for IT help each year (217 average per 1 DoIT FTE staff member)?

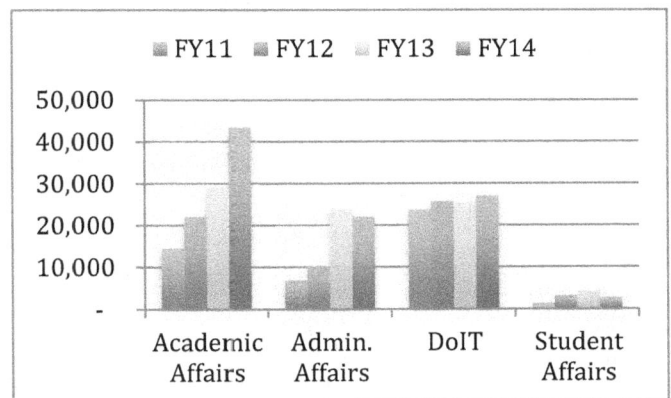

Figure 1. Resolved RT Tickets by Division

A very simplistic exploration of the data provides context. If DoIT's 115 FTE staff members, including 40 FTE students, resolved one ticket per day, there would be no problem. However, consider the following annual trends:

- 48% of all RT tickets are resolved in 12 hours or less;
- Half of the rest are resolved in 2 weeks or less;
- Only 35 DoIT FTE staff resolve more than 200 tickets, only nine (9) resolve more than 500;
- Four years ago, student consultants at our Technology Support Center (TSC) were not allowed to do so for fear they would make a mistake.

At the same time, campus use of the IT knowledgebase was virtually non-existent at 3k page views a year, or little more than 8 per day, which is nothing for a campus with 15k students, faculty and staff. No matter how you slice it, DoIT was simply reaching the limit of its capacity to resolve more customer services requests. Something had to give. Options included hiring more staff (unlikely), getting more production from existing staff (challenging), or reducing user IT support demand (unprecedented).

3. SOLUTION

In 2011, the TSC (formerly Help Desk) that handles all "tier 1" basic IT support moved from the obscure basement of our main DoIT building to the bright, open first floor of our new Information Commons in the Library. Given its proximity and newfound visibility, we knew the role and culture of the TSC needed to change from a mostly remote, but on-campus, call center to a proactive destination for end user support. Since then, the TSC has virtually reinvented itself by also focusing expertly on helping users help themselves.

3.1 Three Key Changes

Specifically, we 1) completely revamped the campus knowledgebase, 2) changed the incentive model for how TSC student consultants used it, and 3) empowered student consultants to do so as an acceptable *initial* resolution to RT tickets that users could always re-open if we were wrong.

3.1.1 Creating FAQs That Show AND Tell

As part of the TSC's 2011 move to the Library, it also changed from reporting to DoIT's Enterprise Infrastructure Support group and began reporting to the Office of Instructional Technology. Among other things, instructional technology staff members were accustomed to promoting and supporting "screencasting," which is typically a short (5 minutes or less), narrated and recorded video capture of any steps, processes or tasks one should be able to complete using a computer. Some may liken screencasting to "lecture capture," which grew in popularity due to "flipped classroom" instructional models. Typically, flipped classroom lectures are moved online to prepare students for working on "homework" problems or projects in class. Khan Academy (http://www.khanacademy.org) is one of the best examples of this kind of short, focused screencasting that often is used precisely in a flipped classroom model.

Starting with Frequently Asked Questions (FAQs) [2] generated from RT tickets and phone calls about our Blackboard Learning Management System (LMS), DoIT staff began creating and publishing online FAQs that mimicked the experience of peeking over the shoulder of an expert, which was not unlike how we consulted with faculty who came into our office for help or when we visited theirs. Examples include:

- How do I export or import my old Blackboard course into a new one?

- How do I make my Blackboard class available?
- Why can't I see my Blackboard class?

The "Show AND Tell" FAQ approach grew, as did the variety of technology topics, which were ideally suited to this form of knowledge sharing.

3.1.2 Tying FAQ Use into Ticket Grading Rubric

Another aspect of instructional technology that began to influence the TSC was the best practice of using grading rubrics, which are nothing more than a way of telling students (in advance) how certain types of effort will be rewarded. In the case of the TSC, we developed a ticket-grading rubric [4] that placed a higher value (and "A" grade) on using the FAQs as an acceptable *initial* resolution to a user's RT ticket requesting help. If our resolution was wrong, users could always re-open a ticket or even give us feedback, after the fact, in our optional satisfaction survey.

However, the key to the rubric's success is that it explicitly reminds our TSC staff to implicitly remind users of where they can likely find an answer on their own, *before* submitting an RT ticket to request help. Exemplary individual effort and customer service is still expected and rewarded with a "B" grade, but if the TSC consultant doesn't refer the user to an FAQ–or recommend the creation of one if it doesn't exist already–then the ticket can only be judged on the merits of the individual resolving it. Remember, given our FTE staff-to-ticket ratio described above, individual capacity alone is challenging to scale. We needed a way to reduce user demand by steering those who were willing to a model that helps them help themselves.

After the ticket-grading rubric was implemented, it was calibrated in a DoIT managers meeting by asking each person to "grade" 3-4 resolved tickets using the rubric. Admittedly, there was some vigorous discussion in the early rounds, but eventually the rubric helped define a consensus standard of effective practice, given user demands and our mostly student-run support desk.

In addition, the exercise essentially gets repeated each week when the TSC coordinator reviews and grades all TSC-resolved tickets for that week (typically about 100-125 per week). This "report card" summary is shared with all TSC student consultants and DoIT managers. Student consultants are also asked to grade themselves upon resolving a ticket, which helps the TSC coordinator: if there is a wide discrepancy between student staff and management, it can lead to a productive coaching session to calibrate an individual consultant's support "radar," but still frees them up to try again. At various times, we've also asked senior student consultants to complete the weekly ticket review, which fine tunes their own radar and ability to provide constructive feedback to peers. No matter who does the weekly ticket review, it typically takes less than an hour to complete.

Finally, for the past few years, we have also completed an annual review of all user support metrics for both the campus and DoIT, to keep an eye on trends. An example is available for FY14 [8]. It can be challenging to pull all of this information together, but it has also helped us monitor and refine important issues such as the ever present and time-consuming bane of all help desks: user password management.

3.1.3 Training and Empowering Student Consultants

Armed with a repeatable methodology for creating effective FAQs, and an incentive model to do so, the TSC has developed an excellent orientation manual and "open door" vs. "sink or swim" supervision style that trains and empowers students with an expectation they will be effective. The current TSC coordinator, a

4-year student consultant veteran who rose through the ranks before being hired full time three years ago, recruits and trains students with a focus on complementing our "self-service" support model.

Having a primarily student-run office leads to a high degree of turnover as students graduate. As a result, we've adjusted our recruitment and training of student employees to focus not on acquiring a deep understanding of our wide array of services but rather on providing them with tools such as the FAQs to troubleshoot and find solutions. With the FAQs, student employees have access to resources and knowledge that might have taken years to learn on their own. Consequently, our recruitment focuses on students who bring an effective communication style. We can teach or equip them with the rest, particularly now that we have a "just in time" knowledgebase supporting both TSC student consultants and users alike.

4. RESULTS

Since we started keeping track in 2011, the FAQs typically generate more than 400k page views annually (see Figure 2). Admittedly, a lot of this traffic comes from the open web, as UMBC users do not have to be logged in to access the FAQ knowledgebase. However, since many UMBC users are in fact logged in, we are often able to track direct referrals from our campus portal, LMS, and other applications that require authentication.

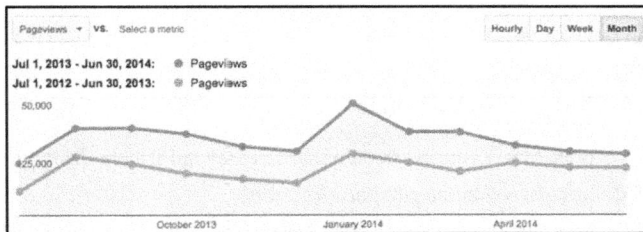

Figure 2. UMBC FAQ Page Views by Fiscal Year

In addition, TSC support phone calls have been reduced 30% as shown in Figure 3, and ticket volume has decreased 3% (since FY10) or remained relatively flat while all other campus support requests have skyrocketed through widespread adoption [3] of our RT ticketing system.

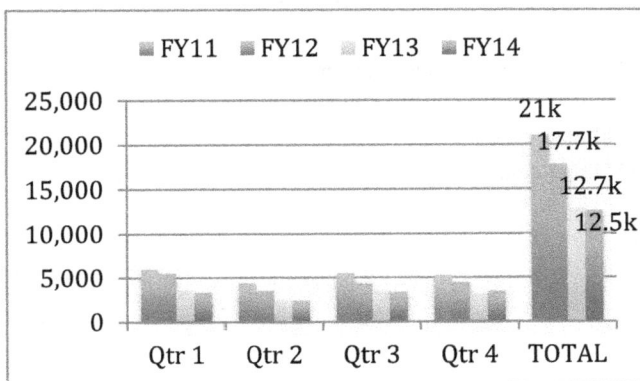

Figure 3. TSC Phone Calls by Fiscal Year

Perhaps more importantly, with just two FT staff and 12-15 student consultants resolving 8k of DoIT's overall 25k tickets annually, the TSC has become a model of efficiency and effectiveness. Overall, DoIT enjoys a 90% "excellent" customer satisfaction rating on an optional survey every customer receives following a resolved ticket.

5. DISCUSSION

Despite the apparent success of UMBC's FAQs, there are still some key challenges to growing adoption, including 1) persuading stakeholders to buy into a central knowledgebase repository, 2) scaling our use of the Confluence wiki, and 3) satisfying the ego of user support stars.

5.1 Buy In

Like very artistically- or technically-minded faculty who prefer to design custom course websites instead of accept the utility of an LMS in their course delivery, many campus departments and support staff still maintain a desire to present a unique documentation experience for their users. Often, this is seen in the myriad ways departments maintain their campus websites. Some have a dedicated webmaster; more often, others throw the responsibility at incoming students. When these well-meaning, but sometimes inexperienced students graduate, they often take their department's site design, information architecture or (worse) server password access with them. As a result, site redesigns are often triggered less by user needs, and more by turnover in student staff.

The same is often true of providing support documentation. If you want to get the word out about a particular business process or service, you have to bring users into your departmental site. Sometimes this impulse comes from a notion of marketing or branding that defines "success" as distinguishing oneself from competitors, and perhaps even peers working at the same institution. Though understandable, the end user is often the forgotten soul who suffers through varying approaches to site design, navigation and usability, just to find answers to frequent questions that support staff probably already know intuitively and answer daily. Until a critical mass of departments buys into a central knowledgebase, the rising tide of adoption cannot lift all users up to a common interface and experience.

5.2 Form vs. Function

Just as staffing support drove DoIT to look at alternative ways to help users help themselves, our FAQ knowledgebase needs to be able to scale, if and as more non-IT departments use it. We would be hard-pressed to give up the "Show AND Tell" approach that has worked so well for most FAQ articles, but sometimes we have had to work around our Confluence wiki platform that runs the FAQs, instead of the other way around. The most frequent objection we hear about the FAQs is that "they aren't pretty." However, few wikis are, since their primary purpose is functional vs. aesthetic, by providing a website anyone can edit while retaining a history of changes if we need to roll back to a previous version.

Admittedly, when we adopted a wiki for the FAQs, we even imagined a Wikipedia kind of experience that would allow the campus community to edit the pages it cared about most, and improve accuracy by directing "many eyeballs" to them. However, the community-editing nature of the FAQs has not played out as we expected, raising a valid question of how long we stay committed to the wiki's potential editing benefit vs. the perceived cost of a less than pleasing aesthetic. We've adopted various third-party plugins to improve the look and feel, only to find they didn't always migrate well when we needed to upgrade the core Confluence code base.

Interestingly, we discovered Atlassian's own recommendation for "Using Confluence as a Knowledge Base" [9] after we'd already started to do so, and then concluded our FAQs did a decent job of implementing their suggested best practices.

Despite some growing pains and things we wish Confluence might do (or even look like), we've yet to find a compelling, effective and efficient alternative that wouldn't require a much deeper financial investment. While it's hard to argue with the results to date, we need to ask if the current wiki platform has impacted our ability to grow wider adoption.

5.3 Ego
Let's face it, there's something gratifying about being perceived as someone who is in the know. Whether it's walking users through the account creation process or solving a problem for a VIP, support staff members who are knowledgeable, empathetic, efficient and effective derive satisfaction from a job well done. They should be highly valued.

However, the scaling question is a relentless taskmaster when it comes to knowledge management, particularly if we depend on the heroic measures of a few. As one might imagine, the variety, volume and sheer repetition of basic IT support can lead to burnout and high turnover. Even some of our DoIT managers who worked their way up through the former Help Desk were skeptical that most users would want to help themselves, let alone whether they could. Again, it's hard to argue with the data that suggests otherwise.

The key is persuading IT support superstars that curating and incorporating a centralized approach to knowledge management can pay off for them. By encouraging a self-service vs. concierge model, support staffers are more likely to get requests from knowledgeable users who are truly stumped and can't proceed without direct intervention from a technical expert. These may not be frequently asked questions or problems, per se, but they are likely to be more difficult, and thus more satisfying to the IT expert who thrives on a challenge.

Admittedly, our FAQs have not yet seen the dramatic growth in campus-wide adoption that typified UMBC's RT ticketing system implementation. However, as other campus groups approach or, in some cases, even eclipse DoIT's 25k annual resolved ticket rate, we predict they, too, will face similar dilemmas about capacity and staffing-to-ticket ratios.

6. NEXT STEPS
Recently, we have begun to experiment with FAQ workshops for non-IT groups who wish to get started. We also maintain a set of FAQs about FAQs [10] that includes templates for knowledgebase

articles and collections of related FAQs as well as how to add the "Show Me" screencasts that people like. Basically, anything involving a computer screen is a good candidate for a "Show AND Tell" article. It's a different way of thinking about "documentation."

Also, in recent years, following a popular presentation at the 2012 EDUCAUSE Conference [11], we've had collegial consults with peers at 3 to 4 other institutions, including the University of Wisconsin, Madison, which runs one of the most popular and ambitious campus knowledge bases in higher education [12]. By no means is UW going to replace its highly respected and frequently used KB with our Confluence wiki. However, like them, we were intrigued by the idea of eliminating the duplication of content and generic knowledge that likely proliferates in most campus IT organizations. This complements our own thinking of how and why departments should get out of the custom documentation business. If so, then how might the same hold true for campuses sharing a central knowledgebase?

Finally, UMBC has long been committed to data-driven decision-making [13], so we would like to sharpen our analysis of the relationship between RT, FAQs and phone support. It may be challenging to do so without investing in a more integrated solution, but as we have done before, we enjoy using innovation to face a challenge.

7. LINKS & REFERENCES
[1]   http://doit.umbc.edu/tsc/

[2]   http://www.umbc.edu/faq

[3]   Kirby, J. and Lefavor, L. 2013. Beyond the IT Help Desk. *EDUCAUSE Review Online*, http://www.educause.edu/ero/article/beyond-it-help-desk

[4]   http://www.umbc.edu/go/ticketrubric

[5]   http://about.umbc.edu/umbc-facts/

[6]   http://research.umbc.edu/fast-facts/

[7]   http://doit.umbc.edu/about/metrics/2014-retreat-poster/

[8]   https://docs.google.com/presentation/d/17ZskLPFBEHaqW66zMd9OQF_4cCyuSwucaQGujgvRNNU/edit?usp=sharing

[9]   https://confluence.atlassian.com/display/CONF57/Using+Confluence+as+a+Knowledge+Base

[10] https://wiki.umbc.edu/x/8gbcAQ

[11] http://www.educause.edu/annual-conference/2012/how-good-faqs-can-change-culture-it-support-inside-and-out

[12] https://kb.wisc.edu

[13] http://doit.umbc.edu/analytics

Deploying and Managing State-of-the-Art Workstation Labs Like a Boss!

Muhammed Naazer Ashraf
Lehigh University
19 Memorial Drive West
Dept. of Mechanical Engineering
Bethlehem, PA 18015, USA
+1 610.758.4093
naazer@lehigh.edu

ABSTRACT

Our PACE Computer-Aided Design (CAD) / Manufacturing (CAM) / Engineering (CAE) Lab is one of our flagship computer labs at Lehigh University. The Lab is uniquely supported by both the Mechanical Engineering & Mechanics (MEM) Department and the IT organization. It is also unique in that we make available pools of virtual workstations to supplement the 60 physical high-end Windows workstations that are critical to our teaching and research missions.

In addition to the PACE Lab, we also have to deploy and support 25 other lab and research environments, each having their own unique software and requirements. The entire university has been using Symantec Ghost for image management for nearly 15 years, but we needed a more flexible and automated solution to create, deploy, and manage Windows Operating Systems. You will learn why we decided to focus our efforts on the completely free Microsoft Deployment Toolkit Lite Touch solution, and how it has increased the efficiency of our deployments.

We are currently expanding these techniques and realizing their time-saving benefits even in our datacenter and support of IT infrastructure. We have also been successful in deploying the Windows 10 Technical Preview in a test lab and are keenly awaiting the final release of the updated deployment tools that will officially support the new Microsoft Operating System.

You will walk away with real-world best-practice workflows that you can immediately implement in your own environment to realize some of the benefits that we have already seen.

Categories and Subject Descriptors

C.5.3 [**Computer System Implementation**]: Microcomputers – *personal computers, portable devices, workstations.*

General Terms

Design, Management, Documentation, Performance, Reliability, Experimentation, Security, Standardization.

Keywords

Automation, BIOS, Deployment, Enterprise, Imaging, Lab, Lite Touch, Monitoring, MDT, Microsoft Deployment Toolkit, PowerShell, UEFI, Windows Deployment Services, Windows PE, Windows Server, Workstation

1. INTRODUCTION

1.1 Lehigh University Overview

Lehigh University is a private research institution founded in 1865 and located in Bethlehem, Pennsylvania, USA. It boasts 600 faculty members, 1,100 support staff, and an enrollment of over 5,000 undergraduates and 1,500 graduate students. Library and computer services are combined in one integrated organizational unit known as Library & Technology Services (LTS). LTS owns and maintains over 500 classroom and lab PCs while also supporting nearly 2,300 departmental PCs.

1.2 PACE Lab Overview

The PACE lab was conceived after Lehigh University received the largest corporate contribution in the University's history, valued at $31 million from the Partners for the Advancement of Collaborative Engineering Education (PACE) in 2005. It was decided that we would try to make available some of the best possible workstations from Dell or HP to our faculty, staff, and students in this Lab. We have a great relationship with both these vendors and find that their superior support and technologies are well worth the extra capital investment to procure these workstations.

Up until 2014, the typical life-cycle of the workstations was three years in the lab. They were then rolled down to the other labs in our Mechanical Engineering & Mechanics department. Starting from 2014, we decided to try extending the life-cycle of the PACE lab to four years, for the simple reason that these workstation have lasted so much longer than we had originally planned. We still have students who are happily running their research on 9-year-old workstation hardware with modest upgrades and able to keep pace with even current generation business-class desktops. We have also fitted consumer-grade solid-state drives in these older workstations to significantly boost their performance. Lehigh University has received our return on investment on these workstations several times over and the decision to continue buying some of the best-available hardware has been easily justified to our stakeholders.

Here is a subset of the applications that are optimized to run on the PACE Lab workstations. We have several other applications that are used in our teaching and research, but priority has been made for running these applications. For instance, if new software is requested that causes conflicts with any of these applications, it may have to be installed in a different lab.

1. ABAQUS
2. Altair HyperWorks
3. ANSYS
4. Autodesk Simulation CFD
5. Autodesk Simulation Mechanical
6. Autodesk Simulation Moldflow
7. Labview
8. Maple
9. Mathematica
10. MATLAB
11. Siemens NX
12. Solidworks
13. Vericut

The current specifications of one of our PACE Lab workstations are as follows:

1. HP Z420 Workstation
2. 16GB ECC 1866Mhz RAM
3. 256GB PCI Express Turbo-Z SSD
4. NVIDIA K2000 Graphics Card
5. 24" UltraSharp Professional Display
6. SpaceNavigator 3D Mouse
7. 5-Year Warranty

2. WHY DO WE NEED A WORKSTATION?
2.1 What Is a Workstation?

A workstation is not just a regular personal computer (PC). It is especially designed to power through high-workload technical or scientific applications, and deliver greater performance compared to mainstream PCs. Dell, HP, and Lenovo workstations are Independent Software Vendor (ISV)-certified and provide features and benefits that simply cannot be matched by conventional PC platforms that enable greater productivity for a disproportionately low cost price. They typically deliver the following three key benefits:

a) Performance – Access to the latest Intel processors, professional graphics cards, and exclusive software technology that further tweaks configurations for critical applications.

b) Reliability – ISV certification provides clear-cut assurance that a specific combination of hardware and software meets key performance and reliability metrics. Rigorous hardware and software testing further ensures problem-free operation. Workstations are built with enterprise-class components including Intel Xeon processors that used to be reserved for servers, and ECC (Error-correcting code) memory.

c) Superior Design – The chassis design provides easy access to individual components. Workstations also feature tool-less entry, which greatly simplifies upgrades and user serviceability.

2.2 Who Needs a Workstation?

Not everyone will require a workstation, but true workstations are purpose-built to create the best possible user experience for a given set of high-level professional applications. If your computing tasks include more advanced applications, architectural modeling, design simulations or complex, detailed analysis, a workstation will be highly advantageous to your productivity and workflow. The performance of the workstation starts with the processor. All workstations will feature the latest Intel Xeon processors, which are designed to deliver the processing and bandwidth power that elite users require. They support professional-grade graphics, expansive memory, and multiple hard drives. The result is a high-performance machine that is faster, is highly scalable, and can quickly deliver results on complex processes, which translate into substantially greater return on your software investments. Dependability is key in any fast-paced professional environment. ISV certification ensures that critical applications will run productively, as well. It is important to find the right tool for the right job.

2.3 Justifying a Workstation

The guidelines for purchasing a computer are no different from those used for purchasing any other capital asset. In the end, the success of any business purchase can be measured by the return it delivers to that business compared to the investment required, also known as the return on investment (ROI).

Workstations are purpose-built to optimize both sides of the ROI equation–maximizing return in the form of higher productivity while effectively minimizing total cost of ownership (TCO) by providing features that standard PCs cannot deliver.

It is also important to note that entry-level workstations are now more comparable to standard desktops and laptops.

Another hidden cost that should be taken into account is what your time is worth. When you add greater reliability, less downtime, and easier maintenance, workstations in professional computing environments are increasingly delivering lower TCO than PCs.

3. ARCHITECTING A PLAN

Efficiencies can be created not just by using new and better tools, but also critically looking at existing workflows to see if there is any room for optimization. For instance, if a technician or student needs to take a USB flash drive to each computer in a lab of 50 computers in order to image them, that process is a prime candidate for an automation and optimization project.

There is a wealth of knowledge in the deployment community and everyone operates by an unspoken code – Steal with Pride. It is just a recently coined metaphor that has been making its rounds online for not reinventing the wheel. We should not be wasting time developing solutions that are already available for free and be taking advantage of other work that has already been done.

What we hope to accomplish in this paper and subsequent presentation is to highlight everything that has worked for us and provide a good starting point for anyone looking at using MDT 2013 Lite Touch for deployments. We have been researching, fine-tuning, and sharing these workflows and techniques with other departments and the community for almost two years. Engaging the online community through social media has honestly been the single most valuable experience in our deployment journey.

We started this project by asking our Client Services Managers and Directors what they thought would be ideal in a deployment solution, which we started using as a preliminary requirements list:

1. Perform bare-metal deployments
2. Upgrade existing workstations
3. Perform Replace scenarios
4. Support Unified Extensible Firmware Interface (UEFI)-based deployments
5. Support our preferred hardware vendors
6. Configure the BIOS at deployment time
7. Permit remote access during deployment
8. Perform extensive logging and monitoring
9. Provide email notification when a deployment is completed
10. Customize the default user profile

4. OPERATING SYSTEM DEPLOYMENT

4.1 Overview of Environment

A broad overview of our recommended MDT 2013 Lite Touch solution involved the following:

1. Creating the necessary Active Directory accounts
2. Installing and configuring MDT 2013
3. Configuring Active Directory permissions
4. Setting up the Deployment Share
5. Adding Operating System images, drivers, applications, and modifying freely available sample scripts from the community
6. Creating task sequences
7. Configuring the Rules Engine (CustomSettings.ini and Bootstrap.ini)
8. Configuring Windows Deployment Services (WDS)
9. Deploying the Windows client

4.2 Microsoft Deployment Toolkit (MDT) 2013

MDT 2013 is the latest release of the free imaging and provisioning toolkit built by Microsoft's Enterprise Client Management team for automating systems deployments. MDT sits on top of the Microsoft Assessment and Deployment Kit, automating these command line tools so you do not have to copy scripts, format disks, and map shares by hand. MDT builds, captures, deploys and configures operating systems and drivers, and even dynamically installs applications. This is Microsoft's seventh generation of deployment tools for IT professionals. It is also more than just an imaging solution; it is an automated deployment platform.

This is a freely available deployment solution from Microsoft. It provides an end-to-end workflow, best practices, and tools for planning, building, and deploying Windows.

MDT has two deployment strategies: the first is called Lite Touch, which is a standalone deployment solution, and the other is called Zero Touch, which is an extension to Configuration Manager (ConfigMgr) 2012 R2. The latter strategy extends the Operating System Deployment (OSD) capabilities in ConfigMgr with 280 OSD enhancements. It is important to note that Lite Touch can be fully automated even though the name suggests some user interaction.

MDT is enterprise-ready and has been built for the enterprise network. It has been downloaded several hundred thousand times from Microsoft and has become the de facto standard for Windows deployments. It is also worth mentioning that MDT is fully supported by Microsoft.

MDT 2013 Lite Touch does not require any management infrastructure, but is still a complete deployment solution that provides the following capabilities:

1. Fully automated deployments – ability to deploy Windows clients and servers and fully automate the process.
2. Create reference images – MDT can be used to create reference images for all the deployment solutions that Microsoft has, including MDT, ConfigMgr, System Center Virtual Machine Manager, VDI, and much more.
3. Install software updates – ability to install software updates, preferably from a local Windows Server Update Services (WSUS) server, as part of the deployment process.
4. Install Applications – MDT can install applications, run scripts and executables, and so forth, as part of the deployment process.
5. Deployment Monitoring – MDT supports end-to-end monitoring of your deployment.
6. Development Framework – MDT provides ready-made functions for many commonly used configurations.

4.3 Configuring the BIOS Like a Boss

If you typically order many workstations from Dell, HP, or Lenovo and forget to tell them how you want the BIOS configured, in general they will come with the factory settings, which include having the Trusted Platform Module (TPM) disabled and no password. We have always relied on a horde of students equipped with running shoes to go to each building and manually perform tasks such as this like when we decided to enforce our Bitlocker Policy.

We recently learned from the blogs referenced in the acknowledgements that we can download the vendor tools, add them to the sequence, and have the sequence configure TPM for us. It could not have been any easier once we saw how it was done.

4.4 UEFI Deployments

UEFI, or Unified Extensible Firmware Interface, is a standard firmware interface that was designed to replace BIOS. It was designed to improve software interoperability and address limitations of BIOS. More and more machines are being shipped either with UEFI enabled or requiring the use of UEFI support. MDT 2013 supports UEFI deployments out of the box.

4.5 Creating a Reference Image

The first order of business once you have a working MDT 2013 infrastructure is to create a reference image. This process can be fully automated using PowerShell. You can also build what is known as an Image Factory using Mikael Nystrom's PowerShell script that can be downloaded from his website indicated in the references. This script goes into MDT, gets all the task sequences, builds all the virtual machines, installs Windows, installs applications, runs Windows Update, runs Sysprep, captures an image, and finally deletes all the virtual machines. The entire process can take a few hours, but it is completely automated and we rebuild the reference images every month.

Think of a reference image as the foundation of a house. If the foundation is shaky and not built well, the rest of the house is compromised no matter how much effort is put into the walls. The house will eventually fail.

Always build your reference images in a virtual machine. It does not matter what platform you use. Building reference images in a virtual environment allows it to be truly hardware independent and produces a superior image. Furthermore, you can take advantage of snapshots, which allow you to instantly roll back any changes, and create your reference images even faster.

The perfect reference image for our environment contains a fully patched Windows 7 x64 OS, .NET Framework, C++ runtimes, and fully patched Microsoft Office 2013 x64. We do not install any drivers in the reference image.

4.6 Creating the Production Images
We then need to put the reference image into production. Every company has a unique way of doing this. Again, we strived to get as close to fully automated as possible, and were successful in achieving this after simulating several deployments.

It is a good practice to have a separate Deployment Share for your production images. The reason for this is that you will typically want the machine to join the domain, be put into a specific OU, and have a list of applications that need to be installed. We do not do this when creating reference images.

There are three types of images: Thick, thin, and hybrid. A thick image includes all drivers and programs. This is the "old school" approach, with very little flexibility. If you are building multiple images per model, it is a thick image. Thin images typically include just the Operating System. This is too far in the opposite extreme from thick images. These images take a long time to update and patch at deployment time. Hybrid images are somewhere between thin and thick providing the Goldilocks sweet spot.

Our hybrid production image for the PACE Lab, which has 60 identical workstations, did end up being close to a thick image because the workstations needed to support a lot of different applications. It did not make sense dynamically installing each of these on the fly at deployment time. Several of the other supported research labs only required a smaller subset of these applications. For those labs, we decided to build directly off our reference image and layer on the required applications during deployment.

An important factor that will determine the type of image you deploy will be the amount of time you have available to deploy the environment. Some of you may have classrooms that you have to deploy twice a day, once in the morning and again in the evening, with only a 2-hour window. For these types of environments, you will need to have a thicker image with the tradeoff that it will be slightly more costly to manage.

It is still important to keep applications like Firefox, Adobe Reader, Java, and Flash out of your image as these update frequently and are very easy to install at deployment time. The more applications you keep out of your image, the more flexible it is and the easier it is to maintain.

4.7 Application Deployment
Applications can be assigned in two different ways in Lite Touch. You can either hardcode them in the sequence, which is called static, or you can have a list of applications, or multiple lists of applications, that you feed into the sequence at deployment time. The latter option allows you to be more flexible and dynamic when you do deployments.

You can further customize MDT to take advantage of databases, web services, external scripts, and frontends, but that is beyond the scope of this paper. However, do keep in mind that the CustomSettings.ini rules engine can reach out to other sources to find those lists of applications and return them to the sequence that is then deploying them.

This is the part that took us the longest time to automate. It would be great if every software vendor supported unattended installations and provided instructions on how to accomplish this. We scrutinized the documentation of all our software to learn about the unattended installations, reached out to the vendor for support when we could not get it working, and created a lot of VBScript and PowerShell wrappers for nearly all the software in our Mechanical Engineering & Mechanics Department.

In addition to creating custom applications, we also decided to create a few thick images, which included all the applications for the Lab.

4.8 Handling Drivers
All hardware on a workstation requires drivers to work with the operating system. Vendors like Dell, HP, and Lenovo now have dedicated enterprise client portals that provide a single, easy-to-find interface for downloading drivers for all their supported models. If, however, you cannot find the driver at the vendor's site, the second best option is to go the vendor's vendor. For instance, if I am looking for a driver to an Intel network card, I would go to Intel's support website. A third option is to browse the Microsoft catalog site, which has drivers for quite a lot of hardware.

It is highly recommended to keep drivers outside the image, in a driver repository, and inject them during deployment. This makes your image very flexible. MDT 2013 can assign drivers in two scenarios:

1. Total Chaos: This is the default method that uses Plug 'n Play ID detection to figure out which is the best driver to inject during deployment. This method is only useful if you support a very limited number of hardware models, typically 3 or 4.

2. Total Control: This is the preferred method, which we adopted, where we organize drivers in a logical structure. For instance, by OS, Make, and Model, from which you selectively have the Deployment inject only the right drivers for the particular model. A couple of default actions need to be tweaked in the task sequences to get this to work.

There are also two different types of drivers: Boot Image drivers, which are WinPE-capable drivers, and OS drivers. Dell, HP, and Lenovo have these readily available on their support webpages. You want to aim to keep your Boot Images as small as possible to ensure it boots as quickly as possible.

4.9 PXE Booting

There are several ways of accomplishing a Pre-boot Execution Environment (PXE), but most will be using either DHCP or IP Helpers. Using IP Helpers is the recommended and more robust method of getting clients to PXE Boot. Windows Deployment Services (WDS) is a role that can be enabled in Windows Server 2012 R2 that allows you to maintain a list of Boot Images that the clients can use to connect to your Deployment Infrastructure. Multicasting can also be enabled in WDS, which greatly increases the speed of network deployment. All of this will be moot if your Network Team has not enabled PXE and Multicast on the switches.

PXE booting your deployments is a lot more fun than running around with a USB stick or DVD, which needs to be updated very frequently.

We were able to reduce our PXE boot times from about 1 minute down to 10 seconds by optimizing the following:

1. Creating the smallest possible Boot Image.
2. Increasing the TFTP Block size to 16384 on the WDS server.
3. Deploying to UEFI-based machines.

4.10 Software Updates with Secunia and ConfigMgr

Secunia is a world-leading provider of Vulnerability Intelligence and has been around since 2002. The company's CSI product has an impressive security database and can be used either integrated with WSUS or integrated with ConfigMgr, which provides the most flexibility for superior patch management and reporting capabilities. We currently have Secunia CSI in production with the dedicated WSUS server configuration. We tested out the ConfigMgr integration and it had much richer management and reporting capabilities, as we expected, but since we did not have ConfigMgr in mainstream production, we decided to use our existing Secunia environment for patch management in our labs.

We are slowly expanding our use of ConfigMgr, as well, but feel we still need a lot more expertise before taking it to production. We hope to publish our experiences with ConfigMgr at a future conference as we certainly see the value in running the System Center suite of tools.

5. CHALLENGES

5.1 Monitoring Your Deployments

When you enable monitoring on your production deployment share, you create a small compact SQL database and web service. You will now have the ability to monitor your deployments in real-time. I highly recommend that you use or purchase an MDOP (Microsoft Desktop Optimization Pack) license, which is something extra on top of Software Assurance. Now you can add the Microsoft DaRT (Diagnostics and Recovery Toolset), which is part of MDOP, into your Boot Images. This gives the ability to remote into the Boot Image and troubleshoot if needed. It is a very powerful feature to have available.

The monitoring information being generated by MDT is an Open Data Protocol (ODATA) data feed, which can be viewed in several ways. You can view it in the MDT monitoring node, but you can get more creative when you connect to it from Excel. Once you have the information in Excel, you can start adding colors, inserting pie charts, and doing a whole lot more with the

table of information. You can also upload the information into a simple webpage.

5.2 Email Notification

There is a neat free VBscript developed by Johan Arwidmark and Mikael Nystrom that sends an email when deployment is completed. They used smtp4dev, which is a small dummy SMTP server to accomplish this. It also grabs the main log file, BDD.LOG, which is an aggregate of all the log files that the deployment generates. There is no better feeling than waking up in the morning and getting an email confirming that every one of your 200 deployments completed successfully.

5.3 Customizing the Default User Profile

It was important for us to be able to configure the default user profile so that every user who logs into a workstation is presented the same desktop environment that the system administrator had carefully customized.

CopyProfile is a feature that was heavily used in Windows 7 and has been around for a long time. It is just one of several methods that can be used to customize the Default User profile, but it was the easiest to implement with MDT 2013. All you have to do is customize the local administrator profile as you want it and then set CopyProfile to True in the Specialize Pass of the unattend.xml file used to deploy that image. It is worth noting that the actual copying of the local administrator profile to the default user profile takes place at deployment time and not during the Sysprep phase.

5.4 Debugging OSD Like a Boss

In Operating System Deployment (OSD), things can go wrong. OSD in both Lite Touch and ConfigMgr is challenging to troubleshoot and you need to learn the order of things when they happen and for different scenarios.

In Lite Touch, when you start a deployment, it will put the log files in RAM in this location:

X:\MININT\SMSOSD\OSDLOGS

After the sequence creates a partition, the logs will then be in the following folder until deployment ends:

C:\MININT\SMSOSD\OSDLOGS

When deployment finally ends, the logs will find their final resting place in this location:

C:\Windows\Temp\DeploymentLogs

So how do you view log files? You use CMTrace. In Lite Touch you do not have it, but in ConfigMgr you do. You can download it from the free ConfigMgr Toolkit and add it to your boot image.

The main log file is BDD.log, but you will also see SMSTS.LOG. SMSTS.LOG is useful in Lite Touch when trying to debug application deployments in a sequence. BDD.LOG is an aggregation of all the individual log files.

The monitoring with DaRT integration gives you the ability to remote into the boot image, which is great since you can be far away and still troubleshoot deployments.

Setting the SLSHARE property in your CustomSettings.ini file in both Lite Touch and ConfigMgr will copy the logs to the server should something go wrong:

SLSHARE=\\MDT01\Logs$

This property is actually very useful as it gathers additional log files to help you troubleshoot depending on the stage when the failure occurred. For example, if Windows setup fails when it reboots into Windows, it will get the DISM log, SETUPACT log, and NETSETUP log. It effectively gathers log files that can help you troubleshoot and even creates a subfolder for each computer, which is easy to find.

So depending on when things fail in Lite Touch, you need to look in different locations for the log files.

6. LAYING THE FOUNDATION FOR WINDOWS 10

We will not need to break a sweat about deploying Windows 10 as it will be officially supported by Microsoft's Deployment Toolkit 2013. Everyone has been waiting for the official update to MDT 2013 that will support all the Windows 10 deployment scenarios.

You will be able to follow nearly everything you have learned in this paper and apply it to Windows 10 deployments. The PowerShell scripts will just need to be tweaked at times.

7. CONCLUSIONS

The workflows and techniques described in this paper are applicable to any deployment scenario and not just to lab environments. We are having more and more departments at Lehigh University moving away from Ghost and adopting this solution for their clients. We have only just scratched the surface of what MDT 2013 as a deployment solution is capable of delivering. There are several more opportunities that are ripe for optimization and we will continue to develop and tweak our solution. It seems like folks are pushing the boundaries with MDT 2013 every day. And it is amazing and impressive how news of novel scripts and workflows travels on social media.

Our next project will be to bring ConfigMgr into production and integrate MDT 2013 to create the ultimate deployment and management solution for Windows assets.

8. ACKNOWLEDGMENTS

I am grateful to my colleagues Timothy J. Foley and Gale D. Fritsche at Lehigh University for their tremendous support of my efforts in training and to Johan Arwidmark and Mikael Nystrom for their invaluable knowledge on Enterprise Deployments and openly sharing it with the community through their blogs.

9. REFERENCES

[1]   Create a Windows 8.1 Reference Image <https://technet.microsoft.com/en-us/library/dn744290.aspx>

[2]   Johan Arwidmark <http://www.deploymentartist.com>

[3]   Mikael Nystrom <http://www.deploymentbunny.com>

[4]   The Deployment Guys <http://blogs.technet.com/b/deploymentguys>

Faculty Development Through Special Initiatives at the University of San Diego

Shahra Meshkaty
University of San Diego
5998 Alcalá Park
San Diego, CA 92110
1-(619) 260-2298
meshkaty@sandiego.edu

Cyd Burrows
University of San Diego
5998 Alcalá Park
San Diego, CA 92110
1-(619) 260-8818
cburrows@sandiego.edu

ABSTRACT

Getting faculty involved and excited about adopting emerging technology in their teaching is an ongoing challenge for the Academic Technology Services (ATS) department at the University Of San Diego (USD). In order to build a stronger following and establish a larger core of faculty partnerships, ATS has designed and deployed a successful series of special initiatives, projects aimed at engaging full-time faculty in the exploration of emerging and mobile technologies. Initiatives are strategically constructed to ensure that faculties achieve desired goals, and our skilled staff are working along side them every step of the way, which reduces faculty anxiety and ensures successful outcomes. Three initiatives are currently operational: the iPad Classroom Project (in its 8th semester) which puts iPads in the hands of all students in the classroom for the duration of a full semester, the Student Technology Assistant Program (in its 9th year) which pairs a faculty member who has a vision with a technologically skilled student employee for an entire semester to develop and bring to fruition a technology-based project that will benefit future classes, and the Summer Innovation Institute (three summer cohorts completed), a two-week long intensive faculty development program focused on achieving pedagogically sound teaching outcomes via the implementation of Blackboard, multimedia, iPads, and numerous other technologies. Learn more about these faculty development strategies and how USD's ATS unit is growing their community of faculty partners through creative, engaging initiatives.

Categories and Subject Descriptors

• **Applied computing~E-learning** • *Applied computing~Collaborative learning* • *Human-centered computing~Collaborative and social computing systems and tools* • Human-centered computing~Ubiquitous and mobile devices

General Terms

Measurement, Performance, Design, Security, Human Factors, Standardization, Theory.

Keywords

Technology initiatives, mobile learning, apps, iPads, faculty development, collaboration, instructional design.

SIGUCCS '15, November 09-13, 2015, St. Petersburg, FL, USA
© 2015 ACM. ISBN 978-1-4503-3610-9/15/11...$15.00
DOI: http://dx.doi.org/10.1145/2815546.2815572

INTRODUCTION

One of the missions of the Instructional Design and Training Team (also known as the iTeam) is to grow and foster a community of faculty whose partnership will assist in guiding the deployment and adoption of new and existing technologies. Historically, a small, core group of faculty members have continuously supported in that role, but the aim has always been to develop stronger ties that reach further into each of the schools at USD.

Over the past several years, the team has produced several initiatives for faculty to become more fluent and comfortable with academic technology integration. Faculty are selected based on their applications or proposals to each program. The Student Technology Assistant Program (STA) was the first of these [7], introduced in 2007, followed by the iPad Classroom Project [4], which began in 2012. The most recent addition to the initiative portfolio is the Summer Innovation Institute (SII) conceived in 2013 and now in its fourth iteration.

An immense effort in marketing and outreach was necessary in order to gain interest of the faculty members for each of these programs, but recent years have shown significant growth in the number of partnerships that have been established and the solid community that can be called upon when needed. The iTeam is constantly deriving more programs and strategies to engage faculty at a deeper level.

1. BACKGROUND

This section offers contextual information about the Information Technology Services organization at the University of San Diego and offers a glimpse into the campus culture and how faculty and students are adopting various technologies. It will provide insight as to the challenges faced in building a strong faculty community of engaged users of technology on the USD campus.

1.1 2014 USD Demographics

USD was founded in 1949 and is a private, Roman Catholic institution with a 2014 enrollment of 5,665 undergraduate students, and 2,656 graduate students. It was ranked amongst the nation's top 100 universities by *U.S. News & World Report* in 2013, ranked number 7 in the category Most Beautiful Campus by *The Princeton Review,* and has an International Study Abroad program that is ranked number 3 for percentage of undergraduate students that participate in study abroad (Institute of International Education's *Open Doors Report*). A total of 897 full and part-time faculty members are on staff supporting seven schools with a total of 42 bachelor's degree programs, 25 master's degree programs, the JD, five LLM, and three doctorate degrees [8].

1.2 Academic Technology Services at USD

Information Technology Services (ITS) at USD is centralized and ATS is one of four major units falling under that umbrella. Within ATS there are 3 business units: Computing Labs, Client Support Services, and Instructional and Media Technology. The Instructional and Media Technology unit is comprised of the Media Services team and the Instructional Design and Training team, or iTeam, who are responsible for faculty support and events such as the initiatives discussed here.

1.3 The Charge of the Instructional Design and Training Team

The Instructional Design and Training team (iTeam) was conceived in 2007 and is responsible for supporting faculty in the identification, implementation, and deployment of new and existing technologies using sound pedagogical methods in curriculum construction. The team also pilots new and emerging technologies and applications and evaluates them for usefulness in higher education.

The team conducts numerous software application training workshops which are offered year round to the entire USD community (approximately 65 sessions each semester) to encourage mastery of university supported technologies including the Microsoft Office suite, Blackboard (USD's learning management system (LMS) [3]), Adobe Creative Cloud, and other integrated technologies that work within the LMS, such as Respondus, Turnitin, etc.

Special events that the team is responsible for include bi-annual Faculty Boot Camps designed to provide just-in-time help to professors at the beginning of a new semester, the annual Technology Showcase highlighting faculty technology accomplishments with an expo style exhibit hall for approximately 250 faculty attendees [2], and a Learn@Lunch series that focuses on trending topics [6], emerging technologies, and the changing dynamics presented by rapid technological developments, new apps, and devices.

Special initiatives round out the team's repertoire of services by engaging faculty with semester long technology-based projects that are goal-oriented, tailored to each individual, and carefully planned with milestones for success. These initiatives include the Student Technology Assistant Program (STA), the iPad Classroom Project, and the Summer Innovation Institute (SII).

1.4 USD Culture

One of the continuous challenges faced by the team is how to bridge the gap between ATS and the faculty community. Many outreach efforts, on-site support events, training workshops and guest speaking events have been offered in the hopes of building a stronger and more engaged faculty partnership, but still the process and growth was slow and inconsistent.

Students entering university campuses come equipped with all the latest gadgets and gizmos and are somewhat technologically savvy. Observations and many years of working with student employees have taught us that while students may be very adept with social media and communication on their electronics, they are not very fluent or prepared to use productivity tools in their studies and research.

Faculty at the university should be prepared to meet students' technological needs and provide them with access to critical materials via the LMS platform, which students can use via the Blackboard Mobile Learn app on their mobile devices. Ensuring that faculty members offer students the best possible learning experience during their time at USD inspires the team to find new ways to reach their target audience and promote technical awareness and proficiency.

2. INITIATIVE FORMATS

Each of the three special initiatives carried out by the iTeam are structured and carried out in unique and different ways. The planning and deployment processes have now been refined into succinct guidelines and documented in shared space so that team members could pick up and lead the project quite efficiently. It took years to get to this point and a lot of learning and bumps in the road along the way as each of these initiatives were developed.

After several semesters offering the STA and iPad initiatives (both individual undertakings by faculty applicants), it became clear that we needed to create a forum where faculty could bond with one another and explore teaching strategies, techniques and approaches to curriculum and assessment. This was the inspiration for the SII.

2.1 Student Technology Assistant (STA) Program

The STA program was the first initiative, launched in 2007. Its aim was to pair technologically talented students with faculty members who had ideas for and/or materials requiring the design and development of technology-based projects that could be used to enhance and augment academic curriculum.

Individual faculty members are invited to apply for either a spring or fall semester STA grant with the accepted proposals, those that most strongly meet the outlined criteria, move forward. The first step in the process is a consultation to determine exactly what will be required, the skills needed to create the project, and to scope the parameters and keep it within manageable boundaries. A student employee is then identified as a match for the project (and given additional training as needed) and the pair meets to identify project milestones and discuss the details in-depth. The student is then responsible for carrying out the work to be done while under the supervision of the STA manager whom they report in to regularly via blog posts and office visits. Students are challenged to be good managers of their own time and to meet expectations as outlined in the initial meeting. They use formal project management software to document all of their tasks and development. They also check in regularly with their faculty partner to ensure that their creation is what the faculty member envisioned, for guidance, critique, and good communication.

A good core group of faculty partners resulted from this offering and anywhere between 5 – 8 projects per semester was completed. These individuals became our "go to" group for many purposes, whether it was evaluating new classroom response systems, speaking as a panelist at our annual showcase event, or providing us with feedback about our products and services.

To date, 62 unique faculty members have taken advantage of this program and a total of 107 technology-based projects have been completed. Of those participants, about a dozen now can be called close partners that work with us on multiple fronts.

2.2 iPad Classroom Project & Faculty Pilot

The preponderance of mobile devices on campus in recent years prompted the team to investigate the pedagogical usefulness of iPads in higher education.

The project is twofold. First, faculty members can check out iPads for an entire semester for the exploration phase, where they investigate how the device and specific apps can be embedded in structured academic curriculum. Some questions that were begging for answers: How can iPads change the way in which students learn? What can be done using the iPads that could never be done before? How can iPads facilitate learning beyond the classroom walls? Enquiring minds wanted to know! In the second phase of the project, faculty applicants that are awarded grants receive iPads for themselves and every student in their class for an entire semester. Faculty must show evidence of having amended their syllabus to include iPad specific assignments and assessments, and identify apps required for the completion of the course materials. Participants must agree to attend monthly brown bag lunch meetings and to present their findings at the end of the semester. In addition, a final written report is required, or a video interview in lieu of the written report.

Initially, many of the same individuals who had participated in the STA program also applied to the iPad project, perhaps because they were in frequent communication with ATS or team members. Eventually proposals began coming in from faculty members whom the team had not had the opportunity to work with closely in the past, which was an exciting milestone. Marketing and promotional efforts (and probably word of mouth) were resulting in a broader community of individuals who were invested in exploring innovative teaching methods through the adoption of new technologies and mobile devices.

To date, 44 unique faculty members have participated in the project and a total of 46 classes of students have been provided with iPads (approximately 856 individual student participants). Of these faculty participants, about 12 – 15 have become individuals we partner with on a regular basis.

2.3 Summer Innovation Institute (SII)

The iPad Brown Bag Lunch meetings provide great opportunities for faculty to brainstorm and share ideas with one another. The premise behind the SII is built on that same foundation, that faculty are interested in what their colleagues are doing and are more receptive to new ideas in a collaborative environment of their peers.

Applicants are screened and are required to attend a consultation prior to being fully accepted. A stipend is offered in the form of either a current generation iPad, $1500 toward approved conference spending, or $1000 cold, hard cash. They are also required to have attended a Blackboard Essentials (two-hour) workshop. One of the desired outcomes is for faculty to walk away with a Blackboard course modeled on the exemplary course rubric that is published by Blackboard. This is used as a foundational repository for many of the other technologies that are explored during the two-week period -- video, graphics, presentations, communication forums, grading and assignment submission, etc. The selected participants come with a very broad range of technical skills, from novice to advanced, and one of the challenges for the team at SII is to ensure that everyone is continuously engaged and interested in the material and content being covered.

The SII contains very structured, daily content, with some flexible time at the end of each day. Daily themes offer insight as to the major topics addressed each day. Themes include Orientation & Pedagogy, Mobile Learning, Bb Hands-On, Flipping/Blended Learning, Multimedia, Plagiarism/Copyright/Open Educational Resources, Social Media, and Surveys & More. The last day is Show and Tell and is framed as a friendly competition amongst the cohort members as they share their course development and newly adopted techniques and ideas with the group. Sometimes a single small idea is a huge hit with the group, and it can never be anticipated as to what that will be. With one cohort it was something as simple as Wordle [9], for another rubric development, and the third group found learning modules and sequential content delivery fascinating.

While the content and structure of the SII is designed by the team, numerous guest speakers, or subject matter experts, are also invited to share their insights on specific topics with the cohort. Representatives from Apple highlight iPad apps that are popular and useful in higher education [1], USD's own Center for Educational Excellence resources offer advice on designing learning outcomes and structuring syllabi, and guests from other universities offer their experience with things like Flipping the Classroom, etc. Previous SII attendees welcome the new cohort on the first day with a panel discussion, offering their experiences and how SII has affected the way they now teach.

The event is held in one of our more flexible classrooms and attendees are strongly encouraged to move to new seating each day and mingle with folks they have not met. Individuals come from one of seven schools on campus so it is a great opportunity for them to learn what is being done outside of their own school and department. There is a mix of indoor vs. outdoor activities, listening vs. hands-on build time, individual vs. collaborative work. More technologically advanced attendees are sometimes paired with less experienced users, and at other times advanced users are grouped together as are the novice users. Group activities are facilitated by one of the four team members present, who provide guidance, examples, answer technical questions and assist with implementation of various apps and technologies explored.

Faculty members were asked to write reflective journals at the end of each day to document their learning and journey through SII and team members routinely scoured those journals for signs of stress, individuals needing additional assistance, to answer questions that arose, and just to inspire and offer encouragement when needed. The feedback to the team's attentiveness was extremely positive and was evidence of the team's dedication and concern for the success of the institute and to the achievement of each individual's goals.

Each cohort is broken up into small groups that compete with one another via a badging system (delivered via Blackboard) to complete certain requirements at SII. Ten badges are available to be earned, and each team member must complete the requirements necessary, so it becomes a bonding experience amongst the small groups as well. Badges include: Content, Course Design, Participation (week 1 and week 2), Graphics, Multimedia, Assessment, Apps, Social Media, and Final Presentation. Each category, or badge, has multiple activities as components, keeping the participants very busy, but on task and fully engaged. The first team to earn all ten badges wins gift cards to the campus restaurant, La Gran Terraza [5].

SII cohort members become our VIPs and are encouraged to apply for the STA and iPad projects once they have defined their teaching strategies and settled on goals and learning outcomes they will move forward with. In addition, ATS supports them and works side by side with them if they are interested in piloting new applications that have been vetted. Their detailed feedback and experiences help the team to further investigate opportunities for larger adoption of these technologies.

To date, the program has been offered to three cohorts of full-time, benefits-based faculty in the summer months (36 individual participants). The program is two full weeks in length, and runs from 9am to 4pm each day. Two 'happy hours' are offered, one each week, and are one of the most loved components where the conversation of the day's content continues. This summer, the program will be offered to a fourth cohort from June 1 through 12, 2015.

SII has by far been the most successful method of building a stronger faculty community and partnership with ATS. Of the 36 individuals that have 'graduated' from the institute, the majority of participants are very responsive to our inquiries, eager to share with others, and generally engaged with the department on a regular basis. At 2015's annual Technology Showcase event [2], a record number of faculty members volunteered as presenters and panelists on various subjects and trending topics. To say the team was pleased with these results is an understatement.

3. FEEDBACK

What did faculty SII attendees have to say about their experience? Here are a few quotes from the wrap up survey:

What did you enjoy most about the Summer Innovation Institute?

"I really don't think I can point to one single element as I enjoyed many things about the program. I enjoyed learning the different tools within Blackboard and the resources. I enjoyed learning about instructional design in both the learning outcomes/objectives and the flipping the classroom instruction. The guest speakers were very knowledgeable. Lastly, I really learned a lot from my fellow faculty colleagues and shared their enthusiasm."

"I really enjoyed seeing all the options of the various types of technology/ tools, as well as seeing the creative ways that people have incorporated these technologies into the classroom. I could see how these tools could enhance classroom engagement and increase student comprehension. I also really enjoyed the camaraderie between the faculty members themselves, but also between the iTeam and faculty."

What was your most valuable take away?

"… simply the amount of information I learned from working with my colleagues and seeing their courses. I think everyone was impressed with Leeva's introduction of color, and Susan's work with the rubric. I think most of us work on our courses in a vacuum or silo so we don't get the synergy of seeing what others are doing."

"Knowledge of the different technological tools, being able to implement some of them for the fall semester - and also the relationship with the iTeam. I would believe that workshop attendees would be much more comfortable reaching out to the iTeam for help."

"Syllabus construction, course development, learning outcomes, how to build a course and incorporate technology the way I want to. How to use Twitter feed. How to use Bb as a faculty and build a Bb course. LOTS of things! This was so incredible valuable!"

Additional Comments:

"I could tell you put a lot of effort into preparation for this institute and it was very much appreciated."

4. LESSONS LEARNED

Of course, there is always room for improvement and the team takes detailed notes throughout the event and holds a formal debriefing session the week they return to the office.

First, the team acknowledged how much learning each member did while spending two weeks with this amazing group of faculty. So much preparation initially goes into the curriculum design and development, the sessions, the materials, the activity plans, the working lunches, guest speaking engagements, and time management. But in the aftermath, the team has learned so much about each of the individuals they have worked with that it provides better context as they return to their day-to-day activities of support and training. It is a great opportunity for professional development for the team members, it's organic, and comes directly from their own campus constituents.

Testing. Testing. Testing. There is never enough testing to ensure that technology will work seamlessly, which was a good lesson also for the faculty member attendees. They were able to see the team fail with technology and move on to Plan B. It happens, just be prepared to handle it.

Team member responsibilities should be defined clearly before the event begins so that everyone knows exactly what to attend to. It was necessary to have somebody review the reflective journals each day, someone to ensure that there were ample snacks, coffee, beverages, someone to prepare the Blackboard content and release it in a timely manner, someone to post homework each afternoon, bring handouts, have office supplies on hand, and a dedicated person to be monitoring the team inbox for other support needs coming in, as that does not stop just because the team is busy with an event.

Faculty reflected a sense of feeling overwhelmed at times. This was fully expected as there is so much content being covered. Making a concerted efforts to take the pulse of the room routinely and ensure that everyone was staying on pace became necessary. Team members often needed to work with a few individuals in a small group to get them caught up and comfortable with a new concept/technology. That way there was no disruption to the flow for others that were technically more advanced and following along nicely. Keeping everyone challenged and engaged became a difficult balance at times.

Providing the perfect blend of sedentary vs. active time was also difficult. More activities were eventually incorporated to encourage participants to move about the room or even outdoors to break up the long periods of being seating in the room.

Maintaining high levels of energy, positive attitudes, and a professional demeanor throughout the two-week period was of utmost importance to the team. Daily debriefs and critique of what went well and what didn't became adopted as a means of keeping the team running as a well oiled machine. The institute required stamina and endurance of every team member and at the same time those people needed to bring inspiration and boost the confidence of the attendees.

In 2014 two sessions of the SII were offered due to the large response by faculty. One was held in June and one in August. This, as it turns out, was a bad idea and will not be repeated. The resources and time needed to put this event together and market it were too intense to make that pattern sustainable.

5. FOLLOW-UP

SII is only the beginning of a semester-long process for these faculty participants. On the last day of the event, the cohort members are divided up amongst the iTeam members so that they each have a specific point person going forward. For the duration of the following semester, team members check in with their faculty groups on a regular basis, meet with them individually, assist with continued course development, continue to work toward identified goals, and advise and consult when necessary.

As our VIPs these folks are invited to special events with the iTeam to discuss satisfaction with current platforms (such as Blackboard), and to identify pain points as well so that those can be improved or eliminated. Their advice is solicited when new product adoption and evaluation is under way. They become our advocates for appropriate uses of technology that serve a purpose and help us reach those that may be skeptical or lacking technical expertise. Because for the iTeam, it's all about, how can technology help you?

6. CONCLUSION

SII has been a very successful means of building a community of invested faculty who are interested and committed to embracing technology and to working with ATS to continue promoting the adoption of appropriate teaching technologies and techniques that foster deeper student engagement and learning beyond the classroom walls.

To date, we have one faculty member who has so fully developed a Blackboard course that it is being submitted to the Blackboard competition as an Exemplary Course and others not far behind. These are truly inspirational individuals that have invested large amounts of their time in order to provide rich and engaging curriculum to their students at USD.

SII alums are now referring their colleagues to join future cohorts, and have gone on camera to provide testimonials about their experience and how the program changed their teaching style, created a richer learning experience for their students, and added

efficiency to the distribution of class materials, also becoming more sustainable through less printing and paper consumption.

Slow and steady, but continuous efforts to engage the faculty community are finally paying off and ATS couldn't be happier about the great group of individuals that now work more closely with the team. Bridging the gap between IT and the faculty community has required great amounts of patience and perseverance, but with a solid group of individual faculty evangelists now on their side, ATS hopes to broaden their horizons even further.

7. ACKNOWLEDGMENTS

We would like to thank our Instructional Design and Training team for all of their hard work in getting these initiatives off the ground and for their continued efforts in marketing, promoting, and deploying these project to the campus community.

8. REFERENCES

[1] Apple. Accessed April 28, 2015. http://www.apple.com

[2] ATS Technology Showcase & Open House. Accessed April 28, 2015. http://www.sandiego.edu/its/teaching/instructional_technology/techshowcase.php

[3] Blackboard Learn. Accessed April 28, 2015. http://www.blackboard.com

[4] iPad Classroom Project. Accessed July 15, 2015. http://www.sandiego.edu/its/teaching/instructional_technology/ipad/index.php

[5] La Gran Terraza. Accessed April 28, 2015. http://www.sandiego.edu/dining/lagranterraza/

[6] Learn@Lunch series. Accessed July 15, 2015. http://www.sandiego.edu/its/trainings_and_workshops/learn_at_lunch.php

[7] Student Technology Assistant Program. Accessed July 15, 2015. http://www.sandiego.edu/its/teaching/instructional_technology/student_tech_assistants/index.php

[8] University of San Diego. *University of San Diego Facts*. Accessed April 26, 2015. http://www.sandiego.edu/about/facts.php

[9] Wordle. Accessed April 28, 2015. http://www.wordle.net

Be the Leader of Your Career: A Self-Centered Approach to Strategic Career Management

Randi R. McCray
Union Institute and University
1+ (203)432-9190
randi.mccray@email.myunion.edu

James L. Rawlins
Pace University School of Business
1+ (203)436.8045
rawlinsjl@gmail.com

ABSTRACT

The role of the Information Technology (IT) professional has changed drastically in the last ten (10) years. Emerging technologies, organizational restructuring, and reduction in IT spending; has not only lead to uncertainty, but opportunity. To maintain relevance in a fast paced evolving field and achieve a high level of career satisfaction; IT professionals must employ the same tactical approach used to implement high-quality IT solutions-- to managing their own careers. While organizations provide a wealth of tools to support career development, key individual elements to ensure career success are: strategy, ownership, and action. A strategic framework for managing one's career, increases the probability for a satisfying and viable career in IT. Professionals should develop a career strategy that merges their career goals with organizational resources to achieve a high-quality optimal career. This paper presents a framework for a person centered approach to career development that leverages organizational resources and individual actions to build a strategic plan for optimal career satisfaction.

Categories and Subject Descriptors

K.4.3 [**Organizational Impacts**]: Employment.

General Terms

Management.

Keywords

Information technology professionals, career management, strategy, career planning, career satisfaction, changing information technology environments.

1. INTRODUCTION

For many IT professionals, career management comes at a slow pace through a combination of organizational tools provided by human resource departments within an organization (i.e; performance reviews, career plans, etc.), supervisors, experience, and passage of time for promotions. There is much debate as to whether these methods are effective in helping individuals achieve career satisfaction. Additionally, the radical changes in

the business environment call for a new framework for strategic career management amongst IT professionals.

Organizations have evolved from complex hierarchies to matrix, virtual, and flat. These new organizational forms have introduced a series of environmental factors which present a new set of challenges for IT professionals. Micro-messaging, organizational inertia, organizational culture, career typecasting and organizational procedures are just a few of the factors that are often over-looked and play a significant role in the IT professional's ability to achieve career satisfaction. Old concepts and models are becoming increasing more inefficient to address these factors. To meet these changes, Chesebrough & Davis (1983) recommend that IT professionals assume responsibility for their own careers [2].

While prior research has clearly demonstrated this need, individuals need a solid framework that merges theory and prior research into a solid plan of action. This paper builds on prior work adding the need for strategic career management in increasing the probability of career satisfaction. Additionally, we propose that the individuals place themselves at the center of the career management process and use strategic actions to manage their careers. Based on prior research and findings, we offer some effective strategies that build upon traditional methods of career planning and are essential to increasing the likelihood of career satisfaction.

2. Theoretical Framework

The first premise of this framework is examines Lent, Brown (1996) social cognitive career theory (SCCT) [3]. SCCT offers an effective approach in understanding the importance of self-efficacy, along with outcome expectations as a foundation for the development of interests, goals, and behaviors. SCCT, which is grounded in Bandura's (1986) general social cognitive theory, emphasizes the importance of personal agency in the career decision-making process and attempts to explain how both internal and external factors enhance or constrain that agency [1]. Consistent with Bandura's theory, SCCT suggests personal attributes, such as internal cognitive and affective states, physical attributes, external environmental factors, and overt behaviors or actions, all operate as interlocking mechanisms that affect one another in a bi-directional fashion. SCCT suggests, career interests directly influence career choice goals, which increase the likelihood of individuals exercising certain actions related to career management. With this triadic causal system, SCCT functions in a framework that emphasizes three social cognitive mechanisms that seem particularly relevant to career decision making and career development. The three social cognitive mechanisms of SCCT are: self-efficacy, which refers to people's judgement about their capabilities, the second is outcome expectations, which refers to personal beliefs related to results of one's behavior, and the third is goals, which are defined as the determination to act to gain a specific outcome.

SCCT suggests that self-efficacy, outcome expectations, and goal setting work together to help individuals exercise personal agency and become self-directed, especially with their career decision making and career development (Lent et al., 1994, 1996). Each element is essential to the career management process. Outcome expectations involve a person's imagined consequences of performing a specific action; goals are a critical aspect through which individuals are able to exercise their personal agency (Bandura, 1997), and self-efficacy which is a central element of personal agency help facilitate a dynamic set of beliefs that are specific to particular performance domains and interact with other people, behavior, environment, and contextual factors.

3. The Traditional Career Planning Process

The traditional career planning process usually involves the employee, the supervisor, career management tools, and resources. An additional third party resource, such as a career counselor can also be included in the process. Within organizations the process involves a bi-directional relationship between the individual and the organization. As illustrated in Figure 1, the organization provides the supervisor with the tools, and the individual brings the skills and competencies, experience, goals and actions. Further, it illustrates that most of the career planning process relies on the individual. While the organization provides a structure and process to facilitate conversations related to career development, accompanied by tools and resources; the individual bears the weight of the responsibility in managing one's own career

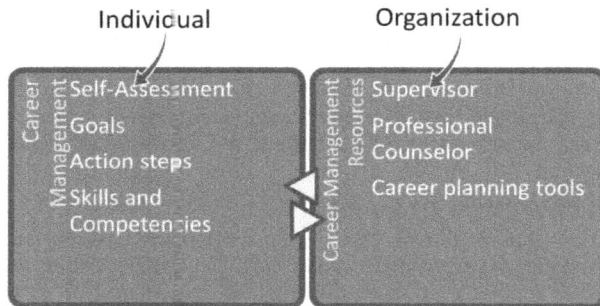

Figure 1. The Traditional Career Planning Process.

Supervisors are instrumental in providing performance feedback, information about roles and jobs within the organization, organizational needs, and the skills required to meet the needs of the organization. A professional counselor can be instrumental in utilizing career aspiration tests, skills assessments, and other tools to help individuals take an introspective approach to understanding their professional goals as it relates to achieving satisfaction in their career. Career management tools are often utilized to document an action plan. The action plan is often the end product generated from the conversation with the supervisor and professional counselor. Tools offered by the organization, such as individual development plans, usually include what steps the individual will take to achieve their career goals.

Both the supervisor and professional counselor provide assistance, but the potential success of career planning depends primarily on the individual's ability to gather and synthesize feedback from the supervisor, the skills and competencies they possess, and developing attainable goals.

4. Environmental Factors and Career Management

As noted in the introduction, there are a series of environmental factors which impact the individual's ability to achieve career satisfaction. Awareness of these factors is an essential element in examining what goals are achievable in the individual's career development plan.

Figure 2 illustrates a series of factors that are present of which many are often unaware of.

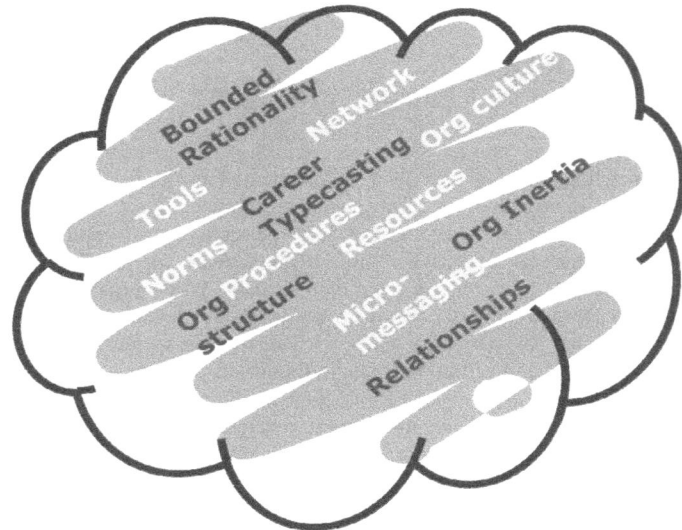

Figure 2 - Environmental Factors that Impact Career Management.

Factors like organizational culture, micro-messaging, the breadth and depth of one's network can have a significant impact on how likely one is able to achieve their intended career goals. While all of these factors may not be present in all organizations, a cocktail of some can be present at any given moment.

These factors often impede the ability for one to successfully attain career satisfaction as they impede career mobility. Career mobility is necessary for individuals who are taking action steps in reaching their career goals.

In is necessary for the IT professional to be aware and to maintain perspective of these factors as they manage their careers. Career typecasting is one environmental factor to which the IT professional must pay particular attention Career typecasting happens when an IT professional is known for a specific skill set. While he or she may have the desire to move into other areas of technology, their potential is only examined through the lens of what they done consistently, or what they are best known for. It is imperative that the IT professional be aware of this factor and develop effective career management strategies that will help them successfully navigate this in addition to other factors illustrated in Figure 2.

5. Strategic Career Management

Strategic career management involves a person-centered approach to managing one's own career. Unlike the traditional process of career planning, strategic career management involves greater awareness additional factors that increase the likelihood for career satisfaction. In the traditional process of career planning, individuals rely heavily upon their supervisors to initiate and facilitate conversations around their career, and their career goals are linked to a specific position within the organization. Additionally, usage of the tools provided by the organization are often leveraged ineffectively and do not operate congruently with the individuals career goals. Often this leads to stagnant careers and dissatisfaction.

This paper recommends modifying the traditional process of career planning with the following points to utilize a more strategic approach to reach career goals. We recommend modifying the traditional process with the following;

Expanded Awareness - IT professionals must not only be attuned to their individual skills and competencies, but they must also be aware of the environmental factors that exist within the organization and what impact those factors may have on their career plans. This is one of the critical elements in taking a more strategic approach to leading one's career. Awareness allows the individual to make adjustments as environmental factors arise and change course.

Solicit targeted feedback - IT professionals should ensure that feedback from their supervisors is useful in helping them achieve their goals. Feedback that is unclear and ambiguous in nature, does not allow individuals to develop methods or goals to grow and adjust. When faced with this challenge, ask clear and concise questions designed to get the feedback that will help you develop actions to address any issues or voids in your skill set.

Set clear, concise, and achievable goals - Be open and clear with your supervisor about your career goals and be prepared to tell them how they can help you achieve those goals. Many supervisors want to help and will. It is up to the IT professional to determine what is needed for them to achieve career satisfaction. It is also up to the IT professional to clearly communicate their needs their supervisor and ask for what they need to achieve those goals.

Effectively leverage tools and resources - Individual development plans are great written documents that will keep the IT professional on task and aware of what their plans are. However, exercised ineffectively, these plans are just written documents which on their own do not lead to career growth. Performance reviews with supervisors can often turn into conversations about if you met your annual goals, how well you did or did not do your job, and what areas you need improvement in. Be proactive in soliciting feedback between performance reviews; ensure that annual goals align properly with your career goals. Take the initiative to ensure that your goals are stretching you a bit more each year, allowing you to develop new skills, and provide opportunities for professional growth.

Contingency Planning – When developing individual development or career plans, include a "what if" for each goal. Do not assume each goal will happen as intended or as planned. If you have identified a specific role within the organization or specific area that you plan to move to, be sure to include in your plan what you will do if that position or role is eliminated. Ask yourself what adjustments are necessary and what will you do as a result of that change. Contingency planning almost never happens using the traditional method of career planning. Often individuals assume that what they desire will happen based on a set of actions identified to meet their intended goal. However, there are environmental factors beyond our control, and they present the need to modify our plans accordingly. Forward thinking is a strategy that is necessary and falls within the individual's responsibility in the career management process. Rapid industry and organizational changes have increased the need for contingency planning as a central tenement to the career management process.

This expanded approach to career management places the individual at the center of the process. The IT professional is exercising strategies to ensure that all of the elements manifest congruently with their desired career goals. In the past, much of this was left to chance, the supervisor, and the human resource functions within the organization; however, given the new landscape of the technology industry, and varied organization structures, IT professionals must now take self-lead approach to strategically manage their careers

6. REFERENCES

[1] Bandura, A. (1986) Social foundations of thought and action. Englewood Cliffs, NJ, 1986.

[2] Chesebrough, P. H., & Davis, G. B. (1983). PLANNING A CAREER PATH IN INFORMATION-SYSTEMS. Journal of Systems Management, 34(1), 6-13.

[3] Lent, R. W., & Brown, S. D. (1996). Social cognitive approach to career development: An overview. The Career Development Quarterly, 44(4), 310-321.

Consistency and Convenience:
Use of Canvas in Help Desk Staff Training

Jessica Morger
University of Wyoming
1000 E University Avenue
Laramie, WY 82071
1-307-766-2842
jmorger@uwyo.edu

ABSTRACT

Training Help Desk staff well is both critical to the success of the Help Desk and time consuming; using Canvas to create an online training course makes that training more consistent and convenient. Quality training creates a superior customer experience, ensures consistent documentation going to other departments in IT, and results in less time spent following up on unclear tickets. However, good quality training is time consuming, difficult to schedule, and needs to be repeated with new staff members often. University of Wyoming IT Help Desk has found that creating an online course with Canvas allows for a consistent, high quality training experience that can be repeated as often as necessary and is available the moment a new staff member starts. Recordings of presentations, screen capture, and quizzes allow staff members to learn at their own rate and test their knowledge before working with customers. In the limited time since launching the Canvas Help Desk course, UWIT has found that tickets are documented more consistently, even experienced staff members have filled in holes in their knowledge, and the time spent training new staff members has decreased and become more focused on individual questions and concerns. Usage of the course is now expanding to other teams and content is always being added. Canvas has proven to increase both our effectiveness and efficiency in training.

Categories and Subject Descriptors

K.6.1 [**Project and People management**]: Training

General Terms

Documentation, Human Factors, Management, Measurement, Performance, Reliability, Standardization.

Keywords

Training, Canvas, Student Staff

1. INTRODUCTION

The University of Wyoming is a land-grant university with 12,000 students and 3,000 faculty and staff. As the only four year

SIGUCCS '15, November 09-13, 2015, St. Petersburg, FL, USA
©2015 ACM. ISBN 978-1-4503-3610-9/15/11 $15.00
DOI: http://dx.doi.org/10.1145/2815546.2815569

university in the state, the University of Wyoming plays an important role both on campus and throughout the state. The Information Technology Help Desk assists students, faculty, staff, alumni, and prospective students over the phone, through email, and by online chat with a broad spectrum of technology issues and services. The IT Help Desk is staffed by one full-time supervisor, several hours a week of full-time consultants assisting, and a pool of 20 to 25 student employees who work in the Help Desk, Service Center (walk-in computer assistance), and Student Lab Support. This pool of student employees can work in any one of those three areas or have shifts in all of them through the course of a week. Normally there are about 15 students who routinely work in the Help Desk.

2. NECESSITY OF QUALITY TRAINING IN THE HELP DESK

Quality training of Help Desk staff improves everyone's experience with the Help Desk. Customers receive better service with more requests being resolved with the first call. IT staff are able to resolve the more complex problems more easily because the initial troubleshooting is thorough and documentation is clear and complete. The Help Desk supervisor spends less time following up on incomplete tickets and can turn around customer requests more quickly. Help Desk staff themselves feel more confident in their jobs. The main problem is how to give Help Desk staff the quality training that they need to accomplish this.

As I moved into the Help Desk Supervisor position, I found that the need for training seemed constant. Student employees graduate each semester, leave for other jobs in their areas of study, and experience changes in their availability due to classes, which leads to regular turnover and a few hiring cycles in each 16 week semester. Students also leave for summer breaks and come back needing refresher training on technical topics and IT procedures. These training situations need to be addressed as quickly as possible for student staff to remain productive.

Retention also seemed to be a problem that was partially caused by lack of good training. Students would prefer to work in one of the other areas that our student techs can work in: our walk in Service Center or our Student Lab support group. This meant I was working with students who often didn't want to be in my area and who were often not performing well in the other support areas. While there are many factors that can affect retention, I felt that training was playing a large part since students were frustrated that they could not adequately troubleshoot customer issues and complete IT processes.

3. HURDLES TO QUALITY TRAINING

I encountered several difficulties to giving my staff the level of training I wanted them to have.

First and foremost, time was the most difficult challenge. Scheduling a training session with all of my staff seemed difficult and I was concerned about how much information my staff could absorb in one sitting or if their attention would wander in a room with so many staff. One-on-one sessions seemed to produce the best results, both in transferring knowledge and creating a culture of customer centered service. However, staff members could start at the help desk at different points in the school year and even when staff did start on the same week, they may start at different shift times. I would have to be available at those times to do each training session and each new staff member needed several sessions to take care of all the basic issues we get at the Help Desk.

Previously, Help Desk staff had completed some training by shadowing and receiving instruction from more experienced Help Desk staff. This caused problems since bad habits were transferred to new staff, the "why" of how we did things was usually missing in their explanations, and all staff had inconsistent knowledge. I had already seen that the result of this method was poor customer service, incomplete documentation, and limited problem solving.

Consistency was another large hurdle even in the one-on-one training sessions that I conducted. I would forget small details or time saving methods even when I was the person training my staff. This led to follow-up training sessions that could leave the information disjointed. It seemed as if I could devote a large amount of time to training and still not be guaranteed the results that we needed to successfully serve our customers and provide quality information for other IT departments.

4. STARTING ONLINE TRAINING

What was needed was a method of training that could easily be repeated and be the same every time, did not require hours of my time with each student, and still maintained the culture of excellence I wanted in the Help Desk. Online training programs could be designed to meet all these requirements and we had access to Canvas an online course management system already being used on campus for the creation and management of online learning.

I started small with the topic of using our ticketing system, since it was an area that every one of my students could benefit from and all new students would need to go through.

I launched the first course module on a small group of students that I could trust to provide open and honest feedback. Their response was overwhelming. Here are just a few of their comments:

- "I have worked here for a year and I didn't know about that feature."

- "This made everything clear for me."

- "Before I had hoped I was doing everything correctly, but now I feel sure that I can."

This resulted in a better Help Desk experience for our customers, our Help Desk staff, and the other IT staff that used our documentation.

Through this implementation, I found a combination of content types and Canvas features that provided a quality learning experience for my staff members every time. I broke my content up into modules that were focused around specific topics. This made it easy for me to assign modules and for my students to review the training areas they knew they needed.

5. COURSE CONTENT

Each module in my Canvas online course was made of two to three elements: a video, a quiz, and in some cases, supplemental reading. Each of these pieces was critical for achieving my training goals.

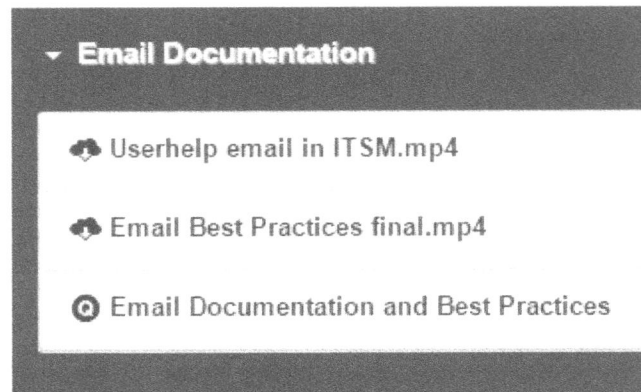

Figure 1. Canvas module about email documentation.

5.1 Videos

Every module contained at least one video and some contain more than one. These videos are simple screen captures of PowerPoint presentations or troubleshooting steps. I used videos instead of simply attaching PowerPoint presentations for the following reasons.

Videos were more engaging and easier to follow. Videos on concepts, such as techniques for writing a quality email, were presented as PowerPoint presentations with me discussing each point. Troubleshooting or procedural videos were screen captures of the workflows that I added highlighting, arrows, and other call outs to. Student staff specifically mentioned that they liked how easy it was to follow the thought process of each video.

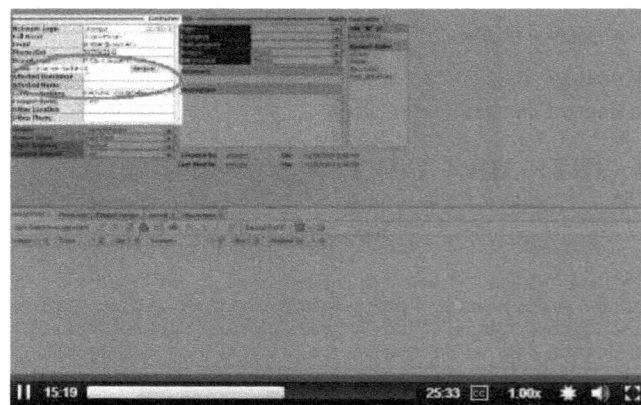

Figure 2. Call outs within a training video were used to direct trainee's attention and make the workflow easier to follow.

Videos gave me a way to convey culture along with information. I could easily stress points and emphasize important steps in a way that other media would not have allowed. Tone of voice and inflection helped me paint a picture of the type of experience I wanted our customers to have when they called the Help Desk.

I found that a couple of short videos worked better than a single long video. It was easier for my students to work through them when they had time. It was also easier for me to edit the videos. Making the editing process easier kept me motivated to continue adding content and expanding the course.

Creating videos was more work than creating Word documents or PowerPoint presentations with lots of bullet points, but it was worth the effort. They kept my students engaged in training while spreading a customer service culture. It made online training one important step closer to those one-on-one sessions that had been successful.

5.2 Quizzes

Each module has a quiz to make sure the staff members understand all of the information from the module. I intended these quizzes to review information and specifically call attention to areas that I knew commonly caused confusion. The quizzes accomplished these goals and a couple of others I had not anticipated.

Quizzes with each module have several straightforward questions simply meant to review the presented information and reinforce areas that have caused confusion in the past.

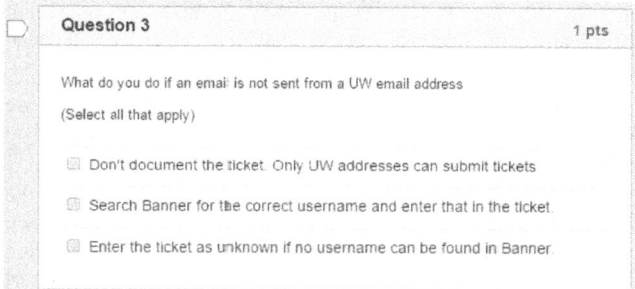

Figure 3: Basic review question in a quiz.

Quizzes also include longer questions meant to give staff members a chance to practice what they have just learned before they are in a customer-facing situation. These are my favorite questions in the quizzes since it is the best chance for me to give staff members specific feedback about their strengths and where they can still improve.

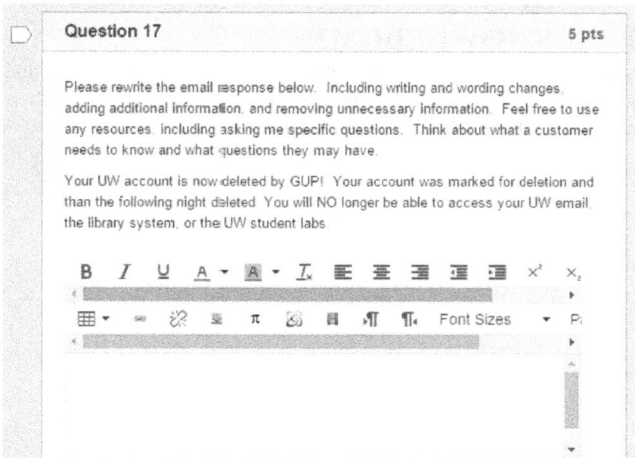

Figure 4: A longer question designed to let staff try out their skills outside of a customer situation.

I also discovered that quizzes had two more advantages that I had not foreseen.

Most of my staff members took them very seriously, possibly because Canvas is the same tool they use to take online quizzes for their classes, and this set the tone for the work that they do in the Help Desk. I noticed a marked difference in how seriously my staff took their work once quizzes were implemented.

Quizzes were also a good early indicator of exceptional and poor performers. While most of my staff performed adequately on the quizzes, normally only missing the questions that tended to be confusing, staff at the extreme ends of the spectrum stood out. I have found that people who performed very well on the quizzes have been outstanding in most aspects of the Help Desk position. Recognizing this potential early has helped me to bring them in on project and committee work more quickly. On the opposite side of the spectrum, the few who have performed poorly tended to be the staff members who didn't take the work seriously to begin with and were not strong Help Desk staff. This early indicator gave me a clear avenue to discuss with these staff members my expectations for their work and concern for the quality I had seen so far.

Once I had some practice with the video editing work, quizzes were by far the most consuming part of the work, but they are worth the creation and the grading time. Quizzes are an element that really let me make the most of the time that I had with each staff member.

5.3 Supplemental Materials

In addition to videos and quizzes, I have also added presentations and white papers to modules. These materials help staff members realize that they are part of a larger industry and adds other voices than just mine to the conversation. Presentation materials from industry experts provide valuable insights and give staff members a larger perspective.

5.4 Additional Canvas Features

Canvas also has other features that are useful for Help Desk staff. I am currently using two of these features.

The first one is the Outcomes feature, which allows the construction of a "grading" rubric. While I do not grade my Help Desk staff, it is helpful for me to break out their performance based on specific areas and see how they compare to a scale in each area. The Outcomes section is accessible to my students; in the future, I would like to use it as a conversation starter in our one-on-one meetings. These outcomes can be weighted and ratings can be broken out as is appropriate for each area. Some areas that I have created are rated pass/fail while others have a wide spectrum of performance possibilities.

Figure 5: Example outcome with a total number of points to denote weighting and various levels of performance.

The other feature I have found use for is the Discussion Board. As a place to pose questions to my staff and to allow them to supply ideas and suggestions, the discussion board has been very helpful. I do review the suggestions and I have implemented a couple of changes based on them. When these changes go into place, I send out emails to all the staff letting them know about the change, the fact that it came from a suggestion, and who made that suggestion, as a way to recognize the contribution those individuals are making.

Figure 6: Example of a discussion board topic. Below the topic, students have a field to post responses.

6. RESULTS

After the initial time investment of creating materials, my time spent on training is minimal. Each new module was a significant amount of work, but then I could use it with students over and over again. Starting a new student took almost no time at all and they could work through training even if I were in a meeting or out for the day. This meant most students in our pool of techs would start work at the Help Desk, rather than one of the other areas, which meant they would complete training in the Help Desk first, ensuring that they were trained with the values I wanted before moving to the other areas. Students coming back from break could easily go through training sessions again to remember processes and troubleshooting steps.

The online training makes it possible for the time that I spend with each staff member to be tailored to their specific questions and concerns. This makes the time much more valuable than when most of it was simply used for reviewing how to fill out fields in our ticketing system. It has also created more of a mentoring atmosphere between my staff members and myself, since my contact with them can be more personal.

Scheduling is no issue at all. There was no need for me to find a time that everyone could attend a training session or conduct multiple sessions. Students could work through the course while they were scheduled in the Help Desk, so there was no need for paid training sessions where students could easily lose focus.

Training staff members went from being a constant struggle to being a non-issue. The quality of the work improved dramatically as tickets were filled out completely and consistently by Help Desk staff members. This also meant I spent less time following up on incomplete tickets and the Help Desk's reputation improved with other IT departments. This consistency also made it easier for others within IT to find the information they were looking for in the tickets.

The Help Desk is no longer losing techs to other areas, but rather has had several instances of techs specifically asking to be assigned to the Help Desk. Overall, student staff members seem happier and are functioning at a higher level. While there are several changes that could have affected this, I believe training was a big element.

7. FUTURE DIRECTIONS

With the initial success of this format, there are several areas for it to grow in the future.

First, I will continue to add and update content in my online course. As IT staff have seen the success of the training, there have been requests for new topic areas to be added to the course to ensure those types of requests are handled more consistently by our Help Desk staff in the future. The list of areas waiting to be added seems to be constantly growing and I expect to be adding content well into the future. I also intend to look for new materials to add from conferences I attend and in industry publications.

The module format also makes it easy for me to update content as needed. We are currently in the process of implementing a new ticketing system, which means that module will need to be updated and edited to reflect the new workflows. Not only is this easy to do, but I believe the updated module's quiz will specifically help students process what these changes will mean for them so they are better prepared to help customers.

I would like to add a gamification element to the training, so we can easily see who has completed what level of training and to add encouragement for staff to complete more training.

Other units within IT have expressed interest in either using the course I have created for the Help Desk or in creating their own courses. With several groups throughout IT needing information such as the basics of our ticketing system, there is a lot of potential for groups throughout IT to benefit from the work done to create this course. Other areas in IT also train large numbers of student staff members and production of their own courses is a worthwhile endeavor for them.

Canvas has made it possible for me to create the kind of training environment that I wanted for my staff, which in turn improves the functioning of the entire Help Desk.

8. ACKNOWLEDGMENTS

A special thanks to my boss Brett Williams for his knowledge and support through this change and to all my student staff for their enthusiasm, honest feedback, and willingness to try new things.

Preparing For Your Software Asset Management Journey

Sean HV Mendoza, EdD
Pima Community College
4905 East Broadway Blvd
Tucson, Arizona 85709
(520) 206-4744
smendoza@pima.edu

ABSTRACT

Developing and implementing a software asset management plan is one of the most important initiatives any institution can undertake. Aside from preparing for the inevitable audit, a Software Asset Management (SAM) plan can create greater consistency of technology services, lower overall operating costs and safeguard the institution's data resources through consistent lifecycle maintenance. By evaluating and standardizing institutional software processes, Pima Community College stepped on the path of discovery by initiating a dialog that nurtured greater opportunities for collaboration and coordination between faculty, staff and Information Technology (IT). The increased dialog among stakeholders enabled the institution to identify and consolidate individualized software, improving the student experience and consistency of resources. With penalties of an audit as high as $150,000 for each software title infringed, the college hoped to prevent the installation of illegal software across its complex technology infrastructure, but discovered so much more on the road to safeguarding its assets. This presentation will describe the challenges of managing software assets in a multi-campus setting and provide an electronic copy of Pima Community College's plan, which can be used as a starting point for any organization. Shedding light on a SAM journey filled with adventure, the presenter will engage in an active dialog to discuss best practices and lessons learned along the way.

Categories and Subject Descriptors

K.5.1 [**Legal Aspects of Computing**]: Hardware/Software Protection – *Licensing*.

General Terms

Management, Documentation, Economics, Legal Aspects.

Keywords

Software Asset Management, Universal Design

SIGUCCS '15, November 09-13, 2015, St. Petersburg, FL, USA
© 2015 ACM. ISBN 978-1-4503-3610-9/15/11 $15.00
DOI: http://dx.doi.org/10.1145/2815546.2815573

1. INTRODUCTION

In the past, Pima Community College's IT organization was complex and decentralized. Each IT group reported directly to campus administration making hardware and software purchases based on the needs of its local employees and programs. With little central coordination, it was not uncommon for the institution to over purchase software based on the projected needs of a campus initiative. Approximately four years ago, IT became centralized and began to prepare for the inevitable audit of approximately seven thousand computers across six campuses and satellite locations across Arizona's Pima County. Organizational infrastructure and the ability to leverage existing technology tools, departmental relationships and business processes played a key role in the SAM journey.

Thinking outside of the box, we utilized existing resources with the ability to display and export a list of applications installed on a computer and alert a department prior to the end of a software asset's lifecycle. At first, we explored a number of options such as Powershell and the Command Prompt [8], but opted to use the information found in Altiris [11] and exported the data to a spreadsheet. With access to so much data, it became difficult to identify utility software that was free or open source versus paid licensing software that could cost the institution a handsome fine if not properly monitored. It was Microsoft's Outlook Calendar that served the immediate need to track license and agreement renewals during the early days of our SAM plan. We successfully tracked software invoices, blanket purchase account, and purchase orders with email documentation by creating standard Outlook calendar entries, adhering to naming conventions and controlling content. The types of information entered into the calendar included:

- Vendor Name
- Software Name
- License cycle: Perpetual/Yearly
- Reminder info:
  - Review: for possible update (comments)
  - Exp:#/#/## (Expiration date)
  - Sub:#/#/## (Subscription date)
  - Eval:#/#/## (Software Evaluation period)
- Location (by Campus)… of responsible party
  - Community
  - Desert Vista
  - District Office
  - Downtown

o East
o Northwest
o West

After gathering all existing software data and licenses, it became apparent the great distance IT must travel in preparation for a software audit. Undaunted, we looked for institutional partners willing to participate in an audit.

With Disabled Student Resources' (DSR) keen interest in minimizing costs and IT's desire to streamline Pima's software inventory, the two departments began a dialog that would lower the cost and the number of software titles purchased by the college, meet the software technology needs of over 90-95% of students with disabilities, and create a Universal Design (UD) culture with "the design of products and environments to be usable by all people, to the greatest extent possible, without the need for adaptation or specialized design." [2] With the college community's support of Universal Design and to lower software maintenance cost, three ADR software licenses were identified, purchased and made available across Pima Community College [9]. These licenses are JAWS [3], Read Write Gold [12] and ZoomText [1]. IT and DSR's collaboration generated over $30,000 in savings the first year and there was an added benefit of making the three software programs available across the institution. The consolidated software as part of Universal Design did not require students with disabilities to self-identify. Faculty did not have a need to ask students if they needed help because the tools provided by the institution essentially made most disabilities invisible.

The creation and adoption of SAM specific business processes and policies by the institution will help support its integration into the culture of the institution. Three documents were created by the IT Community in support of our SAM journey, they are: *The Pima Community College Software Processes and Inventory Manual* [5], *The Software License Policy* [7] and the *Software Audit Procedures* [6]. Designed and created by our IT community, these living documents help guide and capture relevant artifacts that help shape the direction of SAM at our institution. This manual serves as a container of artifacts integral in the development of the SAM solution, including the creation and maintenance of a virtual and media repository, the defined roles and responsibilities of IT Staff, processes and timelines for remediation, guidelines to leverage an existing calendar system as a license lifecycle notification system, and proposed future milestones indicating our journey is moving the institution in a forward direction. Much like any journey into the unknown, keeping a log of where you've been, serves to remind travelers of roads well-traveled. Following this analogy, our manual serves as a reminder to all who read it as evidence of past triumphs and future adventures.

With standardized processes and tools, the college can better leverage its existing resources to meet the software needs of both instruction and college administration. The increased number of partnerships with departments and faculty are a result of the supporting SAM infrastructure. By creating consistent data gathering processes, the centralized management and lifecycle of software assets will continue to improve the availability and increased savings of software resources.

2. SAM MISSION, VISION AND GOALS

Understanding our mission and identifying our specific goals was the key to our success. Once identified, we attempted to take an inventory of existing software across the institution. In an effort to identify our institutional assets, we endeavored to find:

1. tools currently used by the college,

2. current college/campus processes or policies,

3. existing software centric manuals, and

4. individuals with responsibilities and experiences in software assets.

After some exploration, there were no tools specifically designed as a SAM solution. Although some tools were used by the college to gather hardware inventory, there were no tools that could serve as a platform for SAM. As for college processes and policies, there were no specific processes and policies regarding SAM. Campus IT has knowledge and some expertise in software asset management, but not all of them utilized the same tools in the same way. Some campuses IT staff have also developed software processes, but they have not been implemented consistently across the institution. Given the existing SAM knowledge and skill set at the campuses, they helped contribute and play a primary role in the implementation and shaping of the mission, vision and goals.

Based on feedback from the college community and IT staff, our SAM solution mission will:

Develop an infrastructure and processes that provides access to anytime/anywhere installation of software for end users.

Our vision for our SAM solution is:

A process that minimizes IT's involvement in a user's software request. Our SAM solution is a process that is invisible to the user. Users will have the ability to view a list of existing software and submit, via an automated web process, a request to have software installed on their College owned device. Once the request has been submitted by the user, the automated process will verify the availability of existing software licenses. Once verified, the system can offer to the user a time to schedule a software install. If a software license is not available, the department supervisor and/or administrator will be contacted to purchase the appropriate number of licenses. Once the software is purchased and received by IT, the software will be made available to the users as soon as possible. With minimum involvement from IT, users will have control of software installs, times and resources.

Equally ambitious were the SAM goals. The goals of Pima Community College's software asset management solution were designed to:

1. Prepare the college for a future audit

2. Maximize the utilization and consistent deployment of software

3. Connect purchasing practices with our software lifecycle

4. Verify the consistent interpretation and management of software installations

5. Create a proactive approach to software maintenance

Given our past-decentralized model with varying consistency of software management, and software inventory performed with a variety of tools with little or no consistency, implementing the identified goals, mission and vision are truly a herculean task for the college. To prepare for a future audit and maximize the usage of existing software, an initial evaluation of software use and requirements needed to be completed.

3. REVELATIONS OF SAM

Looking for a SAM solution requires an understanding of your existing software assets and culture. After an initial evaluation of data gathered from Microsoft System Center and Altiris, the reviewer made some very compelling discoveries associated with free and licensed software, coordination of software purchases, and use of gathered data.

89% of software installed on evaluated computers was freeware, open source, drivers or applications with no need for license management. The remaining 11% of licenses consisted of a paid single, campus or enterprise license, which would require tracking and management. Given the relatively small number of paid licenses in a sea of open software, finding relevant applications for a future software audit is much like looking for the proverbial needle in a haystack. *Any future SAM solution will require a way to easily filter free and licensed software by vendors.*

Of the paid software, 64.2% had more than one version and 67.8% of software had an undocumented expiration date. This revelation further brought to light the need for consistent processes that govern the lifecycle of software assets at our institution. Through the installation of standard software and a corresponding standard version, the institution would reap the benefits of system stability, improved performance and consistent delivery of resources to its community. *All efforts must be made to create an environment that nurtures the consistent coordination of software purchases and maintenance.*

Pima Community College has a culture of software compliance. All campus IT staff is required to attend SAM training and obtain certification through a company called License Logic [4]. Due to the importance of certification to the administration, IT staff obtained the knowledge to address licensing a wide variety of issues and developed culture of software compliance. Prior to the days of a centralized IT, the zealous culture created an environment that encouraged over purchasing to ensure software compliance. The lack of coordination and absence of data driven decisions across multiple campuses created skyrocketing software purchasing. *Comprehensive data and transparent reporting of software assets to stakeholders will nurture a greater partnership between IT and its administrative and academic partners.* To encourage this partnership, we looked to develop a framework that would support these revelations.

The procedures and policies provided the foundation upon which Pima Community College's culture of SAM was built upon. Providing proof of purchase is one of the most important aspects of a software audit. With the assistance of the institution's business department, a business account was identified and incorporated into the purchasing processes of the institution. Through the use of the business code, IT can centrally gather evidence of software purchases in the event of a software audit. Relevant files and software versions are also gathered centrally to aid in the consistent installation of applications. Partnering with server, firewall and application deployment administrators, a central repository for software assets ensures that IT Staff have access to and knowledge of the latest software version. Campus IT Staff are also provided an inventory and processes manual for best practices of software installations. Within this manual are institutional policies that outline both the importance of compliance and commitment to providing consistent and timely access to software assets. Given these revelations and foundations, we engaged in an active search for a SAM solution.

4. OUR SAM

Guided by our mission and goals, we embarked on finding our SAM solution and started our search on the Internet. Our criteria identified eleven potential companies to review and explore. With price a factor in the selection, two companies emerged from the group. Nearly identical in every way, there was one difference that set the company apart: Customer service. During a call for additional information, one company went the "extra mile" and provided a high value customer service experience for our reviewer. This company was SNOW [10]. With service purchased and IT staff trained, we implemented SNOW as Pima Community College's SAM solution. After our implementation, we learned a few things along the way:

- **Install the inventory server in the DMZ if you want to inventory laptops outside of your firewall.** With the installation of our server behind our firewall, we were unable to inventory remote systems. Moving our server into the DMZ required additional configurations to our firewall and desktop clients after the transition, creating a blackout of data during the transition.

- **Always think of consistency and transparency.** Stakeholders (college community and students) appreciate being provided information about resources that they may or may not need. When a report of all software assets was provided to faculty and staff, many were surprised by all the assets available that often go unused.

- **Stay on top of your goals and timelines.** Software Asset Management is a dynamic process with external forces constantly pushing and pulling goals and timelines. Always make a good faith effort to accomplishing the goals and document steps/challenges towards those timelines. When you reach a milestone, take a moment to enjoy it, but don't forget there's another milestone up ahead.

- **Take the time to build a community.** This project is complex and cannot be completed alone. If you build a community that is aligned with the values of the institution and the individual, you have a better chance of succeeding. Pick individuals who believe in the importance of SAM or inspire others by being the example for this project. At Pima, these individuals are called the "Guardians of SNOW".

- **Look for opportunities to create in data based decisions.** The uses of timely reports to stakeholders play a key role in the success of SAM. The dissemination of reports such as "installed software that has never been used" or "software compliance", has the potential of saving the institution thousands in over purchases or millions in fines, respectively.

The lessons of the past provide a clearer version of the future. Pima Community College considers and actively explores initiatives toward greater alignment to its SAM mission. These initiatives include the use of a keyserver, greater centralized software purchasing, the preparation of a self-audit by the internal auditor, development of a software catalog and the updating of its SAM manual and policies.

5. CONCLUSION

More than just an application that captures software assets data and documentation, our Software Asset Management solution is a combination of technology, processes and relationships with the flexibility and infrastructure to meet the needs of our community. Created initially to meet a future software audit, our SAM journey became more than just a drive down the road of software management. We've created a guide, identified and purchased a vehicle to ease our journey and even acquired a key server to maintain current licensing for additional flexibility. We discovered and created processes and relationships to assist us along the way. Before we took that first step, we had to decide where we wanted to go and how we should get there, so our journey had to be guided by a clear mission, goals and leadership. The SAM team has implemented a number of technical (inventory client, DMZ server) and non-technical solutions (SNOW Guardians Community) to create buy-in and safeguard software assets. A SAM solution and its continued success must include the active participation and collaboration of a team. Once we started taking those initial steps and started traveling down the road, we learned a little more about ourselves and our institution. We discovered that we needed a tool that had could easily identify the difference between licensed and free software; could generate and disseminate reports to make informed decisions easily and on demand; and nurture collaboration and transparency.

Not all SAM challenges can be overcome by technology. Our SAM project's success can also be found in the relationships that are formed with our institutional partners in and out of IT. It is through the customer service provided by the Guardians of SNOW and members of IT, in the form of value added reports and communications, that will mean the difference between the

success or failure of this journey. A journey may begin with the first step, but a successful SAM journey requires a map, some tools and a traveling companion.

6. REFERENCES

[1] AiSquared (2009). ZoomText - Ai Squared - We've got accessibility covered. Retrieved August 5, 2015, from http://www.aisquared.com/zoomtext.

[2] Burgstahler, S (2015). Universal Design of Instruction (UDI): Definition, Principles ... Retrieved August 5, 2015, from http://www.washington.edu/doit/universal-design-instruction-udi-definition-principles-guidelines-and-examples.

[3] Freedom Scientific (2014). JAWS Screen Reader - Best in Class - Freedom Scientific. Retrieved August 5, 2015, from http://www.freedomscientific.com/Products/Blindness/JAWS.

[4] License Logic (2012). License Logic Institute. Retrieved August 5, 2015, from https://licenselogic.com/.

[5] Mendoza, S. (2012). Software Asset Management Manual. Pima Community College - Information Technology. Retrieved August 6th, 2015 from https://drive.google.com/file/d/0B-eQuR_L7mtYbzBPSXc4dVQzdEU/view

[6] Mendoza, S. (2012). Software Audit Procedures. Pima Community College - Information Technology. Retrieved August 6th, 2015 from https://drive.google.com/file/d/0B-eQuR_L7mtYV0I2WGkyZGRTV0s5N1dBSXhmZ29lQmFfTG53/view

[7] Mendoza, S. (2012). Software License Policy. Pima Community College - Information Technology. Retrieved August 6th, 2015 from https://drive.google.com/file/d/0B-eQuR_L7mtYYl9vYlFseVZoc3JWYlJ0Q2I1Q29uNlZWSlNF/view

[8] Patoway, K. (2013). How to Create a List of Installed Programs in Windows ... Retrieved August 5, 2015, from http://www.instantfundas.com/2013/07/how-to-create-list-of-installed.html.

[9] Pima Community College (2014). Faculty Senate Meeting Minutes Apr. 2013 - Pima ... Retrieved August 5, 2015, from https://www.pima.edu/faculty-staff/employee-organizations/faculty-senate/senate-minutes/201304-senate-minute

[10] SNOW (2003). Snow Software: Software Asset Management (SAM). Retrieved August 5, 2015, from

http://www.snowsoftware.com/.

[11] Symantec (2013). Symantec Deployment Solution | Symantec. Retrieved August 5, 2015, from http://www.symantec.com/deployment-solution/.

[12] Texthelp (2011). Read&Write GOLD Features for PC - Texthelp. Retrieved August 5, 2015, from http://www.texthelp.com/north-america/our-products/readwrite/features-pc.

A Real-time Application to Predict and Notify Students about the Present and Future Availability of Workspaces on a University Campus

Shamar Ward
University Of The West-Indies Cave Hill Campus
Department Of Computer Science Mathematics and
Physics
Cave Hill, Barbados
shamar.ward@mycavehill.uwi.edu

Mechelle Gittens
University Of The West-Indies Cave Hill Campus
Department Of Computer Science Mathematics and
Physics
Cave Hill, Barbados
mechelle.gittens@cavehill.uwi.edu

ABSTRACT

The many responsibilities of students require that they access and utilize information about workspaces to facilitate time management. Workspaces such as computer labs, classrooms, and study areas have varying availability. At the University of the West Indies - Cave Hill Campus (UWICHC), students do not have a means of knowing in advance if these areas are unavailable other than to visit the space. If the space is unavailable, the student would have lost time. In addition, an initial survey of the opinions of 100 UWICHC students showed that 72% of the respondents found when a non-class participant entered a room where they were having a class, the activity distracted either them or the instructor. In this paper, we present a system which assesses the availability status of the room and makes a real-time occupancy indicator available to students on and off campus. This indicator avoids cases where a non-class participant interrupts an ongoing class. Additionally, students can query the system for a prediction or estimation on what the status of the space will be on a given day and time based on past conditions. In our survey, 91% of the respondents believed that having a system that relayed real-time or predictive information about class availability would help them, and therefore allow more time for productive activities. We also present an analysis of the use of the system and how students perceived the usefulness of the system in operation.

Categories and Subject Descriptors

H.4.1 [INFORMATION SYSTEMS APPLICATIONS]: Time management (e.g., calendars, schedules).

General Terms

Management

SIGUCCS '15, November 09 - 13, 2015, St. Petersburg, FL, USA
Copyright is held by the owner/author(s). Publication rights licensed to ACM.
ACM 978-1-4503-3610-9/15/11...$15.00
DOI: http://dx.doi.org/10.1145/2815546.2815563

Keywords

Predict Availability, Availability of Workspaces, University Campus.

1. INTRODUCTION

It is a challenging task to plan or organize one's time, if there is no guide as to when required resources will be available. There is no way of knowing when next these resources will become available without being in the physical location. By removing this uncertainty and making predictions as to when they will be next available, students and staff would be better equipped to plan their day and capitalize on the limited time they have available.

The CSL (Computer Science Lab) at The University of The West Indies - Cave Hill Campus is used by students as well as lecturers. There are over 200 students who use the lab in a 24-hour period to do research and course related assignments. However, the lab is also reserved by the university for two hour lab/practical sessions.

As a result, the lab is busy and a common problem occurs when the lecturer or instructor is teaching a lab and students enter because they do not know that there is an ongoing practical. This can be a distraction for both the instructor and students. Paper-based notes have been placed on doors, however, because of the dynamic nature of space scheduling, the occupancy facts may change. Therefore, there is currently no method of knowing when the lab is occupied or in use without entering.

Another problem occurs when a student needs to use one of the machines in the lab to perform some activity. They may walk an extended distance to get to the lab due to the geography of the campus, only to realize that all machines are in use. This wastes time for the student on they came to campus for the sole purpose of using the lab. They may also have passed other labs on campus which they could have used. If the student was able to access information indicating the lab was full, occupied or is normally full at that time based on prediction and estimation, they would have been able to make a more informed decision, hence saving time.

2. SYSTEM REQUIREMENTS

We surveyed the students at the UWICHC with the following research question in mind: "Can a mobile application be developed to aid students with their time management by notifying them in real time and also giving predictions on workspace availability?"

The following questions were asked:

- Which faculty are you from?

- Do you sometimes require the uses of a lab and it is either full or in use?

    o If yes, how do you realize it is full or in use?

- Were you ever in a class or a lab and a person came in checking if there was a class?

    o If yes, did the person distract you or the lecturer/ instructor?

- If you could access information from a website or mobile application informing you about the availability of a lab space, would this assist you?

- Which mobile platform would you prefer the mobile application to be deployed on?

Figures 1 to 3 show summaries of key responses from our survey: Figure 1 shows that 97% of the students surveyed have indicated the only way they know if a lab is reserved or full is to visit the location and look into the room. From the results we gathered, students who require the use of a lab are required to be at the physical location of the lab as they also need to open the door (look in) to assess the status of the room which can be either full, reserved or available. In addition, this can be a disadvantage for students having to travel to a lab with the uncertainty of if the lab will be accessible.

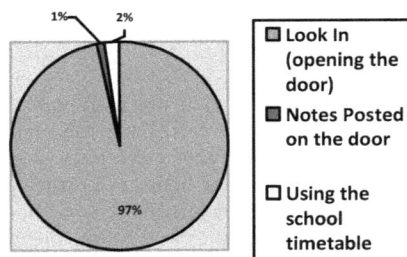

Figure 1: Students' responses to: Do you sometimes require the use of a lab and it is either full or in use? If yes, how do you realize it is full or in use?

In Figure 2 we note that 67% of students are distracted when the interruption occurs. Figure 2 results show students as well as the instructor become distracted when students open the door to look in and asses the status of the room. We view this as a significant problem since results from this study shown in figure 1 also show the method used by most students to assess the status in the room distracts majority of students and instructors.

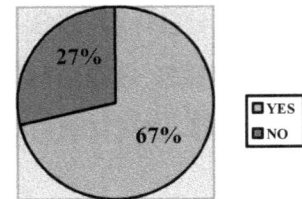

Figure 2 Students' responses to: Were you ever in a class in a lab and a person came in checking if there was a class? If yes did the person distract you or the lecturer/ instructor?

In Figure 3, 91% of the respondents believed that having a system that relayed real-time or predicted information on lab availability would assist them in having more time to perform productive activities. This result indicates the need for an automated system which can provide real-time or predicted information to students.

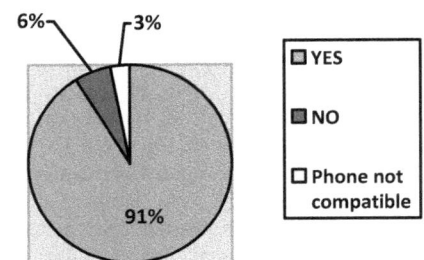

Figure 3: Student's responses to: If you could access information from a website or mobile application informing you about the availability of a lab space, would this assist you?

Based on these results we recognized that the system should:

1. Provide users with predictions on estimations based on past conditions.

2. Provide real-time information on current conditions and situations at any given time.

3. Have a physical indicator outside of the lab showing its current status (for example, full, not full, reserved, class in progress).

3. RELATED WORKS

Based on the answers given by the students we have found that the work most relevant to the required system fell into two categories. A system is needed that:

1. Relays information to students.

2. Captures and stores data which will be used to give real-time information on room availability as well as to give predictions.

We will summarize these relevant works here.

3.1 Relaying information to students

At Carnegie-Mellon University (CMU) [6] Salber et al. implemented a system to aid students in being more efficient. The system was referred to as the Portable Help Desk (PHD). The Portable Help Desk gives students information on resources around the campus such as printer queues and the current stock of vending machines. By providing this information, students are better informed about the resources without having to visit them at their various locations around campus. The paper showed the need for a system that provides information about the availability of resources remotely. However, Salber et al. did not address the question for computer lab spaces. In addition, no prediction or estimation methods were used since no data was stored for analysis. Therefore, students only had real-time information and could not plan ahead. Salber et al. used both audio and visual methods via web interface to inform the student on the status of resources through the PHD system.

In the work by Kestranek et al. [3] a mobile application was developed to deliver real-time information to the user. This system was comprised of networked noise level monitors which collected the amplitude of the noise in the area and compared those values of an acceptable amplitude stored in the database. This information was then displayed to the user via a mobile application along with features of the room such as types of furniture and availability of a white board and projector. The system would deliver this information along with a Google map. However, if the user did not have a mobile phone capable of using this feature they would be able to use the SMS service the system provides. This system is similar to the system needed at the UWICHC by offering information to students without them being physically there. However, there are a few differences. The first difference is that Kestranek et al. [3] used noise level monitors to gauge both the noise level and the availability. It was not clear how the audio received was processed to give an approximation of the number of persons in the room at a given time. Also, we are not sure how the system would perform in an environment which is generally noisy in terms of constant footsteps or people talking. The work by Kestranek et al. is similar to Salber and colleagues' work in that it shows that [6] students need to have the information about the resources around campus. This supports the need for such a system at UWICHC. While, Kestranek et al. [3] revealed a mobile application that can be used to relay information to the student about resources, this system did not offer predicted or estimated information to students so they could plan. Only real time information was available.

We therefore gathered that both a web interface and a mobile application are useful to deliver real-time information to students.

3.2 Storing data about the status of the room

In the research by Kestranek et al. [3] they mention their application required an Apache web server, PHP, MySQL database and wireless routers. We decided to use the same implementation to store our captured data.

3.3 Capturing Data

Pengfei et al. [4] proposed a bus arrival time prediction system based on bus passengers' participatory sensing. They used the cellphones of passengers to estimate and predict the bus arrivals at bus stops. This however relied on the cellphone users manually entering information via their mobile phone. The work by Pengfei et al. [4] indicated it was possible to use the users' cellphones to capture data and then do a prediction or estimation. However, although this may be applicable to the bus scenario, the approach may be burdensome to students. The approach used with the buses would also not indicate if there is a class in session in the room.

Power [5] described the implementation of Pal Mickey devices at Disney resorts. Pal Mickey used 400 different infrared transmitters located throughout the Walt Disney Theme Parks to advise visitors to Disney on activities taking place close to their current location. Power went on to mention that Pal Mickey was also used by the resort to analyse customer movement and therefore was used as an analytical tool for its developers at Walt Disney Theme Parks. From this paper we gathered that devices such as infrared transmitters can be physically attached to areas of interest which can be used to detemine the location of the user. We then asked if a similar system could be used to determine activity within the lab.

Power's work [5] showed it was possible to use a physical device (infrared transmitter) to also gather information on the user's location. In our case we could use the computer terminals within the lab to determine the number of persons in the lab. With our data collection method in mind we can now design our system.

4. SYSTEM DESIGN

The system needs to perform the following tasks:

1. Provide users with predictions on estimations based on past conditions.

2. Provide real-time information on current conditions and situations at any given time.

3. Have a physical indicator outside of the lab showing its current status (for example: full, not full, reserved, or class in progress).

In order to satisfy these requirements, we recognized that the necessary components of the system were:

1. The Database

2. Estimation and Prediction

3. Mobile Application

4. Door Indicator

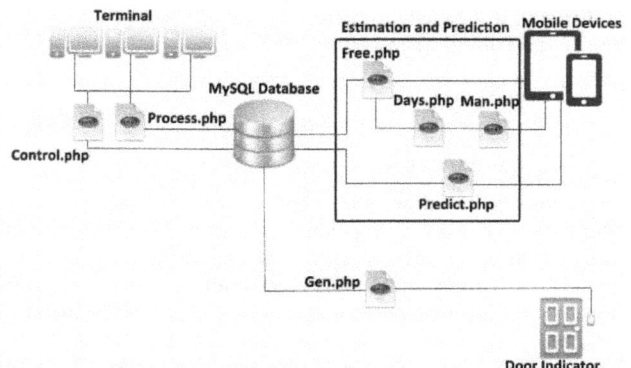

Figure 4. The system.

4.1 The Database

A database was designed to store lab activity data collected from the terminals as well as to store the times the lab would be reserved for a class. Kestranek et al. [3] used a MySQL database to store noise level data. We chose the same database management system since it is open source and capable of storing the necessary data. The database contained the following five tables:

- Compc: Stores the number of active lab computers.
- Cslat: Contains the classes times for the lab.
- Csll: The table contained the number of computers logged in at any given time.
- Cslm: This table stores the unique id of each computer operational in the lab.
- Cslsl: Contains a log of every log in, log out or shutdown event which occurred.

4.1.1 Database Manipulation and Management

PHP scripts were used to insert and retrieve information from the MySQL database.

Getid.php: This script when queried issues a unique id to each machine on the first run of the C# application.

Control.php: This script adds an entry to the csll and cslsl tables for the event which occurred, e.g., login, logout, and shutdown.

Process.php: This script was responsible for removing the mid (machine id) from the csll on the logout or shutdown event it also makes an entry to the cslsl table.

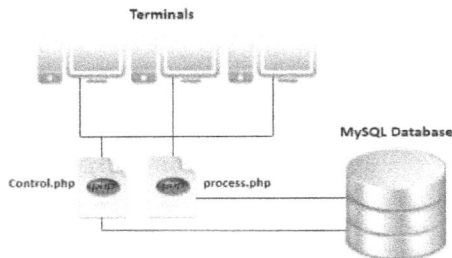

Figure 5: Communication between the database management and manipulation files.

4.2 Data Collection

Based on the context as well as protocol restrictions within the university, three methods were identified for collecting data on the lab availability. These were:

- Camera
- Application installed on the terminals
- Laser Counter

We chose to install an application on the terminals in the lab since it would incur no additional cost when compared with the camera and laser counter method. In addition, it satisfied the policies of the university since it allowed the network security team to test the application and monitor the data collection and analysis. The primary operating system used at UWICHC for campus networks is Windows. We therefore chose C# as the programming language for the application because of the ease of interface between technologies. The C# application installed on the terminals followed the flowchart seen in Figure 6.

4.2.1. Testing and Optimization of C# Application

The C# application was designed to run in the background and therefore the user had no interaction or communication with the application. By doing this the user would not be interrupted when an event occurred, and it reduced the possibility of the user either terminating running the process or entering information which could affect our result. However, the initial C# application used loops and it was believed that a better alternative could be designed since it was still possible for users to experience sluggish behavior from other applications.

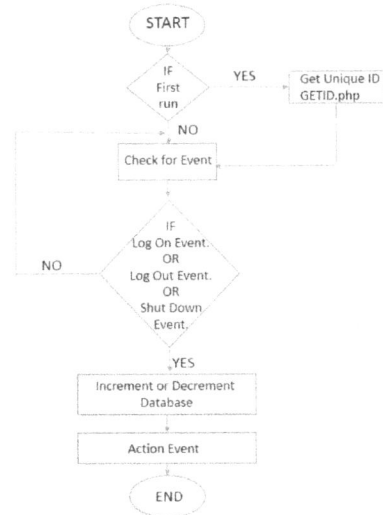

Figure 6: Flowchart of C# program.

We therefore optimized the application by removing loops and replacing them with event listeners so it would use less memory. During testing the application used 2000 KB of memory and this was deemed acceptable, since the user would not experience any effects of having the application running while they were performing their usual lab tasks.

4.3 Prediction and Estimation

We approached the usage of the terminals in the lab as a queue to provide the prediction and estimation feature of the system. We noted that there was no physical line outside of the lab (queue), however, with persons still monitoring the status of the room through our application there was actually a virtual queue. Queuing theory appeared to be most appropriate to this study of waiting lines [8]. Queuing theory uses the arrival of persons and applies probability to compute the demand of the resource over a time period. However, in this initial attempt to solve this lab space issue, the data collected did not take into account the wait times or queue lengths which are required by the queuing theory models. Based on the type of information that we were able to collect for this initial solution, we decided that SMA (Simple Moving Averages), a time series qualitative forecasting method [1], would be suitable. To compare results attained we also used trend-line forecasting and compared results to the SMA. The formula used is shown below:

$$SMA = \frac{D1 + D2}{N}$$

The SMA formula was implemented in PHP. A PHP class queries the database for all data on each day and time and returns the SMA. Whereas, with the trend-line forecasting the data was generated and entered into MS Excel® which generated a chart. PHP was then used to implement the trend line formula by changing the x value to generate an estimation for that day and time. Figure 7 shows the chart which was used to generate the trend line for Saturday based on two weeks of data with each day highlighted in red and blue.

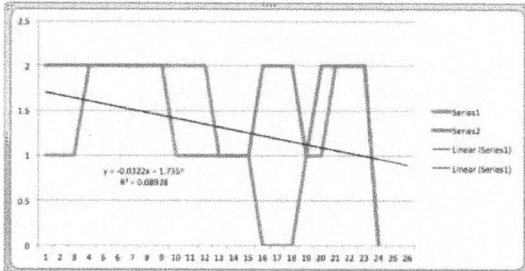

Figure 7: Trend-line graph of data for two Saturdays.

The PHP files used to calculate the SMA and trend-line forecast are described below.

Free.php: This script compares the times for scheduled classes in the database to the current time of the day and decides if the current time falls between any of the booked times.

Days.php: This script contains a class which is used to store the number of machines logged in or out during hours 0 – 24 (24-hour clock). Each hour states the number of machines available.

Man.php: This script controls and manipulates the class days. It populates the class from the logs in the database.

Predict.php: When this script is queried it requests two variables, which are the day, and time, which are used to estimate the number of occupied machines.

Gen.php: This script communicates with the door indicator it checks the database for the availability/status of the class.

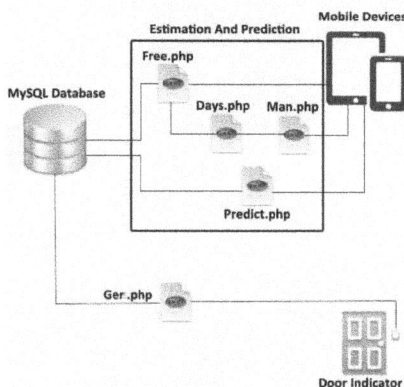

Figure 8: Communication between the database mobile application and door indicator

4.4 Mobile Application

From our survey, 71% of respondents use Android devices. However, since it is possible to build one application and deploy it on multiple platforms with the use of Cordova, we chose to use this interoperable technology. Apache Cordova is a set of device APIs that allow a mobile application developer to access native device function such as the camera or accelerometer from JavaScript. Combined with a user interface (UI) framework such as jQuery Mobile, Dojo Mobile or Sencha Touch, this allows a smartphone application to be developed with just HTML, CSS, and JavaScript [2].

However, Apache Cordova would not give the full functionality that a user would require. Users also need to have a user friendly interface. For this reason, without the aid of a graphic designer to assist in the interface, we began a search for possible templates or frameworks that we could integrate with Cordova. The developers of Cordova [2] mentioned some UI frameworks such as jQuery Mobile, Dojo Mobile and Sencha Touch. However, we used Ionic framework for its attractive interface and, unlike other UI frameworks such as Sencha touch and Kendo UI, it is open source. The mobile application that was developed using Cordova and Ionic framework offers the following features.

- Checks for the presence of either a data or Wi-Fi connection
- Checks for a server connection
- Checks the server for whether a class is active in the lab
- Checks the server for availability of machines in the lab real-time
- Checks the server for availability of machines in the lab estimation or prediction

4.4.1 Connectivity check

Figure 9: Application notification screen after checking for a data plan or Wi-Fi connection.

The mobile application checks for either a data connection or a Wi-Fi connection. If there is no connection, the user is notified giving them the opportunity to rectify the problem. As seen in figure 10 below a red indicator is displayed if the user either has no connection or the server is unreachable.

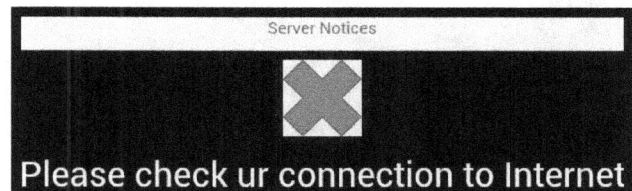

Figure 10: Application notification screen after checking for a data plan or Wi-Fi connection.

4.4.2 Availability check and prediction

On making a successful server connection with Wi-Fi or data, the application will query the database for the status of the lab workspace. If a class is currently in the lab, there is no need to calculate the availability of the machines or prediction for that time period. Therefore, to let the user know of the current class status the appropriate message and available function is displayed. Shown in Figure 10 is the message displayed when a class is in progress and occupies the workspace.

Figure 11: Class in progress display.

In Figure 12 we see the message and function which is displayed when the lab is available for use. It will now allow the user to check the availability of the lab as well as see the prediction/estimation based on past weeks.

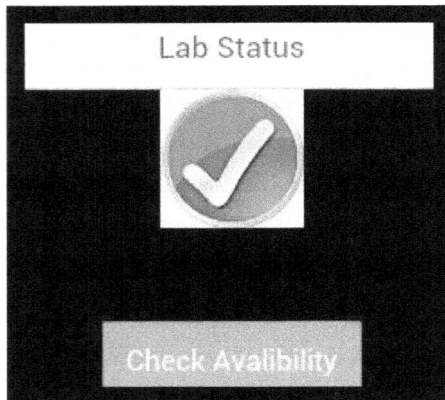

Figure 12: Showing the lab is available for use.

Figure 13 shows the real time availability, estimated availability based on simple moving average and predicted availability using trend line forecasting.

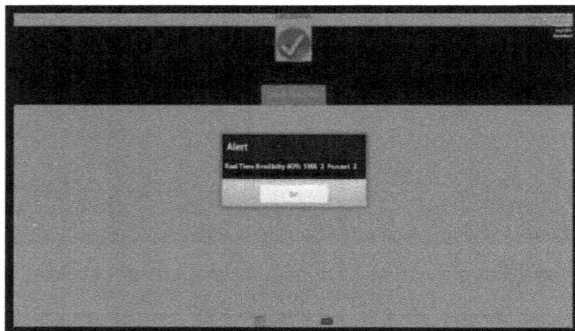

Figure 13: The requested SMA and trend-line estimation.

4.5 Door Indicator

To address the case where the user does not have an active cell phone, a physical indicator should be placed outside of the door where persons wishing to enter can see the status of the lab.

In the literature, the first solution discovered was that of a sliding notice board. However, that would have been too costly for this study. We noted another possibility in the use of used Smartphones. For this study we recycled a Blackberry 8520 (posted on the outside of the workspace door) as the Door Indicator to notify students of the classes' status without requiring them to have their own device. However, all Blackberry® backlights time out after two minutes of inactive use. This was not favorable since the user should be able to see the class status without performing any action. Therefore, a solution was pursued and we discovered an application which could be installed to keep the backlight on indefinitely. The indicator was developed using Html CSS and JavaScript. However, the Blackberry operating system version 5 browser caches pages which are repeatedly called. After 2 calls the application started to record incorrect values. A random generator was then used to pass random values to the page so it was not cached by the browser. The application displayed 4 states of the workspace which are listed below:

- Class in progress (red)
- No Class But full (blue)
- No class Not Full (green)
- System Error (orange)

Figure 14 shows how the indicator shows the class status using color codes and a brief text.

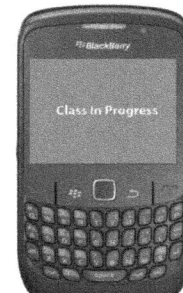

Figure 14: The Cordova application Door Indicator application running on Blackberry 8520.

5. RESULTS

Beta testing was used to check the application performance in real world situations as well as to gauge the performance of the SMA and Forecasting Formulas. Six Android testers participated. We were unable to use Apple devices due to the restrictions imposed by Apple for developers to subscribe to their developers center. An Android application package (APK), which is used to install the application on an Android, was distributed to each subject which was then installed on their phone to be tested. They were each asked to fill out an assessment sheet which highlighted the following sections:

1. Overall comments and usefulness.
2. Accuracy of real time, SMA and trend line forecast.

3. Recommendations or improvements.

Subject #1

Overall: The real time aspect was helpful and useful and accurate when used.

Accuracy: The SMA and forecast were off by 1 or 2 but never exceeded 2.

Improvements: Improve the accuracy of SMA and Forecast.

Subject #2

Overall: It was useful since I could sit at home and see how many persons were in the lab and at what times so I could decide to go or not.

Accuracy: The real time was accurate when tested but the SMA and forecast values were off.

Improvements: Offer information on who is in the lab and doing what.

Subject #3

Overall- The application was really useful since it allowed me to be more comfortable when relaxing knowing that I can tell when the lab is available without having to physically go and check.

Accuracy- The real time was accurate however the SMA and forecast was not accurate.

Improvements- none

Subject #4:

Overall- The application was really useful since it allowed me to be more comfortable when relaxing knowing that I can tell when the lab is available without me having to physically go and check.

Accuracy- The real time was accurate however the SMA and forecast was not accurate.

Improvements- None

Subject #5

Overall- The application was super useful since I no longer had to ask other students entering the lab if they had a class. I could now just check the app to see if a class was in the lab and also it seemed to give the warning 10 minutes before (cool).

Accuracy- when tested it was hard to tell if the application was giving the correct reading since it was given in a percentage.

Improvements- Give actual statistics of who is in the lab that would be more useful than a percentage.

Subject #6

Overall- The application was nice.

Accuracy- Was accurate but not the SMA and forecast

Improvements- More platforms.

Analysis of Results

As expected the SMA and forecast was not accurate enough for the subjects with only 2 weeks of data used to create the trend line or average. The other functions of the application, such as the class availability indicator, were useful, in ways not anticipated. One subject said they appreciated that the class full indicator changed ten minutes before there was a class. Initially that was not designed as a feature but was actually a defect in

the system since classes do not begin on the hour but at ten minutes past. The system truncates the minute's section of the time and just uses the hour. Other faults which subjects identified were that the application be more accurate as it relates to the predictions and estimations.

6. CONCLUSIONS AND FUTURE WORK

In this paper we successfully designed a system capable of providing real time workspace availability information to students as well as predicting and estimating workspace availability via a mobile device and a door indicator. This application can be very useful to the UWICHC and its students by helping them to be more organized and plan their time better. This was noted in the comments provided in a follow-up survey of users of the labs space. In addition, it can also reduce workspace distractions with the door indicator feature by reducing the number of persons opening the door during a class or reserved period.

In the future, we will explore other methods of prediction such as queuing theory and Exponential Moving Average (EMA) since SMA does not give accurate predictions in all cases. We will also seek to improve the prediction feature by including parameters in our calculations such as time of the semester and weather conditions which would have an impact on the workspace availability. There were limitations in the data collection in some instances. For example, someone may be in the workspace using a chair but not using a terminal. Our system would indicate the availability of a terminal. However, since the chair coinciding with the terminal is in use, a student would not be able to use the terminal. In future work, we will focus on identifying other methods of not just identifying available terminals but also identifying how many persons are actively using the various aspects of the workspace.

7. LIMITATIONS OF THE STUDY

During this study some complications and limitations were encountered. Some of these include:

1. Data collection
2. Protocols and restrictions of the campus
3. Time
4. Parameters
5. Platform testers

7.1 Data Collection

Due to time constraints, the data was limited to two weeks of logs. Therefore, each day of the week had reoccurrences, which were compared and analyzed. Preferably more data would have led to a more accurate estimation/prediction. In future we will collect and relook how the data is stored so other prediction algorithms such as queuing theory mentioned before can be used.

7.2 Protocols and Restrictions of the Campus

The University Of The West Indies where the test case was conducted has an obligation to protect the interest of its staff (records), students (records), and the assets of the campus (in this case, the computer systems). Therefore, to ensure their obligations were met the system had to be tested and reviewed before it could be installed on the campus' network. This process involved:

1. Acquiring permission to conduct the research on the premises.
2. Review of the C# application which stored the data in the database.
3. Setting up a server on campus network to accept data sent by C# script.
4. Moving scripts and MySQL tables from external server to local server on campus.
5. Second review of the C# application which stored the data in the database.
6. Running/Testing C# application on the campus network to detect any issues or conflicts with other applications.
7. Implementing the application on computers connected to the campus network.
8. Submitting a request for the server to be accessible from outside of the campus. This is so users who would be using their data plan would still be able to access the information since they would not be on the campus network.
9. Adding a firewall rule to allow external access to the server on Port 80 (http).

We addressed the protocol and restriction limitation by selecting a method of data collection which could have easily been monitored and tested by policy enforcers on the Campus IT Services team. By selecting C# which is native to Microsoft Windows the standard operating system at UWICHC, this reduced the testing time of the application and also ensured compatibility with all the terminals. In future we will attempt to reduce the monitoring and testing time even further by studying other methods of data collect keeping within the protocols and restrictions.

7.3 Parameters

Parameters such as semester, time of semester, number of assignments due and the weather could be used to better aid in the prediction and estimation by comparing the lab usage to these parameters to see if a trend or a pattern exist. In the future, we wish to use these parameters to see if they can improve the accuracy of our prediction since these parameters would affect the usage of the lab.

7.4 Platform Testers

Only Android testers were called upon since other platforms such as Apple's require paid subscriptions to the developers platform in order to be able to deploy the application on the physical device. In future we wish to have the application tested by a wider audience which would not limit our study to only Android users.

8. ACKNOWLEDGMENTS

We would like to acknowledge Dr. Thomas Edward, Dr. Adrian Als, and Dr. Paul Walcott for their suggestions on aspects of the research project. We would also like to acknowledge all the participants of the survey and the members of CITS (Campus IT Services), in particular Mr. Austral Estwick, Carla Nurse and Corey Hinds for providing permission and reviewing the application. We also thank Mr. Maurice Beckles FST (Faculty of Science and Technology) IT technician for providing us with a server and installation of the application.

9. REFERENCES

[1] Alsultanny, Y., 2012. Successful Forecasting for Knowledge Discovery by Statistical Methods. In *Information Technology: New Generations (ITNG), 2012 Ninth International Conference on*, 584-588. DOI= http://dx.doi.org/10.1109/ITNG.2012.160.'3

[2] Apache Software Foundation, 2013. About Apache Cordova.

[3] Kestranek, D., Clark, R.J., Sanders, M., Poole, E.S., Marquartdt, P., Rabun, J., and Rhodes, J., 2011. Spaces Without Faces. In *Proceedings of the Proceedings of the 13th International Conference on Human Computer Interaction with Mobile Devices and Services* (Stockholm, Sweden, 2011), ACM, 2037490, 703-705. DOI= http://dx.doi.org/10.1145/2037373.2037490.

[4] Pengfei, Z., Yuanqing, Z., and Mo, L., 2014. How Long to Wait? Predicting Bus Arrival Time With Mobile Phone Based Participatory Sensing. *Mobile Computing, IEEE Transactions on 13*, 6, 1228-1241. DOI= http://dx.doi.org/10.1109/TMC.2013.136.

[5] Power, D.J., 2004. Decision Support Systems: Frequently Asked Questions. *iUniverse.*

[6] Salber, D., Siewiorek, D., and Smailagic, A., 2001. Supporting Mobile Workgroups on a Wireless Campus. *IBM T.J. Watson Research Center.*

[7] Sperry, B., Bradley, A., and Lunch, M., 2013. Start Building With Ionic Drifty.

[8] Sztrik, J., 2010. Queueing Theory and its Applications, A Personal View. *Proceedings of the 8th International Conference on Applied Informatics 1*, 9-30.

Understanding Windows 10

Gale D. Fritsche
Lehigh University
EWFM Computing Center
8B East Packer Avenue
Bethlehem, PA 18015
01-610-758-5038
gdf2@lehigh.edu

ABSTRACT

Windows 10 was released in July 2015 as a free upgrade for Windows 7 and Windows 8 customers. With any operating system upgrade, there are many steps that need carefully planned and many questions answered in order to reduce problems for the technical staff as well as end users. What does the arrival of Windows 10 mean to your organization? How are you going to plan for a smooth transition to Windows 10? How should your organization approach its implementation? Since Windows 10 is free and distributed to Windows users, how will you support the various users who are prompted to install it – especially home users and users on campus who are not in active directory? This paper will outline the new features of Windows 10, will discuss its improvements as well as the anticipated issues and challenges that may be faced during a campus wide implementation.

Categories and Subject Descriptors

K.8.3 [MANAGEMENT AND MAINTENANCE]; C.5.3 [MICROCOMPUTERS]

General Terms

Management, Documentation, Performance, Security

Keywords

Windows 10, Operating System, Upgrades

INTRODUCTION

Lehigh University Overview

Lehigh University is a private research institution founded in 1865 and located in Bethlehem, PA. With an enrollment of approximately 4,700 undergraduates and 2,000 graduate students, Lehigh employees 600 faculty members and over 1,100 support staff.

SIGUCCS'15, November 9-13, 2015, St. Petersburg, FL, USA.
Copyright ACM 978-1-4503-3610-9/15/11 $15.00.
DOI: http://dx.doi.org/10.1145/2815546.2815577

Both library and computer services are combined in one integrated organizational unit known as Library and Technology Services (LTS). LTS supports and maintains maintains 450 public site computers, 2500 faculty/staff computers and various independent equipment and specialized computing labs. Approximately 70% of the PCs are managed and updated by use of Microsoft's Active Directory. The other 30% are managed by the individual user or department. Approximately 70% for the staff and faculty desktops are running some version of the Windows operating system; most of these are Windows 7. The remaining 30% of faculty and staff desktops are either Macintosh computers or desktops running some form of the Linux operating system. As for Windows Desktops, Lehigh has a Microsoft campus agreement that allows for the upgrade of all faculty/staff Windows computers on campus to the newest version of the Operating System. Since Lehigh has a Microsoft campus agreement, Students are eligible for a free download of Microsoft Windows 10 from the Kivuto web store. Microsoft Office 365 is available at no cost to students as well as faculty and staff for home use.

WINDOWS 10 OVERVIEW

Most Colleges and Universities vary significantly from corporations in the way desktop upgrades are managed. For profit entities tend to focus on standardization of hardware and software platforms while Universities tend to support a wider range of platforms. This means that in most cases, the operating system lifecycle in higher education (for faculty and staff) tends to be longer than in corporate environments. College students, especially incoming freshman arrive each year with the latest hardware and operating systems. Some students also run older operating systems than university standards. Therefore, staff who support student owned computers need to be up to date on new software offerings at the early stages, as well as be up to date on older operating systems.

The Windows 10 Operating System has been available to the general public since July 2015. The Windows 10 upgrade planning process at Lehigh has been in progress for a very short period of time. The University plans on rolling out Windows 10 as a test to a small subset of public site computers during the fall semester 2015. If no major problems are encountered, we will continue to roll out to the remaining public site computers in January 2016. The faculty and staff upgrades will take place on an as needed basis until incompatibilities are addressed and software and driver problems are solved. Our plan is described in greater detail in Section 5 of this paper

Versions

Windows 10 offers six different versions, each designed to fill specific computing needs. There are four versions of the Windows Desktop operating system (Home, Professional, Enterprise and Education - See Table 1 [4]) and two Windows Mobile versions (Mobile and Mobile Enterprise). The Home based products such as Windows Home have the basic Windows features but do not include advanced security and compatibility features that are needed in the corporate or business environment. Windows Professional is a step up from the Home version and includes many advanced and security features such as Bitlocker Encryption, Remote Desktop and Group Policy Management.

Windows 10 includes an Education version specifically designed for Educational institutions. This version has many of the same features included in the Enterprise version but has a slightly different upgrade path (can be upgraded from Home, Pro and Home where Enterprise can only be upgraded from Pro and Enterprise). Another major difference is that Education versions cannot use the Long Term Servicing Branch (LTSB) which allows for the suspension of automatic updates. In Windows 10, one of the new security features is that updates and security patches will be forced (users will not have the option the install) unless an organization selects a more flexible service branch. This is described in greater detail in the next section.

In addition to LTSB, the Enterprise version allows for volume license and windows activation to occur automatically over the network with a local server call to a Key Management Server (KMS). This type of environment allows for streamlining the installation and activation process for end users. Lehigh University utilizes the Enterprise version of Windows 10 and has the activation process automated through Active Directory.

Service Branch Versions

Microsoft has introduced a servicing model for Windows 10 referred to as "Service Branches." Service Branches allow for automatic updating of the operating systems based on what version of Windows 10 is installed. These branches give organizations the flexibility to test updates and patches within their environment to make sure there aren't any problems with integrating the changes prior to releasing them. There are three different levels of service branches being implemented [1]:

Current Branch (CB) – Windows 10 Home (Pro version is optional) uses the current branch option. This option has no flexibility. Security fixes and new features will be updated to the operating system automatically and the end user will not have the ability to postpone or avoid the updates.

Current Branch for Business (CBB) – Windows 10 Pro and Education versions that are managed by an upgrade service such as Windows Update for Business or Windows Server Update Services have the option to use Current Branch for Business. This option gives administrators some flexibility to delay the implementation of updates, but they cannot do so indefinitely.

Table 1. Windows 10 Desktop Versions

	Home	Professional	Education	Enterprise
Architecture	IA-32 and x86-64			
Availability	OEM Retail	OEM Retail Volume Licensing	Volume Licensing	Volume Licensing
Max RAM	4 GB (32bit) 128 GB (64)	4 GB on 32 bit 512 GB on 64 bit		
Continum	Yes	Yes	Yes	Yes
Cortana	Yes	Yes	Yes	Yes
Hardware Device Encryt	Yes	Yes	Yes	Yes
Edge	Yes	Yes	Yes	Yes (LTSB)
Windows Hello	Yes	Yes	Yes	Yes
Bitlocker	No	Yes	Yes	Yes
Group Policy	No	Yes	Yes	Yes
Windows to Go	No	No	Yes	Yes
Virtual Desktops	Yes	Yes	Yes	Yes
Business Store	No	Yes	Yes	Yes
Enterprise data Protect	No	Yes	Yes	Yes
Hyper V	No	64 Bit Only	64 Bit Only	64 Bit Only
Remote Desktop	Client Only	Client & Host	Client & Host	Client & Host
Device Guard	No	No	Yes	Yes
Direct Access	No	No	Yes	Yes
Credential Guard	No	No	Yes	Yes
Applocker	No	No	Yes	Yes

Long Term Servicing Branch (LTSB) – Windows 10 Enterprise has the option of using the Long Term Servicing Branch. This Branch allows organizations to postpone updates (other than security updates) indefinitely. It gives administrators a great deal of flexibility in implementing and testing updates prior to applying them to an organization's infrastructure.

Administrators can divide their organization into different Brach groups (CB, CBB or LTSB) and manage a heterogeneous environment if desired.

Windows Support Lifecycle

Microsoft does not provide support, security patches or updates for operating systems indefinitely. For example, Microsoft ended support for Windows XP on April 8, 2014 and no longer provides security patches and updates for Windows XP systems. Microsoft announces when it will stop supporting operating systems well in advance. The current schedule is detailed in Table 2 [1]. Education institutions need to be aware of when operating systems will no longer be supported due to the many security concerns of having unpatched systems connected to a campus network.

Table 2. Windows Support Dates

	Date Released	End of Mainstream Support	End of Extended Support
Windows XP	October 25, 2001	April 14, 2009	April 8, 2014
Windows Vista	November 8, 2006	April 10, 2012	April 11, 2017
Windows 7	October 22, 2009	January 13, 2015	January 14, 2020
Windows 8	October 26, 2012	January 9, 2018	January 10, 2023
Windows 10	July 29, 2015	October 13, 2020	October 14, 2025

When Microsoft ends Mainstream support and transitions an operating system to Extended support, an organization is limited to paid and self service support options. For example, you can not just call Microsoft with a support question after mainstream support ends. At the end of Extended support, security patches and updates will no longer be supplied. This means that expired systems connected to a University network will become vulnerable to malware and other attacks due to security holes not being patched.

Since Extended Support for Windows 7 continues to 2020 and for Windows 8 to 2023, most institutions are not in hurry to perform a mass operating system upgrade to Windows 10. However, planning needs to begin, decisions need to be made, and testing needs to be performed to determine the best course of action for your institution. As mentioned previously, Higher Education is a diverse and heterogeneous environment made up of a variety of departments with varying computing needs. Many departments and labs use specialized software that will not work with newer operating systems. Some departments have specialized

instruments with hardware that do not have drivers for newer operating systems.

Even though an institution may not be in a hurry to upgrade, the helpdesk and desktop support personnel need to be prepared to support Windows 10. Students will arrive with Windows 10 systems and faculty and staff will upgrade their home computers more rapidly than in the past because Windows 10 is free and will be provided through a windows update feature.

NEW WINDOWS 10 FEATURES

As mentioned previously, Universities need to plan for the arrival of Windows 10, yet have a little flexibility as to when it should be necessary. There is little doubt that Windows 10 will be the logical transition from Windows 7 given the lengthy support cycle of Windows 7, as well as being better designed for desktop use than Windows 8 (for example, the return of the desktop, start menu etc.). In addition, a new feature set, security improvements and enterprise management enhancements make Windows 10 an attractive transition path from Windows 7. Table 3 [5] outlines some the general features that are new to Windows 10. As mentioned previously, the desktop has returned along with the Start Menu. The Start Menu is slightly different in Windows 10 because it incorporates small tiles as part of the menu instead of text menu options. Other notable features include the Cortana personal assistant brought over from Windows phone, Continuum that provides an easy transition from Tablet to PC desktop, and Microsoft Edge which replaces Internet Explorer. Features like Cortana require a microphone and may be more useful on a laptop with an integrated microphone.

Table 3. New Features in Windows 10

Feature	Description
Start Menu	The Start Menu was removed in Windows 8 and returns in Windows 10
Cortana	Personal Assistant that will help you find files on your PC, manage your calendar, chat with you as well as many other tasks
Continuum	Allows you to easily switch between Tablet mode and Desktop mode
Forced Updates	Users will no longer have the option to postpone or avoid critical patches and updates
Window Hello and Passport	Biometric Authentication that gives access through the use of a fingerprint, Iris or face recognition
Device Guard	Allows enterprises to lock down devices to guard against Advanced Persistent Threats
Microsoft Edge	The new web browser to replace Internet Explorer

SECURITY IMPROVEMENTS

Windows 10 has many new exciting features designed to make the operating system more secure. Biometric Authentication is now integrated with the new feature called Windows Hello. Windows

Hello has built in capabilities to allow you to unlock your Windows 10 computer with fingerprint, iris or face recognition. For a laptop, you will need to purchase a camera with an Infrared (IR) sensor to take advantage of these features. Some manufacturers indicate they will start shipping new Windows 10 computers with Intel's RealSense 3D cameras that include IR sensors and can be used for face and iris recognition. For a phone, some manufacturers of Windows phones and tablets are starting to outfit them with IR equipped cameras as well. Windows Hello uses a technology called asymmetric key cryptography which is used in devices like Smart Cards.

Another security feature in Windows 10 is called Microsoft Passport. Once Windows Hello authenticates you, Microsoft passport is unlocked and instantly allows you access to online services that require authentication using your Microsoft Account. This technology works by binding your private encryption key to your device and only thing stored online is your public encryption key – thus eliminating the ability for a hacker to steal your password.

Device Guard is a new feature that gives enterprises the ability to lock down devices to guard against Advanced Persistent Threats. It will block anything other than trusted applications as a way to guard against zero day threats. This tool is flexible and can be configured to different levels. For example, it can be set to authenticate applications from specific vendors, custom applications, Windows Store etc.

Upgrade Plan

At Lehigh, it was determined that a Windows 10 committee was needed to organize policies and procedures, make planning and implementation decisions as well as develop a communication plan for the campus. A group of Lehigh Computing Consultants were brought together to develop a plan and project timeline.

The committee began to determine the scope of the project and how to proceed in order to reduce end user frustration and loss of time. It was determined that the best approach was to test Lehigh's applications and hardware and if few problems are encountered, upgrade the public computing sites and technology classrooms first. Then as a long term goal, focus on the individual faculty and staff members who use the public sites on a regular basis, and then beginning the process of upgrading faculty and staff computers.

Communication and Timeline

The first step is to communicate to the campus community an outline of the project timeline with our intention to upgrade a pilot public computing site to Windows 10 in Fall 2015 and upgrade the remaining public sites and classrooms before the Spring 2016 semester.

We are currently formulating guidelines outlining Library and Technology Services upgrade plans and will communicate them through various channels to campus. These guidelines will outline the timeline and plans for gradual campus upgrades. Since the Windows 7 support lifecycle extends to 2020, there is no rush, and we need to make it clear to faculty and staff that there is little urgency to upgrade quickly to Windows 10.

Anticipated Issues and Challenges

Lehigh desktop computers are normally imaged with a Windows 7 image using a tool named Universal Imaging Utility. This tool houses a variety of drivers for systems and allows for a standard image to be deployed to a variety of PC hardware configurations. The Computing Consultant team is currently developing a faculty/staff Windows 10 image and testing newer deployment methods to see if the Universal Imaging Utility is the optimal way to deploy Windows 10.

Since Windows 10 is a free upgrade, the Help Desk and Computing Consultants who support residential networking need to be prepared for the arrival of the many student Windows 10 systems. Student computers at Lehigh are not managed by Active Directory, therefore many students will be taking advantage of the free upgrade to Windows 10 on their own. Incoming freshmen will also be arriving with new Windows 10 computers and will be downloading and using Lehigh applications, anti-virus as well be connecting to the campus network. Under Lehigh's Microsoft campus agreement, students are also entitled to a free copy of Microsoft Office 365 which should be fully tested prior to students' arrival.

Preparation also needs to be made for the home computers faculty and staff will be upgrading along with the many computers on campus that are not managed by Active Directory. At Lehigh, it is not requirement for on campus computers to be managed by Active Directory, and many faculty and staff opt out of being part of Active Directory for one reason or another. Therefore, many faculty/staff will be upgrading these computers on their own and may encounter upgrade and compatibility problems.

Finally, Lehigh maintains 2 virtual computing sites - a virtual public site (Windows 7) configured with identical software offerings as the public computing sites. The second virtual site, is an administrative public site that offers various administrative software tools such as Banner, Argos and other specialized tools used for reporting. These sites are powered by VMWare and accessed by using the VMWare View client. These public sites will also need to be eventually upgraded to mirror the desktop experience of users so that we maintain consistency. We believe the work of our Windows 10 committee will minimize Windows 10 support issues this fall. I hope to report on our progress and the results of our public sites pilot at later time.

ACKNOWLEDGMENTS

The members of the Lehigh University Library and Technology Staff

REFERENCES

[1] Microsoft Corporation http:///www.microsoft.com. (August 2015)

[2] Microsoft Windows Blog http://blogs.windows.com/ (August 2015)

[3] Trusted Reviews http://www.trustedreviews.com/opinions/windows-10-vs-windows-7 (August 2015)

[4] Wikipedia, https://en.wikipedia.org/wiki/Windows_10 (August, 2015)

[5] Wikipedia, https://en.wikipedia.org/wiki/Windows_10_editions (August, 2015)

New York University Steinhardt Information Technology Group's New Methodologies for Developing Student Worker Skillsets

Lendyll Capitulo
Academic Technology Specialist
New York University
246 Greene Street
New York, NY 10003
1-212-998-5377
Lendyll.Capitulo@nyu.edu

ABSTRACT

In light of resource constraints and the strong push for new university technology initiatives, an increasing number of Information Technology (IT) and Academic Technology (AT) teams must create more efficient ways to support staff, faculty, researchers, and students. This demand affects IT/AT professionals and student technicians alike. While hiring student technicians can be a cost effective alternative to retraining and/or hiring more IT/AT professionals, expecting efficient quality work from this population creates its own set of unique managerial challenges. Such challenges demand a new, integrated methodology that both trains and develops student talent.

Using his experience as a student leader and Resident Assistant in NYU's Office of Residential Life and Housing Services (ORLHS), the author has fostered his student technicians' skills while creating a pervasive culture of customer service and support. This paper will discuss how student-focused development plans, modular trainings, and goal setting has positively impacted the NYU Steinhardt School of Culture, Education, and Human Development IT group's ability to fulfill its mission: "To empower members of Steinhardt to efficiently and effectively incorporate technology in their academic and professional work". The author will also discuss measures of the training method's effectiveness, as well as future challenges of the student development model at NYU and the higher education community at large.

Categories and Subject Descriptors

K.6.1 [**Project and People management**]: Training

General Terms

Human Factors, Design, Experimentation

Keywords

Student workers, development.

SIGUCCS '15, November 09-13, 2015, St. Petersburg, FL, USA
© 2015 ACM. ISBN 978-1-4503-3610-9/15/11 $15.00
DOI: http://dx.doi.org/10.1145/2815546.2815568

1. INTRODUCTION

The future of higher education is uncertain. With emerging technologies constantly redefining the experience of being in a classroom and financial constraints limiting the decisions of many educational institutions, new strategies have been proposed to save money while giving educational institutions the flexibility needed to keep up to constantly evolving technologies. One popular strategy in many technology organizations is to use student technicians as a way to remain flexible and cut costs.

While student workers offer a cost effective alternative to retraining and/or hiring more IT/AT professionals, expecting quality work from this population creates its own set of unique managerial challenges. In order to describe these challenges, I will break this paper into three major parts. First I want to create the context by describing the demographics of NYU, the Steinhardt School of Culture, Education and Human Development and Steinhardt IT. Next, I will describe the three unique challenges of working with student workers. Finally, I will discuss the three strategies that Steinhardt IT used to address these challenges.

2. ORGANIZATION DESCRIPTION

2.1 Demographics

New York University (NYU) is one of the largest private universities in the United States. The university is comprised of 20 schools, colleges, and institutes [1]. In terms of technology support, service models fall into one of two major classifications, either a central technology resource or a distributed (non-central) technology resource. Steinhardt IT is considered a distributed technology resource as it works more closely with the Steinhardt School of Culture, Education and Human Development.

2.2 Steinhardt IT Organization Structure

Steinhardt IT is a technology group that serves the needs of the Steinhardt School of Culture, Education and Human Development. The group is comprised of one director, two full-time staff members and fewer than 10 student technicians. The student technicians are divided into two categories: core student technicians and non-core student technicians. The group manages the needs of 290 full-time faculty, 5,952 students, and approximately 275 staff [2]. On the more technical side, this equates to around 850 unique endpoints (desktops, laptops or other devices) with two data centers.

To manage our customer service, Steinhardt IT uses a Zendesk ticket tracking system. All issues from request to solution are tracked and managed through Zendesk. Zendesk allows the Steinhardt IT leadership team to collect metrics on the performance of members of the team in regards to resolving customer service requests.

2.3 Student Technicians and Core Student Technicians

When tracking student technician development, Steinhardt IT management makes a distinction between core student technicians and non-core student technicians. Core student technicians are considered to be the student technicians who have a technical and interpersonal skillset to resolve complex (i.e. tickets that take between 1 to 8 hours to solve and have a moderate risk to the organization) tickets on behalf of Steinhardt IT. Core student technicians play a vital role in the development of non-core-student technicians. One goal of the student development plan is to transition non-core student technicians into core student technicians.

2.4 Metrics Used to Determine Performance

Steinhardt IT management uses two specific metrics to measure the effectiveness of the Steinhardt IT Help Desk. These two metrics are Average Time to First Response (measured in business hours which are 9 AM- 5 PM Monday through Friday) and the Time to First Resolution (measured in regular hours).

2.4.1 Average Time to First Response

The average time to first response is a metric that Steinhardt IT uses to track the average amount of time it takes between a ticket being initiated and an agent making the first response on the ticket. This metric describes how quickly the team responds to Steinhardt community members.

2.4.2 Average Time to First Resolution

The average time to first resolution is a metric that Steinhardt IT uses to track the average amount of time to solve a ticket from when the ticket is first submitted to the help desk. This metric describes how quickly problem and incident tickets are resolved.

3. THREE CHALLENGES REGARDING THE DEVELOPMENT OF STUDENT TECHNICIANS

Steinhardt IT has identified three particular challenges that they wanted to address when working with student technicians: limited skillset, organizational buy-in, and work/school balance. Each of these challenges will be discussed more in-depth in each subsection.

3.1 Limited Skillset

For many of the Steinhardt IT student technicians, the position might be the first major technical job they ever have. As they are students primarily, many do not have the same depth of technical knowledge that a full-time team member, who has worked in the industry several years, would have. Additionally, the skills they may have are consumer level skills, a far cry from the enterprise level skills needed to effectively serve the Steinhardt community.

The challenge for Steinhardt IT is to cultivate the skillset of the team's student technicians to reach a baseline level. The three skills that are the primary focus for management are tier 1 technical support, basic understanding of NYU and Steinhardt's technology systems, and proper customer service. After all three of these skills are developed, the students can be successful in their roles as student technicians.

3.2 Organizational Buy-In Issues

Student technicians may not have the same level of organizational buy-in as a full-time employee because of different motivations for holding their positions. There appears to be three major motivations for wanting to be a Steinhardt IT student technician. Firstly, some of the student technicians view this position as a way to make a little extra money, as they would any student position. Secondly, Steinhardt IT has a few international students who see the student technician position as a way to build work experience in the United States. Finally, some student technicians see IT in higher education settings as a viable career path that they would want to pursue after finishing their degrees.

Regardless of the motivation, the challenge for Steinhardt IT management is to demonstrate the value of the student technician position as a stepping-stone to whatever future career goals that a student technician may have.

3.3 Work/School Balance

At Steinhardt IT, there is a saying that "student technicians are students first". This means that student technicians are expected to make their studies their priority above work. This requires special scheduling needs. For example, a student might need flexible scheduling when studying for midterms and finals. Additionally, student technicians' work schedules tend to follow the academic calendar. Many student technicians might not be able to work during the summer months because of other commitments (e.g., internships, trips home, and study abroad).

The challenge for Steinhardt IT management is to remain operational while still accommodating for these special scheduling needs. In order to achieve this, Steinhardt IT has to instill in its student technicians that the privilege of flexibility comes with responsibility. This responsibility is firstly, letting the managers know of rescheduling as far as in advance as possible and secondly, to be good colleague to their fellow student technicians by not "dumping" last minute work when they are rescheduling.

4. THREE STRATEGIES TO ADDRESS THE CHALLENGES

In order to address these three challenges, Steinhardt IT uses three strategies: student focused development plans, modular trainings, and goal setting. When all three are used, Steinhardt IT is able to effectively resolve all three previously mentioned challenges. Each strategy will be discussed in the following subsections.

4.1 Student Focused Development Plans

Student focused development plans are roadmaps that Steinhardt IT management use in the career development of student technicians.

4.1.1 Goals of the Student Development Plan

The core purpose of the student focused development plan is the student technician onboarding process that starts the first day that a student technician arrives at Steinhardt IT. This onboarding process establishes the goals of student development in the context of building the skillsets needed to be successful. The student technicians are presented with the four roles they would play at Steinhardt IT (See Table 1). In order to achieve those goals, they will need to build their skillset in a way that targets growth in first tier support, knowledge of NYU and Steinhardt systems, and experience in customer service. The goal of the onboarding process is to develop the student technician's skillset to the point where the student technician can move from solving simple requests to solving complex tickets and performing advanced tasks.

Table 1. Steinhardt IT Student Technician Roles

Role	Definition
Customer Service Representative	You are the first point of the contact between the SIT Group and the Steinhardt Community.
Level I IT Support Agent	You are our first line of defense when resolving short-term issues.
Operational Agent	You are responsible for facilitating the behind the scenes work that keeps the SIT Group running.
Innovator	You contribute to the academic technology conversation by making recommendations that help us carry out our mission statement.

4.1.2 Constant Check-Ins

Steinhardt IT uses constant checks as a way to evaluate and communicate progress to all student technicians. During the onboarding process, the new student technicians meet regularly with core student technicians and full-time Steinhardt IT employees on the first day, 2 week, 6 week, and 3 month milestones. During these check-ins the new student technicians have a chance to process their experience at Steinhardt IT including what they like about the job, what is challenging them, and where they see themselves improving. Involving the new student technician in this process establishes the value of the position. Instead of a position that is static and is only a means to an end, the constant check-ins maintain the dynamic nature of the Steinhardt IT team. Not only can they achieve their original goals by working as student technicians, but they also can grow in their careers along the way. This growth mindset is key in establishing buy-in from the new student technicians.

In addition to the student onboarding process, the entire team of student technicians has a biweekly staff meeting. At the staff meetings the students give updates regarding what they see in the field. This culminates in management asking three questions to the team: "what's hot?", "what's not?", and "what do you need?". This process has allowed the student technician team to evolve from a reactive group that simply resolves issues to a proactive group that is critically assessing the needs of the community and anticipating what the team needs to improve service. By incorporating student technician feedback, Steinhardt IT management hopes to emphasize the value of the student technician in the organization, thus increasing buy-in, instilling accountability of being on the team, and all the responsibilities that come along with it.

4.1.3 Mentoring

Mentoring is another component to the student development plan and goes hand in hand with constant check-ins. Between check-ins, student technicians regularly meet with core-student technicians and fulltime Steinhardt IT employees. During these meetings, the student technicians are encouraged to talk about their experience at Steinhart IT. The mentors offer their own perspectives regarding the student technician's experience while offering advice. The goal of mentoring is two-fold. The student technicians get another perspective of what it's like to work at Steinhardt IT. For the mentors, they are able to shape the future of the organization in a way that they would like to see it grow.

4.2 Modular Trainings

Modular trainings and associated documentation further develop student technicians by building on the base skillset as a result of the student focused development plans. Modular trainings are written to be given multiple times throughout the year by both Steinhardt IT management and core student technicians. These trainings give Steinhardt IT the flexibility to provide the training that is necessary while saving time and energy by not having to rewrite material each time a training needs to be given.

4.2.1 Goals of Modular Trainings

The goal of modular trainings is two-fold. The first goal is to increase the student technicians' technical toolkit (by expanding their skills of first tier support, knowledge of NYU and Steinhardt systems, and to sharpen their customer service acumen) while the second goal is to instill the student technicians with the culture and expectations of working at Steinhardt IT. In order to achieve these two goals, modular trainings have been divided into two sub categories: technical trainings and cultural trainings.

4.2.2 Technical Training and Documentation

Technical trainings and associated documentation allow for core student technicians to increase the skillset of the student technicians. These trainings and associated documentation describe the business processes of Steinhardt IT in a way that is easily digestible for new student technicians. While the training first instills the knowledge of the technical process, the documentation is vital as a reference that the student technicians can use until they fully internalize the process.

One example of a technical training that Steinhardt IT gives student technicians is the Ticket Priority Training. In this training, Steinhardt IT management describes the rationale for setting ticket priorities in Zendesk. The student technicians are taught that there are two primary factors which are taken into account when setting ticket priority. These two factors are urgency (measured by internal time deadlines) and impact (measured in working hours lost). After this training is given, the student technicians are then given the Ticket Priority Matrix. The Ticket Priority Matrix lays out the important information given during the training in a manner that the student technicians can easily reference. See Table 2 for the Ticket Priority Matrix.

**Table 2: Ticket Priority Matrix
(Part of Technical Documentation)**

	Low	Normal	High	Urgent
Time Deadline (Urgency)	No Hard Deadline	Less than 1 week	Less than 3 days	Less than 1 day
Working Hours Lost (Impact)	Less than 1	Up to 7 hours	7 to 35 hours	Greater than 35 hours
Example Issues	Browser Issues Software Installations	Single Computer Crash	System Crash	Server Crash
VIPs	All VIPs get an automatically +1 increase in priority (Low priority becomes Normal, Normal becomes High, High becomes Urgent)			

4.2.3 Culture Training and Documentation

The culture trainings and associated documentation are other vital tools that Steinhardt IT Management uses when developing student technicians. Cultural trainings describe the culture of working at Steinhardt IT. The trainings lay out explicitly the shared values of working at Steinhardt IT while also explicitly laying out the expectations of working on the team. Cultural trainings differ from technical trainings in that they are less flexible (need to be formally given by someone who is trained in facilitating them) and require the entire Steinhardt IT team (all full-time and part-time employees) to attend.

One example of a cultural training that Steinhardt IT presents once a year is the Steinhardt IT Standard Operating Procedure Seminar. During the training, members of the IT team meet and discuss the shared values of working on the Steinhardt IT team. Steinhardt IT management lays out the expectations for student technicians, particularly the privileges of having a flexible schedule and the responsibility of informing Steinhardt IT Management when they know they are going to be out and to make sure that they do not burden their colleagues with their work while they are out. The student technicians get a chance to voice their views about working on the team. They usually discuss the workload, how it's divided, and how they like to work (e.g. some student workers prefer more hand holding than others). This back and forth discussion ensures that the expectations the Steinhardt IT team has for its members are explicitly laid out. The supporting documentation is the Steinhardt IT Standard Operating Procedure. This document records all of the expectations discussed during the seminar as a reference for the expectations of working at Steinhardt IT. See below for examples of what is in the Steinhardt IT Standard Operating Procedure.

4.2.4 Examples of Culture Training from the Internal Communication Standards Section from the Steinhardt IT Standard Operating Procedure

The following are pillars of internal communication at Steinhardt IT. These pillars were derived from a seminar held with the entire IT team in the summer of 2014. Notice the phrasing of the expectation and how it incorporates what the team as a whole does.

- **Respect:** Regardless of the circumstances, the major underlying expectation in all interaction is the mutual respect between both parties. This respect takes many different forms.

- **Respecting for the Person:** While everyone might not have the same job title, all team members have the ability to meaningfully contribute towards the mission of the group. All team members should respect everyone's role towards working towards the mission statement. **At Steinhardt IT, we recognize the importance of every member of the team and every member from the student technicians to the executive director deserves the same amount of respect.**

- **Respecting Time:** Everyone on the team is busy with their individual tasks and projects. When assigning tasks it is important that a balance between what needs to be done and what has already been assigned should always be taken into account. **At Steinhardt IT, we do not micromanage each of our team members. We trust that when a team member agrees to a task, they will**

complete the task or ask for further assistance if necessary.

- **Respecting Abilities:** Everyone on the team plays an important role and has unique abilities at Steinhardt IT. When we combine our roles and abilities, we are able to achieve much more than what we would be able to do if we all work alone. **At Steinhardt IT, we want to create an atmosphere in which individual abilities are celebrated in context of what each member's ability is able to contribute to the Steinhardt IT Mission.**

- **Be Present:** When communicating with each other, it is important that team members give each other their full and undivided attention. Communicating is not just listening; it is also engaging, connecting, and empowering. For this reason, we use the phrase "Be Present" or "Being Present" to represent the idea of engaged communication. **At Steinhardt IT, we strive to actively and critically engage each other as we communicate with each other. We strive to "Be Present" during a conversation.**

- **Accountability:** There are times when we come together to work on a ticket, problem, or project and we all have assigned tasks. During these times, team members should hold each other accountable by engaging a conversation that follows up on the task. **At Steinhardt IT, we believe that accountability does not just come from top down, but instead is a shared value. As such, we strive to hold each other accountable to the high standards that we hold for ourselves.**

4.3 Goal Setting

Goal setting is done formally at Steinhardt IT once a semester as a modular training during one of the bi-weekly student technician meetings. The goals are written down with clear action steps needed to achieve the goals. After the goals and action steps have been written, they are posted in the Steinhardt IT office so that student technicians can hold each other accountable to each other's personal growth.

4.3.1 Goal of Goal Setting

The primary goal of writing and posting goals is to increase student technician buy-in by showing how Steinhardt IT can help them reach their professional, academic, and personal goals. Steinhardt IT stresses the "flatness" (the importance having goal setting at all levels of the organization) of this growth model by having Steinhardt IT Management post their goals alongside the student technicians' goals. This solidarity once again emphasizes the importance of student technicians on the team.

4.3.2 CLEAR Setting Model

Steinhardt IT uses the CLEAR goal-setting model. CLEAR is an acronym that stands for Collaborative, Limited, Emotional, Appreciable, Refinable [3]. The piece that is stressed the most is *collaborative*. Steinhardt IT Management stresses the need to work together and rely on each other to achieve goals. Since the goals are posted, team members can check in with each other and hold each other accountable for their success. This group cohesion increases student technician buy-in and also shows that everyone on the team is responsible for maintaining a positive work environment.

4.3.3 Examples of Steinhardt IT Clear Goals

Below are example CLEAR Goals set by Steinhardt IT Student Technicians. Notice the breadth of the goals ranging from personal goals to academic goals.

- Learn how to prioritize and manage my time.

- Raise GPA by 0.4 points

- Build a habit of keeping track of the type of work done at the end of the day, in order to reflect on any new skills acquired.

5. CONCLUSIONS

While these three strategies seem to work in isolation, in practice each of these strategies build off each other. Student-focused development plans are the bedrock of giving students the skillset necessary to support the Steinhardt IT operation while first exposing them to culture and expectations of being a Steinhardt IT team member. Once the student technicians have the basic skillset, modular trainings start to grow their skillsets so they can tackle more advanced problems while they start to reflect on their role on the team, thus increasing buy-in and a shared sense of responsibility. Finally, goal setting allows the student technicians to start thinking of how Steinhardt IT can help them achieve goals outside of work. Taken together, these three strategies can dramatically shape how a student technician views the student technician position and how seriously to treat the job.

Now the final question to answer is: does all this theory-crafting actually work? When Steinhardt IT first implemented these three strategies in September of 2014, Steinhardt was going through a transition period. One of the full-time members of Steinhardt IT left the organization and Steinhardt did not have the resources to replace him. In order to keep the operation running, a new strategy needed to be implemented to achieve the same high level of service that the community has grown accustomed to.

Chart 1: Time to First Resolution August 2014 to June 2015

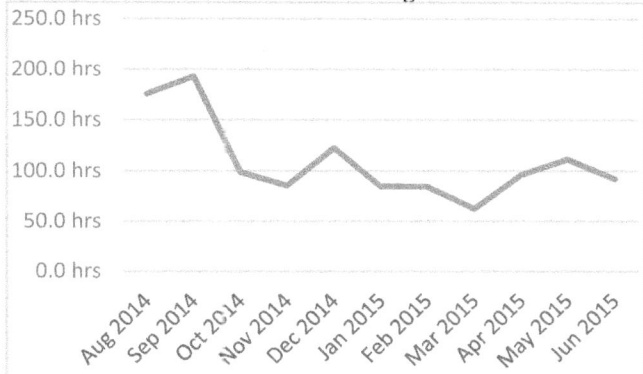

Since implementing these new strategies in developing student technicians, not only has Steinhardt IT been able to maintain the same level of service, but service has actually improved. The primary measurement of service is how quickly a problem ticket is resolved and is measured by the Average Time to First Resolution. Average Time to First Resolution dropped sharply between September 2014 and October of 2014 and has remained

lower ever since (See Chart 1). While there might have been other factors affecting this metric such as quicker ticket routing and the volume of tickets received, these factors do not necessarily compensate for being down a full-time person. Additionally, the dividends of having highly trained student technicians are still being recognized. Steinhardt IT is still collecting data on how highly trained student technicians are able to efficiently and effectively support a helpdesk operation.

6. FUTURE CHALLENGES

While the future is bright for student technicians at Steinhardt, there are two future challenges that have to be addressed. The first challenge is what happens when core-student technicians graduate or leave Steinhardt IT. Since much of Steinhardt IT's operation relies on student technicians, there is a larger operational impact when a student technician leaves the team. Replacing a student technician is more complicated than finding a new student to take on the role. The new student has to build the skillsets and competencies needed at Steinhardt IT by completing the student development plan. During the time needed for the new student technician to complete the student development plan, Steinhardt IT will be short on personnel resources.

While being shorthanded might appear to be anecdotal, there seems to be a trend as seen in Chart 1. During times of the highest student technician staffing in March 2015, Average Time to First Resolution reached a yearlong low. As student technicians prepared to graduate and work less time during the months of April 2015 and May 2015, Average Time to First Resolution increases. The metric starts to show a decrease in June as new student technicians are trained and Steinhardt IT starts to return to a baseline staffing level.

The second challenge is, if a student is hired full-time, how the student navigates the transition from casual employee to professional employee. This is a transition that most students have to make after they graduate, but working at Steinhardt IT there is special emphasis that is placed on this transition. Hiring a student means working with that student's history at the organization. It is not as easy as having a "clean slate" after the hire. This is an important consideration for management to consider if they are considering hiring a graduating student employee to become a full-time employee.

7. ACKNOWLEDGMENTS

I would like to thank my supervisor, Ben Vien, at Steinhardt IT for giving me the resources to write this paper. I would like also like to thank our student workers Sunaina, Kamran, Lucas, Kevin, Nick and Kenny for being patient as we try new ways to improve the student technician experience.

8. REFERENCES

[1] About NYU. New York University. New York University. Retrieved June 26, 2015. https://www.nyu.edu/about.html

[2] About NYU Steinhardt. NYU Steinhardt. New York University. Retrieved June 26, 2015. http://steinhardt.nyu.edu/about/

[3] Economy, Peter. Forget SMART Goals -- Try CLEAR Goals Instead. INC.com. Retrieved June 26, 2015

Improving Communication and Building Communities with Google

Sean HV Mendoza, EdD
Pima Community College
4905 East Broadway Blvd
Tucson, Arizona 85709
(520) 206-4744
smendoza@pima.edu

ABSTRACT

With assistance from the Academic Technology arm of Information Technology (IT), Pima Community College staff and faculty have been improving communication and building learning communities to meet the growing academic demands of our community. Utilizing Google Hangouts, college employees can quickly and easily communicate with struggling students, offering a variety of services including counseling, advising, and tutoring. Faculty have explored Google's ability to share relevant documents, images and videos to create personalized learning environments for students and peers. Employee groups have also explored the use of Google+ Communities as a means to storing departmental artifacts and chronicling the evolution of departmental processes. When used as a knowledge base for current and future employees, Google and its variety of apps create synergy of learning, collaboration and services between faculty, staff and students. This paper describes how IT has worked with stakeholders to leverage Google tools and address a variety of concerns to improve communication and build communities. The presenter will provide how-to examples to using and implementing these tools and hands-on activities for session participants.

Categories and Subject Descriptors

K.3.1 [**Computing Milieux**]: Computers and Education – *collaborative learning*; K.6.1 [**Management of Computing and Information Systems**]: Projects and People Management – *training*.

General Terms

Management, Documentation, Design, Security, Human Factors, Standardization.

Keywords

Google, Communities, Universal Design, Learning Objects, Personalized Learning, Accessibility, Intellectual Property, Security.

1. INTRODUCTION

One of the largest drivers to innovate instruction and institutional processes comes from our need to meet the needs of our students

SIGUCCS '15, November 09-13, 2015, St. Petersburg, FL, USA
© 2015 ACM. ISBN 978-1-4503-3610-9/15/11 $15.00
DOI: http://dx.doi.org/10.1145/2815546.2815574

in the STEM (Science, Technology, Engineering and Mathematics) fields. Integrating cultural values, innovative assessments and relevant contexts with the learner's goals within the STEM community, we may find a pathway that cuts through the current educational malaise of standardized testing. The urgency of the shift in expectations of society and student demographic can be best described in ACT's report, "The Condition of STEM 2014" [2].

> "Students who enter a major that matches their interests are more likely to remain in their major, persist in college, and complete their degree in a timely manner than students whose major and interests do not match."

We must strive to meet this challenge in education. In response, Pima Community College's IT department is leveraging expertise in learning technology by forming relationships with academic departments and providing training to faculty and staff that introduces innovative concepts and redefines processes towards student success.

In an effort to anticipate and prepare for an institution's technology infrastructure, an associate once asked me, *What will classrooms and learning look like in the future?* I responded with, *The future of learning will be mobile, virtual, personalized, and connected to a community.* Google's apps and combination of services can be used to nurture communities [5]. Available on both desktops and mobile devices, learning and teaching can occur from wherever and whenever the student is ready. Pima Community College offers access to a variety of software resources providing the greatest possibility of academic success for our students and employees. Through the tools and services provided by Google, college employees find ways to leverage technology to improve communication that nurtures communities. At the heart of each community are the leaders that build relationships and an infrastructure that scaffolds standard access for its followers. Recently migrated to Google, Pima Community College leaders and its infrastructure have been exploring Hangouts, Google+ Communities and Learning Objects to improve employees and students communication. To maximize efficiency of faculty and staff, training is offered to departments and employees on demand and an overview of Information Technology's best practices are integral to the institution's new employee orientation. This paper will build a common awareness of security, intellectual property, accessibility, document sharing and best practices that nurture collaboration and communities.

2. POINTS OF IMPORTANCE

With more of our lives becoming digitized and available on the Internet for the convenience of our friends, family and students, **security** plays a large role in safeguarding our physical and virtual presence. Not only should we be aware of our technologies limitations, but also knowledgeable of our institutions policies and best practices to safeguarding data. Google's web based tools allow for the collaboration of teams from virtually anywhere on the planet. Because of this level of access and availability, educators must be aware of the potential security dangers inherent in a world that is always on, available and searchable. In an effort to prepare college employees to create a safe and collaborative experience for students and peers, new and veteran employees are provided training opportunities that include the institution's acceptable use policy, best practices for sharing data on the Internet, and identifying technological and agreement limitations. Prior to working at the institution, all employees must read, agree and sign the Technology Acceptable use Agreement. Available on the Pima Community College website, this document clearly defines prohibited behavior of college employees; and state and federal standards that protect the institution [9]. The institution's new employee orientation increases security awareness by highlighting a theoretical cost of a data breach running easily into millions of dollars. College employees are encouraged to use and leverage Google's highly collaborative tool to improve student and/or institutional success. Training also emphasizes the potential of inappropriately shared documents to be viewable and searchable to anyone on the Internet with a click of the button. With the power of every employee and student to share documents with the world instantaneously, a firm grasp of college policies, practices and abilities of Google, can best guide them to appropriately share their document.

College employees (specifically faculty) generate **intellectual property** as a part of their day-to-day activities. Sensitive to the needs of employees, the college provides training and the infrastructure to support the development of copyrighted work for the benefit of our students. Under our current agreement with Google, college employees who develop intellectual property under our current infrastructure will not lose rights over developed content. Pima Community College's legal counsel further confirmed that under the institutional terms of service and our existing Board Policy (2702) college employees would not lose intellectual property rights over content [8]. Protected by the practices and policies of the institution, employees can develop instructional materials and processes to create a personalized learning experience sensitive to the needs of students and designed to be accessible to our college community. With the integration of Universal Design at Pima's New Employee Orientation, and the adoption of Google as a unified communication and collaboration tool, Pima Community College is nurturing a culture sensitive to the personalized learning and accessibility needs of students.

The ability to provide **accessible** instruction and resources to students for success is what will differentiate Pima Community College as a premier institution. Nurturing a culture of Universal Design, we have deployed three standard applications that empower students to engage in academic activities "without the need of adaptation or specialized design" [7] and provide to all faculty and staff a program to caption instructor/student generated videos. The three desktop applications available across the Pima Community College are Read Write Gold, ZoomText and JAWS. According to our partners, Access and Disability Resources (ADR), the combination of standard applications and Google's willingness to provide alternatives and additional resources is a step towards greater accessibility [3]. Generating recorded videos and uploading them to YouTube, the Camtasia application provides to all faculty and staff the ability to caption videos prior

to upload. The availability of institutional resources such as video editing software (Camtasia) and staff training described in earlier sections have played a significant role in nurturing interest and creating a culture of Universal Design. Encouraging honest dialog and providing training to college employees nurtures a culture of security that safeguards student data, intellectual property and accessibility.

3. SHARING DOCUMENTS, IMAGES AND VIDEOS

Pima college's training of faculty and staff encourage the use of mobile devices as dissemination of documents, images and video using Google Apps is a key part of our effort to provide a foundation of anywhere learning and access. The following example illustrates how our training program helps encourage best practices when sharing content via Google Drive on a mobile device.

1. Find the Google Drive Application on your mobile. If you don't have the application already installed on your device you can download the program from Google [4]. Select the icon and you'll be presented with a menu (See Figure 1).

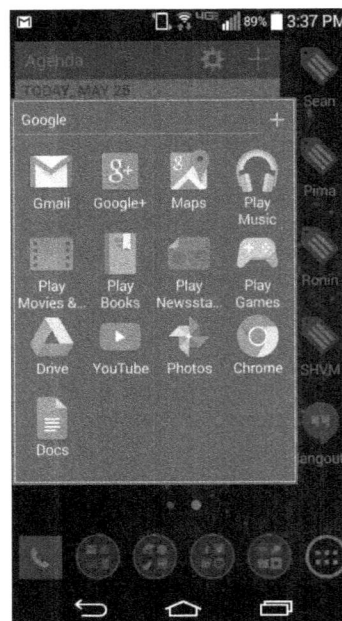

Figure 1. Google Application.

2. From the menu, there are a variety of different options that allow you to navigate to a desired document via My Drive, Shared with me, Starred and Recent. Find the file you want to share. In this example, the file to be shared is a Google presentation and happens to be a recent addition to the drive (See Figure 2).

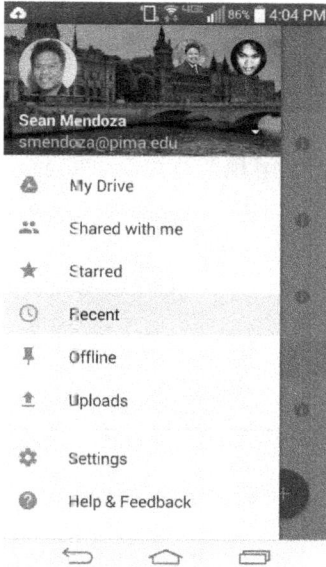

Figure 2. From the menu.

3. **Find the file titled "Capturing and Building Objects". Given the length of the title, some of the middle text will be removed.** To the right of the viewable title is an icon with the letter "i" in a field of black. Select that icon by clicking it with the mouse (Figure 3).

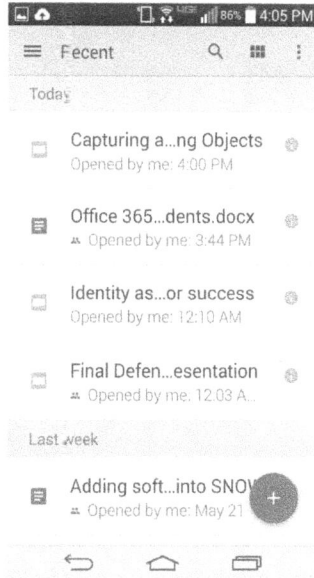

Figure 3. Find the file.

4. **Selecting the icon will open the screen that allows you to Add people and share a link with other google users.** Choose the Add people option (See Figure 4).

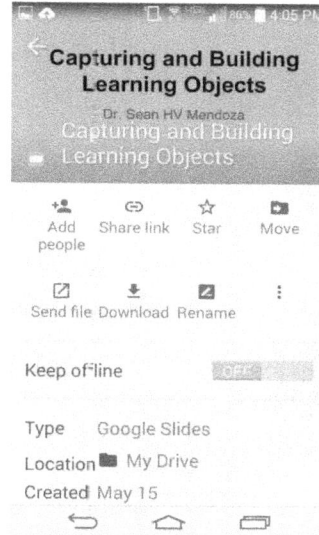

Figure 4. Selecting the icon.

5. **The first field provides the ability to enter the name or email address of individuals (See Figure 5).**

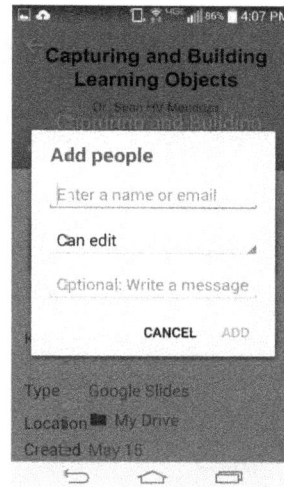

Figure 5. The first field.

6. **The second field governs the type of access each user will have on this specific document.** *Can Edit* rights provide users the ability to make any change to the document. *Can Comment* rights allow the addition of text to the document that is highlighted in a unique color and are not completely incorporated until approved by the owner of the document. *Can View* rights provide the ability to view and read the document only (See Figure 6).

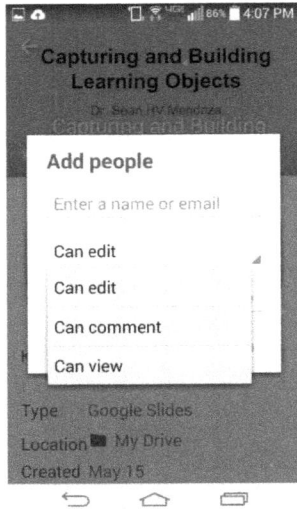

Figure 6. The second field.

7. Once you've entered the email address and rights attributes of contributors or viewers of your document, you can type a short message to participants in the third field and press the "Add" text on the screen. In the event you choose to share a document with someone outside of your organization, Google Drive will confirm you intend to share a document outside of your institution with a "Confirm Sharing" dialog box (See Figure 7).

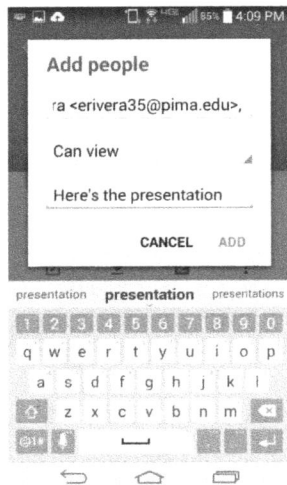

Figure 7. Entered email address.

As described earlier, sharing images or videos on mobile devices are essentially the same and typically vary based on the navigational differences between Android and iOS devices. Sharing images via a mobile device can be done from within the video or camera app. In this example, the gallery application on an android mobile device is used to post an image directly to Google Drive. From within the application the center icon at the bottom allows you to share an image; choose it and you will be given a variety of options (See Figure 8).

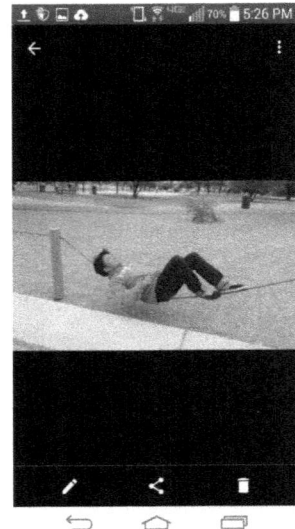

Figure 8. Sharing an image.

Find the Google drive icon to upload your image and select it (See Figure 9).

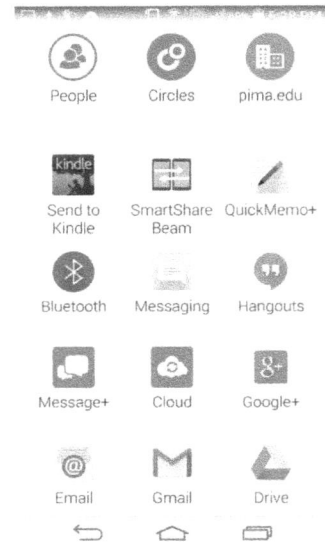

Figure 9. Google Drive icon.

Once selected users can (See Figure 10):

- verify the image to upload is correct (see preview on the top right),
- change the name of the image/video to be uploaded and
- change the location of the folder to be uploaded.

88

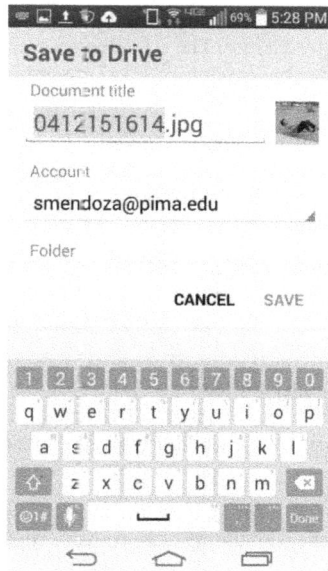

Figure 10. Verifying image.

Depending on the size of the file and your connectivity to the Internet, it may take some time for the file to be available for sharing (See Figure 11).

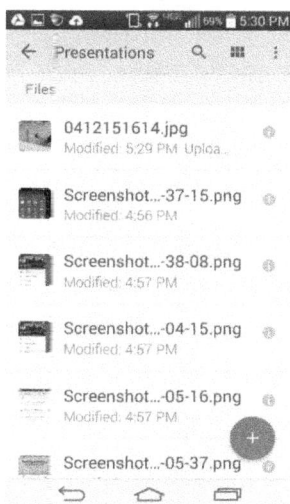

Figure 11. Depending on the size of file.

Once the file has been uploaded, sharing the image or video is the same as sharing any document created in Google drive. Each file and video are potential artifacts any employee can contribute to benefit their community.

4. GOOGLE HANGOUTS AND COMMUNITIES

More than just a video conferencing tool, we have used Google Hangouts to improve communication between employees and the students we serve. Since its introduction, the college community has used this tool for individual and group dialog in the form of real-time text, audio and video. Student services staff and departments such as Advising, Counseling and Financial Aid have used a number of Hangouts' features to support online students or clients unable to visit a traditional campus. Features such as desktop sharing enables students to "show" their individual screen/college experience and be guided by a student services or faculty member. With the increasing use of mobile devices by students, texting is often the best way to reach students. However, college employees fear sending their cell phone numbers along with a text to a student. Google Hangouts eliminates this fear as text messages are connected to our institutional Google mail address and not personal cell phone numbers. In addition, both desktop computers and mobile devices can use Google Hangouts. Given the range of services provided by Hangouts, Pima Community College staff has used Hangouts to:

- improve student retention,
- deliver training,
- advise students,
- assess student comprehension, and
- capture lecture or meeting presentations via Hangouts on Air.

Google+ communities provide an opportunity for individuals and groups to engage in asynchronous communications via communities. Through this service Google+ provides college employees an opportunity to:

- collectively store relevant community specific artifacts such as videos and manuals;
- share and explore ideas and concepts;
- poll the community on relevant topics;
- capture discussions for future comment; and
- connect with individuals with varying perspectives.

5. CONCLUSION

As educators and leaders we must not be afraid to play and learn with technology that bring us closer to students and our communities. Mindful of our security, we must be ever vigilant to safeguard our student and intellectual data, while providing the greatest possible access to our community. Taking an active role to improving our community by sharing our skills, knowledge and abilities, we transform our followers by developing curriculum that elicit lived experiences. By engaging in activities that have relevancy in a community and appropriate context, behaviors and values begin to align with social norms and appear with greater frequency [6]. Willing to guide, change, and transform their followers, they are not only excellent problem solvers, but leaders who are charismatic, inspirational and empathetic to the developmental needs of their community. As educators, we must regularly review our institutional processes, resources and instruction for accessibility. Given the litigation facing some of our most prestigious institutions [10], we must commit to creating a culture of Universal Design that provides access to learning and services to all members of our community.

The college continues to explore opportunities that encourage staff and faculty to share artifacts relevant to local and global partners. Committed to success, Pima College has implemented community centric Google applications, innovative employee training and learning centric concepts in and out of the classroom. With the collective support from IT and the office of the Provost, a growing awareness of academic technologies potential for positive change may become an example for the state of Arizona and other Community Colleges. Pima Community College is willing to change the world because, "the ones who are crazy enough to think they can change the world, are the ones who do." [1]

6. REFERENCES

[1] ABC News. 2011. Steve Jobs Death: 20 Best Quotes - ABC News - Go.com. Retrieved August 2, 2015, from http://abcnews.go.com/Technology/steve-jobs-death-20-best-quotes/story?id=14681795

[2] ACT. 2014. The Condition of STEM 2014 | Key Findings | ACT. Retrieved August 1, 2015, from http://www.act.org/stemcondition/14/findings.html.

[3] Google. 2014. Get started in Google Docs with a screen reader. Retrieved July 30, 2015, from https://support.google.com/docs/answer/1632201?hl=en.

[4] Google Play. 2012. Google Drive - Android Apps on Google Play. Retrieved July 31, 2015, from https://play.google.com/store/apps/details?id=com.google.android.apps.docs.

[5] Mendoza, S. 2009. The trinity of community: Google, Facebook and Twitter. In *Proceedings of World Conference on E-Learning in Corporate, Government, Healthcare, and Higher Education.* (Vancouver, CA, October 2009) Association for the Advancement of Computing in Education (AACE), 3555-3562.

[6] Mendoza, S. 2014. Massively multiplayer online games as a sandbox for leadership: The relationship between in and out of game leadership behaviors. Ed.D. dissertation. Pepperdine University, Malibu, CA.

[7] NCSU.EDU. 2011. What is Universal Design-Principles of UD. Retrieved July 30, 2015, from http://www.ncsu.edu/project/design-projects/sites/cud/content/principles/principles.html.

[8] Pima Community College. 2013. Copyright Resources | Pima Community College, Tucson ... Retrieved July 30, 2015, from https://www.pima.edu/privacy-policy/acceptable-use.html.

[9] Pima Community College. 2013. Privacy Policy | Pima Community College, Tucson ... Retrieved July 30, 2015, from https://www.pima.edu/privacy-policy/acceptable-use.html.

[10] Schaffhauser, D. (2015). Harvard and MIT Face Lawsuit for Lack of Online Captioning ... Retrieved August 2, 2015, from http://campustechnology.com/articles/2015/02/12/harvard-and-mit-face-lawsuit-for-lack-of-online-captioning.aspx.

"TBD": A Flexible Technology Training Model for Smaller Campuses

Julio G. Appling
Lewis & Clark College
Portland, OR
(503) 768-7221
jappling@lclark.edu

ABSTRACT

When scheduling training workshops on small college campuses, it can be difficult to accommodate the varied schedules of faculty and staff. In 2012, the IT department at Lewis & Clark College moved from a pre-determined schedule of training classes to a mix of scheduled workshops and "TBD" (To Be Determined) classes scheduled based on interest and availability. This change, along with adding on-demand resources such as screencasts and lynda.com, has enabled us to respond better to the training needs of our campus community and created opportunities for long-term engagement. This paper examines the factors we considered when making these adjustments to our training workshop schedule and the campus response (which has been mostly positive). Also it will discuss plans to further integrate face-to-face training with on-demand resources through "curated" lynda.com lesson plans used in conjunction with 1:1 individual consulting.

Categories and Subject Descriptors

K.6.1 [**Management of Computing and Information Systems**]: Project and People Management – *Training*

General Terms

Management, Documentation, Human Factors

Keywords

Training, Educational Technology, Liberal Arts

1. INTRODUCTION

In the Fall of 2014, Lewis & Clark Information Technology underwent a re-organization. Client Services, the division of IT responsible for educational technology, software training, and tier-two user support was dissolved. The Service Desk took responsibility for all desktop support and an Educational Technology division became responsible for faculty training. IT training is offered to address support staff and general training needs through a combination of curated on-demand training videos, twenty-minute mini-sessions, and knowledge-based—rather than skill-based—workshops.

2. THE OLD MODEL

2.1 Training Workshops

Our training offerings for staff, faculty, and students prior to Fall 2012 consisted of three options: eighty-minute workshops, special request "gather five" classes, and online video training through lynda.com. Training was provided by the four consultants in the Client Services division of IT, whose staff also provided tier-2 user support and educational technology consulting.

In-person software training workshops were offered in single, eighty-minute sessions, with more extensive subjects such as InDesign and Photoshop offered in two sessions. Workshops covered basic and intermediate skills for applications on IT's supported software list, as well as other IT topics such as "iPad Tips and Tricks" and "Storage & Backup Options." Classes used one of our two computer labs, which are primarily used by students, but are available for academic use as well as faculty and staff training purposes.

IT offered ten to twelve workshops over the course of each academic term. Classes were scheduled either in the morning at 10:00 AM or the afternoon at 2:00 PM, with rarely more than two classes scheduled per week. Class attendance had a minimum of five, and classes were cancelled three days prior to the class date if they did not meet the minimum registration. In the event of a cancellation, instructors would offer to meet with users individually if they had specific (or time-sensitive) training needs, or direct them to on-demand training resources.

2.2 Lynda.com

For specific training needs not addressed by our scheduled workshops and not among our officially supported software, we offered the option for users to check out a temporary Lynda.com license. Lynda.com offers a full and open library of training courses to subscribers. While these courses have always included software, lynda.com has recently expanded into general business concepts such as best practices for presentations, change management, project management, and office organization.

Five licenses were available for users to check out for two weeks at a time, along with a sixth license available reserved for IT staff training. If demand was low, the user had the option to retain the license, and continue taking courses for another two-week period.

2.3 Advertising

IT advertised training workshops in four locations, including two print publications. A brochure including the full schedule of workshops as well as a general IT newsletter which included the training schedule was mailed to all staff and full-time faculty in the first two weeks of the term. The print publications were also distributed at new employee orientations, as new employees were frequent registrants for training workshops. Events also appeared on display monitors around campus, which aggregated all campus events published to our course website. Finally, in our frequent interactions with our staff and faculty, IT would regularly promote upcoming training workshops and events via word-of-mouth.

Online, IT published our full workshop schedule and descriptions to the IT website. Using LiveWhale, our content management system, we tagged training events by subject, which helped target to specific campus users groups, such as graduate school faculty, academic departments, student organizations, and department admins. Lastly, classes were promoted via the school's social media outlets on Twitter and Facebook within two weeks prior to the class date, one week prior, as well as the day before. While IT's Twitter followers primarily consist of other Lewis & Clark campus departments and organizations, it allows another back-channel to directly target our training updates to specific groups.

2.4 Registration

Registration was (and still is) done through a form on the Information Technology website, or by sending an email directly to our training email. Drop-ins were allowed, though discouraged, since pre-registration numbers determined whether or not classes would be cancelled. Following our Google Apps transition, IT began confirming workshop registration using the "IT Training" Google Calendar, which included all IT training workshops. This practice of adding our events directly to users' calendars reduced, but did not eliminate, no-shows, since some (faculty in particular) did not use Google Calendar.

If specific user groups or departments needed more specialized training, Client Services offered a "gather-five" policy, in which users could put together rosters of at least five attendees, for which we would schedule and offer a class on a requested topic, provided the topic was one that could be reasonably covered by one of our staff. This practice typically addressed the needs of departments seeking training for new processes or to address a specific issue.

On average, workshop attendance ranged from six to eight attendees, and day-of cancellations were common. Following a sharp spike in IT training during the Spring 2012 Google Apps Transition, when the campus community relied heavily on us for Google training, workshop attendance waned dramatically to an average of fewer than five per class.

While it is unclear why a sharp decrease in class attendance correlated with the completion of our Google Apps transition, a few possibilities may be offered. Microsoft Office training made up our most heavily attended workshops, largely due to the dramatic changes between Office versions which led to a one- to two-year period of adjustment. While Google Apps contributed to a large increase in class attendance upon release, Google updates were small and frequent. Once trained, users rarely returned for future training on the same Google application. Instead, users more commonly sought answers to one-off questions regarding Google Apps functionality and capability.

Decreased attendance fed into additional problems with our training workshop model. Since training classes were held in the computer labs, we preferred to avoid shutting down the computer labs for an under-attended class. While we could leave them open, it made things awkward for students wanting to use the labs, and printing during classes was loud and disruptive. Additionally, last-minute cancellations made it difficult to anticipate how much effort for instructors to put into class prep, when classes could be cancelled or few attendees showed up.

3. CHANGES
3.1 TBD Classes

To become more flexible, beginning in Fall 2012 we introduced TBD (To Be Determined) classes. TBD incorporated the "need based" scheduling model of the gather-five policy, with courses advertised as a catalogue of unscheduled workshops open for registration. When the registration reached a minimum of five, the instructor would contact those registered, requesting general availability, including best days of the week, and their preference for a morning or afternoon class. A class occurs around registrants' schedules, and were added to our public training calendar where any others interested in the topic may also attend. Remaining TBD registrants for classes not meeting the five-person minimum are contacted following the completion of the final scheduled class in the term and offered training via lynda.com courses with a one-on-one follow-up if necessary.

3.2 Results

Initially, we offered a roster of four TBD classes alongside a shortened offering of our more reliable scheduled classes. This gave us an opportunity the gauge the interest of new workshop topics while still offering our more established classes. Classes receiving requests, but failing to meet the minimum required attendance, would be the first offered in the next term as scheduled classes, since we knew there was already some interest.

TBD classes were well-received by faculty and staff, though buy-in was initially slow. In the first term they were offered, ten faculty signed up for four different TBD classes. Two of these (both advanced Excel topics) would be added to the schedule and both exceeded our minimum attendance goal with around eight in attendance. Since classes added to the schedule often reflected immediate needs, attendee cancellations declined and class cancellations were rare. Additionally, registration numbers for TBD classes allowed us to gauge interest in new course offerings without committing an instructor to class prep and sucking up a block on the room schedule.

Scheduling classes often proved to be a challenge, particularly when interest was high. At times, even despite a six-week window and ten possible times per week, an agreed-upon time could not be found. In these cases, we requested more flexible times from the requestors with more difficult schedules, or offered lynda.com training. While part of this effort is balanced by the reduced amount of time spent arranging the calendar and reservations at the beginning of the term, our numbers on the campus were small enough that we rarely had more than seven individuals to schedule for.

Unfortunately, while this reduced last-minute cancellations, it did not eliminate them. Flexibility is also a culture, and we were fighting an established culture of flakiness. The source of our cancelling classes before had been last-minute cancellations on the part of the attendees, and this problem continued into the TBD classes. Even when classes were worked around schedules and were confirmed via Google Calendar, we inevitably had at least one cancellation per class. Fortunately, we were typically able to pick up additional registrants during the time the class appeared on the public schedule of training courses. For our future TBD classes, we are considering raising the minimum to six or seven, to further maximize attendance.

4. REORGANIZATION

4.1 Changes

Following our Fall 2014 IT department reorganization, much of what had previously comprised IT Client Services now made up the Educational Technology division. While some responsibilities of Educational Technology included training and consultation for faculty, the new-and-improved IT Service Desk—now with two full-time professional staff—would provide software support for staff and students. Staff training, as well as training classes in general, was not included in the departmental re-organization, with the assumption that future training would be primarily offered through on-demand resources such as lynda.com and other online resources.

Given the low attendance and frequent cancellation of our training courses, it was easy to see the logic behind the change. Why offer a service if so few attend? In offering general blanket training courses, we often watered down our training to the point that the knowledge was often either easily accessible through other means, or not specific enough to meet the needs of those in attendance. In addition to services such as lynda.com, straightforward answers were both easy to find (e.g., Google it) and easy to provide through screencasts. Additionally, software applications have grown so robust that it was difficult to address the needs of our users with a single class, leaving them often approaching us afterwards with varied follow-up questions.

4.2 Training Post-Reorg

In response to the re-organization, we've grown to rely more on our web-based and on-demand trainings and to seek increased opportunities to integrate both the creation of training resources as well as training outreach into our existing procedures. Our overall goal is to maximize the quality of face-to-face contact without consuming too many IT staff hours.

We've shortened training classes to 20-minute lunch-&-learn classes. Attendees are free to bring their lunch, and classes are primarily demonstration. In these classes, we provide focused demonstrations of a single concept or task. For example, rather than providing a general overview of Gmail functionality, we focused on what could be done with email, such as setting up advanced filters and labels to auto-route email, which created the excitement and interest that often encouraged our users to seek answers themselves, or sometimes determine that they didn't need such features, but knew they were there. Likewise, Excel classes on specialized concepts such as pivot tables, formulas, and functions, could often be shortened to feature demonstrations, given the abundance of existing YouTube demonstration videos.

Since training workshops (particularly for staff) no longer fell under the responsibility of any IT staff, the training workshop schedule moved almost entirely to TBD classes, offering a catalogue of possible training workshops with no pre-scheduled classes. With minimal faculty on campus, no trainings were scheduled for Summer 2015. While Educational Technology expects to offer faculty-focused Lunch & Learn sessions again during the Fall, we received no inquiries regarding the absence of training workshops, scheduled or otherwise. Faculty questions are handled by Educational Technology, and staff inquiries are directed to the Service Desk.

4.3 "Flipped" workshops

During the Spring, we experimented with offering Photoshop, one of our more challenging classes, in a flipped class format...sort of.

The classes were offered in two parts, where the first session involved working through a list of specially-curated lynda.com classes in our lab with the instructor present. Attendees would use the lynda.com exercise files, and the end goal was to provide the same type of general training offered through or previous "getting started" workshops. The second workshop would be an open Q&A workshop building upon the skills gained in the first session, and applying them to the individual needs of the users. Ideally, this also gave attendees the opportunity to see how skills gained from the foundation workshop applied to different scenarios and projects.

While we considered offering the users the option to take the video-only session on their own, we decided against this for a few reasons. Firstly, being a small campus community, our users have grown accustomed to face-to-face interaction and we prefer to meet with our users personally whenever possible. Also, our users have expressed in the past that they enjoy the opportunity to get away from the distractions of working at their desk. Lastly, this arrangement allowed us to keep the lab open to students, as all training happened over headphones. Our only class offered in this manner thus far has been Adobe Photoshop.

The result of our first offering were mixed. We still experienced several last-minute cancellations, and, in the end, out of five registrants, only two attended the class. Having not offered instruction in the form of curated video, we underestimated the amount of clarification needed. Neither attendee followed the list of courses, which was not discovered until most of the way through the class. This was partly due to misunderstanding of directions, but the automatic progression of lynda.com videos also contributed to this problem, as users often did not realize videos had progressed to the next video in the sequence. This naturally made the second session more difficult, as it was intended to build upon the knowledge from the first session. While not a total loss, the second session did spend more time reviewing the basics than the instructor would have preferred.

In the future, we plan to modify our moderated video sessions to include a general in-person overview of lynda.com functionality and operation at the beginning of the workshop, which will include instructions on how to disable auto-play. Upon review, we were reminded how easy it is to miss transitions between videos, particularly while in the midst of a course. Additionally, we're researching a site license for lynda.com rather than individual subscriptions for checkout. With this arrangement, we would consider making the curated courses available to our users, giving them the option of taking training on their own schedule.

5. CONCLUSION

While ideally, employees would be hired with all required skills for their position, changes in procedures, new applications, and unexpected staff turnover inevitably leads to new training needs. Modern software applications expect users to be quick learners with a reasonable level of operational attunement. Today's users must also be flexible in adapting new and emerging digital tools to new processes. These skills aren't fostered through how-to workshops and step-by-step worksheets, but rather through developing a culture of continued learning and adaptation. While TBD classes allowed us to better match training to user needs, the overall eighty-minute workshop model we have relied upon for so long does not appear to be the wave of the future.

While the face-to-face culture of small, liberal arts colleges makes in-person training an attractive option, the abundance of easily available desktop software applications and mobile apps makes it a difficult model to scale. Particularly in a higher education environment, software applications can be highly specialized, and the multitude of offerings may lead to five different departments performing addressing the same needs with five different tools. While some regulation of supported software is to be expected, this addresses only part of a larger issue.

IT support has expanded beyond mere training and fixes, and more into providing consulting for users looking to find the correct tool to address their needs. Given the right atmosphere, most of our users are willing to explore on their own, but such an atmosphere must be treated as the norm, rather than a one-off exception. Ways to foster such a culture include readily available digital modules, application-specific user groups, and group training events that allow users to learn from each other. This has less to do with scheduling the right workshops, and more about establishing and sustaining open communication with users. IT now serves as the guide and facilitator rather than the sole keeper of the knowledge.

6. ACKNOWLEDGMENTS

My thanks to my colleagues at Lewis & Clark Information Technology, as well as the many faculty, staff, and student users that we support who consistently challenge us to seek new knowledge and explore new approaches in helping them succeed.

7. REFERENCES

[1] Appling, Julio. We're going Google!: Making the most of marketing. In *SIGUCCS '12 Proceedings of the 40th Annual ACM SIGUCCS Conference on User Services* ACM, New York, NY, 223-226.
DOI=http://dl.acm.org/citation.cfm?doid=2382456.2382511.

Women in IT: The Endangered Gender

Vicki Leigh Noles Rogers
University of Georgia
and University of West Georgia
24683 Georgia Highway 100
Roopville, GA 30170
678-378-1248
vickir@uga.edu

ABSTRACT
Information technology (IT) careers continue to grow and yet the number of women in them continues to decline. The gap is even more profound in leadership positions. This paper is a review of existing literature, information and statistics concerning women in higher education information technology leadership. It is a call for recruitment, professional development, and retention aimed at helping women overcome systemic exclusion from IT management. It combines the topics of women, higher education, information technology, and leadership and considers them through the lens of professional development and adult education. Finally, it discusses and endorses ideas for initiating change in our field to increase our diversity and therefore meet the growth demands.

Categories and Subject Descriptors
K.6.1 [**Management of Computing and Information Systems**]: Project and People Management – *Staffing and Training.*

General Terms
Management, Performance, Human Factors.

Keywords
women in information technology; women in leadership; women in higher education; women professional development; IT gender; gender leadership; higher education gender

1. INTRODUCTION
Technology is growing at a truly remarkable rate. One estimate proposes at this rapidity we will only have the resources to fill half of the open technology positions by the year 2018 [9]. In fact, because technology plays such an important part in essentially every sector of our economy, computer related jobs are considered to be one of the 10 fastest growing US occupations. That said, it is well documented that men greatly outnumber women in the Information Technology (IT) domain [5], [7], [11], [30], [31]. Allen et al [6] observed that while women's participation was on the rise in many traditionally male-dominated occupations like accounting and medicine, the percentage of women in IT was actually declining. The Bureau of Labor Statistics reported in

SIGUCCS '15, November 09-13, 2015, St. Petersburg, FL, USA
© 2015 ACM. ISBN 978-1-4503-3610-9/15/11 $15.00
DOI: http://dx.doi.org/10.1145/2815546.2815558

2012 that women now make up 26.6 percent of the total computer and mathematical occupations. This is down from the Information Technology Diversity's report from reported women at 34.9 percent in 2002 down even more from 41 percent in 1996 [6]. These statistics are shocking and actually do not require great interpretation. The percentage of women in IT is shrinking.

There have been many reasons postulated for the dwindling number of women in IT in general, which may or may not be the same reasons for women in IT in higher education. McKinney et al [22] attributed the lack of women in IT fields to a "throughput problem," meaning too many women are leaving the field, and an "input problem," meaning lower numbers enter the field. Beyond this, other reasons are cited for the lack of participation and advancement of women in technology. These include organizational practices such as masculine work environments, hiring and promotion biases, a lack of role models and mentors, family issues, leadership stereotypes, work-life balance, inequities in performance and promotion procedures and inflexible work policies [10]. Orser, Riding, & Stanley [26] found personal barriers were most frequently mentioned by women when considering their success in technology based careers. These personal barriers include gender-influenced self-efficacy, a lack of social capitol, networking opportunities and a sense of belonging. Given all these reasons and ideas, there is still a great deal to research and understand about the general topic of women in IT.

In addition to the incredibly low number of women in the field, there are a disproportionately high number of men in management. [32] Beyond knowing men outnumber women significantly in IT and in IT leadership, we know very little about the current and potential systems of support for women within higher education IT roles interested in leadership. This manuscript focuses specifically on existing research and calls for more research in the area of women's professional and career development in higher education IT. Bierema said many years ago, "Organizations need to understand that women's career development is different" [12]. I believe women's career development is different, but women's career development in higher education IT is even more distinctive.

2. METHOD
For this article, I am interested in the relationships and overlap of the topics of women in leadership, women in technology and women in higher education. These general topics will give background in the field and lead to greater understanding on how to better support and encourage women in higher education technology careers.

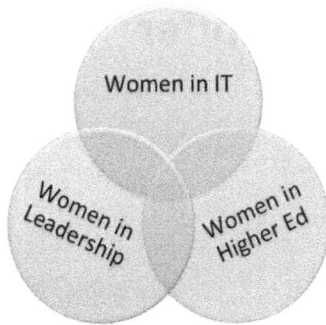

Figure 1. Contributing Bodies of Knowledge Concerning Women in Higher Education Information Technology Careers.

The search for relevant literature on these topics was conducted using the University System of Georgia's Galileo library portal. GALILEO stands for "GeorgiA LIbrary LEarning Online" (GALILEO). It is an initiative of the Board of Regents of the University System of Georgia. GALILEO is an online library portal to authoritative, subscription-only information that includes access over to over 100 databases indexing thousands of periodicals and scholarly journals.

My search consisted of the following keywords:

- Women AND information technology
- Women AND leadership
- Women AND higher education

3. RESULTS

The knowledge about women in IT, higher education and leadership is increasingly more plentiful. However, there is an obvious lack in information specifically about the intersection of these three larger bodies. Very few empirical studies exist in combination of these topics beyond knowing that women in higher education IT are few and women in higher education leadership roles are fewer. [5], [7], [11], [30], [31] I have chosen to highlight some of the predominant ideas around the three topics as well as illuminate the rather small amount of information about the intersection (Figure1).

3.1 Women in IT

Information technology as a career stems from the early computing profession that began in 19th century – men that built nautical tables, calculated trajectories, and reconciled financial accounts. These original careers were almost exclusively male. This is a significant point as it established the tradition that computing and IT were male roles from the foundation. As women entered these jobs, they were more often in support roles. Support roles tend to be the jobs that require soft skills, such as service desk roles, customer service, and "non technical" work. Supporting roles by nature are assistants, not responsible for what is considered the core work. The masculine nature of IT was established in the formation and the androcentric culture persists today. This is true in the profession as a whole and in the climb to leadership [14].

McKinney et al [22] noticed there are few given reasons for the obvious difference in the numbers of women and men in IT. Some possibilities were offered – less ability in the "hard" sciences, educational experiences dissuade women from these careers, less

comfortable because of the male environment. None of these possibilities had been tested prior to the McKinney [22] study. Research since that time has shown that IT women are susceptible to gender discrimination as well as other issues in advancement opportunities, quality mentoring, and assignment choice that their male counterparts may not experience. In addition, they tend to receive lower salaries and are filling fewer management positions [5]. This is especially interesting given 59% of the overall American workforce in 2007 were women [26].

Beyond the existing lesser numbers of women in information technology are significant statistics of women leaving the field. Wentling [34] found that women are nearly three times as likely as men to leave IT. The reasons cited for leaving include cultural fit, expectation gaps, lack of role models and mentors, career satisfaction, organizational commitment, role ambiguity, and role conflict. Williams, Muller, & Kilanski [34] consider the changes in the social organization of work in the last few decades. Since that time we have faced downsizing, restructuring, computerization, and globalization. It is a time of great change for both women and IT.

Wentling [34] observed that while there are some women achieving success in the IT field, they are actually the exceptions. Women's participation in information technology careers is low overall, but it declines even more as they attempt to climb to higher positions. D'Agostino [16] quoted Betty Spence, president of the National Association for Female Executives in saying: "the glass ceiling exists and is stronger in IT than in any other field." The US Bureau of Labor and Statistics reports 30 percent of computer and information systems managers are female however, an in-depth study by Educause, a higher education IT professional organization, found an even lower number of 23 percent are actually in the leadership positions of CIO or senior management [8]. There is clearly a disproportionately high number of men in management [32].

3.2 Women in Higher Education

As this discussion is about women in information technology with higher education settings, it is important that we also discuss the position of women in higher education. Women are now surpassing men in all degree levels, earning 60 percent of the master's degrees and 50.4 percent of the doctoral degrees. Women make up 57 percent of total college students and yet they are only 26 percent of full professors, 23 percent of university presidents, and 14 percent of presidents at doctoral degree granting institutions [32].

Acker [1] believes that hierarchies take on gendered constructs. I believe there is nowhere this is more evident than the academy. Madden [20] states that education is founded on hierarchies and observes that women are not only in the minority in higher education, but also in the smallest proportions at the most prestigious colleges and positions. Savigny [28] says, "Despite the considerable advances of the feminist movement across Western societies, in Universities women are less likely to be promoted, or paid as much as their male colleagues, or even get jobs in the first place [28]. Male leadership continues to endure in higher education. This shows us a challenge for women exists in higher education without the additional specialty of IT. Facing the challenges in both realms equates to a difficult road for women that want to grow and advance in higher education information technology.

3.3 Women in Leadership

Beyond the discussion of women in IT and women in higher education is a sizeable amount of information about women and leadership. While the first two sectors seem to be the greatest challenge, the consideration of trials women face in leadership development should not be ignored. Leadership has been defined and conceptualized in many ways. Northouse [23] observed that the commonality of leadership definitions is the belief that leadership involves influencing others toward the attainment of a goal. Leadership is a topic with a vast body of knowledge. The information from this segment of our discussion is important and helpful.

Men have traditionally held leadership roles in any sector [29]. While the number of women in the workforce continues to grow, the path for women to develop as leaders continues to be narrow. [2] [13]. Women earn more than half of all bachelors, masters and doctoral degrees and make up half of the US labor force [33], and they still fill less than five percent of top management positions [21].

Historically, the research on women's underrepresentation in leadership focused on intentional exclusion. In recent years this body of knowledge has shifted to research what has been termed second-generation gender bias, the "powerful and yet often invisible barriers to women's advancement that arise from cultural beliefs about gender, as well as workplace structure, practice and patterns of interaction that inadvertently favor men" [18]. These invisible barriers can easily be related to the potential barrier for women in IT. Further research should consider leadership theory and application in addition to any information gathering in the areas of women in IT and women in higher education.

3.4 The Intersection

The intersection of women in IT, higher education, and leadership is the area I am most interested. This body of knowledge is rather small. Educause has done a small amount of research on women in higher education IT. They said, "Most research and statistics on IT organizations and workers either examine aggregate data or concentrate on a corporate perspective" [14]. The same publication noted that there is very little data on women IT leaders in higher education. They argue that more research is needed for several reasons. As technology becomes more prevalent in our lives, it is reasonable to question if such a homogenous group, as IT seems to be, can create and support technology that will serve everyone. In addition, higher education itself is becoming more diverse – students, faculty, and staff. IT within the institutions should seek to do the same. [14]

4. DISCUSSION

Now that we recognize the low numbers of women in leadership, in higher education and information technology, and the intersection of the three, it begs the question of why and how can we make change? The fact that there is very little information about the intersection of these topics is extremely telling. There have been several articles calling for more research on the topic. In fact, Igbaria & Baroudi [19] said: "…future research should explore the potential barriers to promotability among women who have aspirations to information systems upper management and executive careers. We need to look at the reasons for the existence of barriers and possible ways to overcome them." Morris [23] presented literature concerning women in information technology and observed that few empirical studies have been conducted to see why and how women persist in IT careers. Ahuja [4] answered that call and presented a model of social and structural determinants of women's career choices, persistence and advancement in IT. Her model serves as a framework for exploring the many issues surrounding women in IT. Drury [17] said, "There is a need to study the lived experiences of women in higher education IT" [17]. All of these calls are still mostly left without further research and most definitely without application.

Research should be initiated within a higher education information technology setting for the purpose of understanding the lack of female leaders and the lack of development opportunities. It is my belief that an action research study would be well suited for this topic. Reason and Bradbury [25] define action research as a "participatory process concerned with developing practical knowing in the pursuit of worthwhile human purposes. It seeks to bring together action and reflection, theory and practice, in participation with others, in the pursuit of practical solutions to issues of pressing concern to people, and more generally the flourishing of individual persons and their communities." This combination of action and research, theory and practice would work well for a working group of IT employees in a higher education setting. I believe the process of action research that encourages intervention and solutions, while observing and reflecting would also be significantly beneficial to the higher education and IT. I believe this process will reveal great opportunity for women, higher education and leadership development.

5. ACKNOWLEDGMENTS

Many thanks to ACM SIGUCCS for considering this paper and big love to the family and friends that continually support me in my journey.

6. REFERENCES

[1] Acker, J. (1990, Jun). Hierarchies, Jobs, Bodies: A Theory of Gendered Organizations. Gender and Society, (2), 139-158.

[2] Acker, J. (2006). Inequality regimes: gender, class and race in organizations. Gender and Society, 20(), 441-464.

[3] Agosto, D. E., Gasson, S., & Atwood, M. (2008). Changing mental models of the IT professions: A theoretical framework. Journal of Information Technology Education, 7(), 205-221.

[4] Ahuja, M. K. (2002). Women in the information technology profession: A literature review, synthesis and research agenda. European Journal of Information Systems, 11(), 20-34.

[5] Allen, M. R., Riemenschneider, C., & Armstrong, D. (2004). The role of laughter when discussing workplace barriers: Women in information technology jobs. Sex Roles, 50(3/4), 177-189.

[6] Allen, M. R., Riemenschneider, C., & Armstrong, D. (2006). Making sense of the barriers women face in the information technology work force: Standpoint theory, self-disclosure, and causal maps. Sex Roles, 54(11-12), 832-844.

[7] Arora, A., & Athreye, S. (2002). The software industry and India's economic development. Information Economics & Policy, 14(), 253-273.

[8] Arroway, P., Grochow, J. M., Pirani, J. A., & Regenstein, C. E. (2011, October). The higher education CIO: Protrait of today, landscape of tomorrow. . Retrieved from http://www.educause.edu/ecar

[9] Ashcraft, C., & Blithe, S. (2009). Women in IT: The facts. Retrieved from http://www ncwit.org/sites/default/files/legacy/pdf/NCWIT_TheFacts_rev2010.pdf

[10] Ashcraft, C., & Blithe, S. (2010). Women in IT: The facts. Retrieved from http://ncwit org/pdf/NCWIT_TheFacts_rev2010.pdf

[11] Beise, C., Myers, M., VanBrackle, L., & Cherli-Saroq, N. (2003). An examination of age, race, and sex as predictors of success in the first programming course. Journal of Informatics Education Research, 5(), 51-64.

[12] Bierema, L. L. (1998). A synthesis of women's career development issues. New Directions for Adult and Continuing Education, 80(Winter), 95-103.

[13] Black, A. E., & Rothman, S. (1998). Have you really come a long way? Women's access the power in the United States. Gender Issues, 16(1/2), 107-134.

Clark, E. (2012, October 16, 2012). Women CIOs in higher education. EDUCAUSE Center for Applied Research. Retrieved from http://www.educause.edu/ecar

[14] Current population survey, annual averages, household data. (2010). Retrieved from http://www.bls.gov

[15] D'Agostino. D. (2009). Where are all the women in IT. CIO Insight, 32(76).

[16] Drury, M. (2011). Women technology leaders: Gender issues in higher education information technology. NASPA Journal about Women in Higher Education, 4(1), 96-123.

[17] Ely, R., Ibarra, H., & Kolb, D. (2011). Taking gender into account: Theory and design for women's leadership development programs. Academy of Management Learning & Education, 10(3), 474-665.

[18] Igbaria, M., & Baroudi, J. J. (1995). The impact of job performance evaluations on career advancement prospects: an examination of gender differences in the IS workplace. MIS Quarterly, 19(), 107-123.

[19] Madden, M. (2011, Fall). Four gender stereotypes of leaders: Do tey influence leadership in higher education? Wagadu: A Journal of transnational women and gender studies, 9(), 55-88.

[20] Man, M. M., & Skerlvaj, M. (2009). Is there a "glass ceiling" for mid-level managers? International Journal of Management and Innovation, 1(1), 1-13.

[21] McKinney, V. W., Brooks, N., O'Leary-Kelly, A., & Hardgrave, E. (2008). Women and men in the IT profession. Communications of the ACM, 51(2), 81-84.

[22] Morris, L. (2002, November). Women in information technology literature review: recruitment, retention and persistence factors. Paper presented at the Mid-South Educational Research Association, Chattanooga, Tennessee.

[23] Northouse, P. G. (2013). Leadership: Theory and practice (Sixth ed.). Los Angelos: Sage.

[24] Orser, B., Riding, A., & Stanley, J. (2012). Perceived career challenges and response strategies of women in the advanced technology sector. Entrepreneurship & Regional Development, 24(1-2), 73-93.

[25] Reason, P., & Bradbury, H. (2008). Handbook of Action Research (2nd ed.). London: Sage.

[26] Quensenbery, J., & Trauth, E. M. (2007). What do women want? An investigation of career anchors among women in the IT workforce. Procedings of the ACM SIGMIS-Computer Personnel Research, 122-127.

[27] Savigny, H. (2014). Women, know your limits: cultural sexism in academia. Gender and Education, 26(7), 794-809.

[28] Stelter, N. Z. (2002). Gender differences in leadership: current social issues and future organizational implications. Journal of Leadership Studies, 8(4), 88-100.

[29] Sumner, M., & Niederman, F. (2004). The impact of gender differences on job satisfaction, job turnover, and career experiences of systems professionals. Journal of Computer Information Systems, 44(), 29-40.

[30] Trauth, E. M., Neilsen, S. H., & VonHellens, L. A. (2003). Explaining the IT gender gap: Augstralian stories for the new millinnium. Journal of Research and Practice in Information Technology, 35(), 7-20.

[31] Truman, G. E., & Baroudi, J. J. (1994). Gender differences in the information systems managerial ranks: an assessment of potential discriminatory practices. MIS Quarterly, 18(), 129-141.

[32] US labor force, population, and education. (2011). Retrieved from http://www.catalyst.org

[33] Wentling, R. M. (2009). Workplace culture that hinders and assists the career development of women in information technology. Information Technology, Learning & Performance, 25(1), 25.

[34] Williams, C. L., Muller, C., & Kilanski, K. (2012, May 23, 2012). Gendered organizations in the new economy. Gender and Society, 26, 549-573.

Who Says You Can't Go Home?

Jen Servedio
Colgate University
13 Oak Drive
Hamilton, NY 13346
1-315-228-6814
jservedio@colgate.edu

Jon Beers
Colgate University
13 Oak Drive
Hamilton, NY 13346
1-315-228-6453
jbeers@colgate.edu

ABSTRACT

When is it time to bring an outsourced service back in house? The field of information technology is ever changing. Outsourcing may be good today, but what about tomorrow?

Nearly ten years ago, outsourcing our helpline was the perfect solution. We were dealing with an IT personnel shortage and as a result, we were unable to meet the needs of our faculty and staff.

As we grew during those ten years, it became very clear that there was a huge disconnect between the outsourced level 1 helpline and our level 2 and level 3 support. Statistics showed that call volume per day was low and that there were several hours each day that we were paying to have 2 full time employees but couldn't utilize their time for anything other than level 1 phone support. Logistics were also our enemy. Having the outsourced technicians off-site also meant they couldn't go to offices and perform level 1 tasks. We desperately needed to centralize into a fully functional service desk model.

During this session we will share how our IT department evolved and why it was the right time to insource. It took time and hard work to gather the necessary information to even consider making this change. You will see how we convinced our upper administration why this would be a good move, how we handled push back from the campus community, and how we successfully brought our helpline back home.

Categories and Subject Descriptors

K.6.1 [**Management of Computing and Information Systems**]: Project and People Management – *Management techniques (e.g., PERT/CPM), Staffing*

General Terms

Management, Measurement, Documentation, Performance, Design, Economics, Reliability, Human Factors, Standardization

Keywords

Insourcing; Service Desk; Incident Management; Service Requests; Level One Support

1. INTRODUCTION

Technology support needs at Colgate had grown but the underlying structure providing the support had not. The tactical component of our service structure was outsourced and, as a result, wasting valuable time and resources within Information Technology Services (ITS). Bringing the help desk back to campus gave us the flexibility to transform Technology Support Services into a fully functioning service team that will be able meet the needs of faculty, staff and students and strategically manage them in a way that more closely aligns with the business processes of the University.

This paper outlines three specific areas of concern: the ITS Help Desk, the internal organization of Technology Support Services (TSS), and event support.

2. ITS OUTSOURCED HELPDESK
2.1 Previous State

The ITS help desk that serviced faculty and staff was outsourced to a company who provided a combination of dedicated and non-dedicated staff. Dedicated staff primarily answered calls for Colgate and had basic knowledge for supporting our standard hardware and software Non-dedicated staff answered calls for several clients in addition to Colgate and offered very limited troubleshooting. Non-dedicated staff often obtained information from callers and escalated help requests to dedicated staff for follow up the next day.

2.1.1 Hours of Coverage

According to our contract, two full-time dedicated staff answered calls Monday through Friday from 7 a.m. until 4 p.m. One dedicated staff member took a lunch break while the other covered the phone. Non-dedicated staff then took over until 10 p.m. Weekend coverage on Saturdays and Sundays from 10 a.m. until 10 p.m. was covered by non-dedicated staff.

2.1.2 Cost of Outsourcing

Outsourcing our level one phone support came with the following expenses:

- monthly fee $9,995
- Colgate-provided equipment
  - 2 HP laptops ($2,000)
  - 2 MacBook Pro laptops ($3,000)
  - 2 Cisco 7941 VoIP desk phones ($1,200)
  - 1 Cisco 2851 VoIP router ($3,500)
  - All Colgate standard software installed on the provided computers (most are part of site licenses, estimated additional software $2,500)

The cost of equipment (divided by a 5-year life-cycle) and contact center fee equals $122,380 annually.

2.1.3 Contracted Support Agreement

The following is taken directly from our contract.

- Assist users with application issues, operating system issues, and other issues as indicated for supported products - refers to the supported hardware and software list that is supplied to university owned computers.

- Assist users with questions and troubleshooting relation to installation, configuration and setup of application software.

- Assist users with basic hardware issues, as we are able.

- Direct personally owned equipment and home repairs to Colgate.

Full support:

- Assist with software installation

- Troubleshoot software problems

- Conduct walkthroughs of documentation and training

- Escalate to tier 2 (Colgate) where applicable

Limited Support:

- Assist with software installation

- Troubleshoot basic software problems

- Direct people to appropriate documentation and training

- Escalate to tier 2 (Colgate) where applicable

Specialty Support:

- Install the software as we are able

- Offer advice as we are able

- Escalate to tier 2 (Colgate) where applicable

- Non-supported software

- Not install or support the software

- Direct end user to tier 2 support or product manufacturer

2.1.4 Statistics

Data taken from our Footprints ticketing system indicates that there were 2,956 tickets opened between May 2013 and May 2014. The average monthly call volume is 240; per day is less than 10. Since the average call time is ten minutes, there are less than two hours of work performed. The most calls opened in one day were on the first day of classes (8/29/2013). On that day there were 41 calls. The majority of them were password resets.

Further analysis of the data collected shows these top five types of calls. They are all entry-level technical problems.

- User cannot log in to the portal, email, network - password reset

- Voicemail setup

- Voicemail - change pin

- Printing issues

- Spam

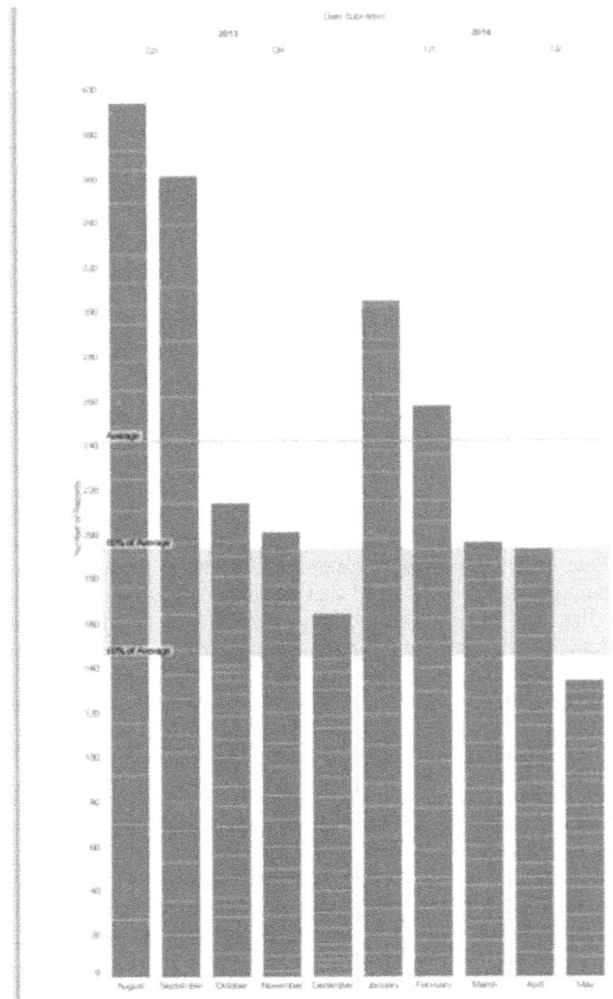

Figure 1. Monthly Call Volume August 2013 - May 2014.

The diagram above shows the monthly call volume from August 2013 through May 2014. Trends can be easily identified with the most calls taking place at the beginning of the semester and then gradually decreasing as the semester comes to a close.

2.1.5 Other Issues

The outsourced help desk did not serve our students. As a result, ITS maintained a separate help desk run by two FTEs and student workers. This duplication of effort was costly and created a communication barrier between problems that the students are experiencing and those that faculty and staff are experiencing. It was proposed that merging the two support models would break down that barrier and enhance communication. Second, since the outsourced call center was not on campus, they escalated level 1 support calls when a technician is needed on site. Our level 2 Technology Support Coordinators (TSC) were taking time away from higher-level problems to address these calls. These types of calls should be handled by level 1 support and/or trained student workers.

The level of satisfaction with our outsourced company had declined since we originally outsourced several years ago. Although our contract with them states that they will answer "80% of all calls within 20 seconds" as a service level objective, there had been complaints about the time users are were kept on hold. When this was brought to their attention, they could not offer good reason for the delay. Further investigation revealed that one of the outsourced agents was spending an exorbitant amount of time on the phone with callers where it would be more productive to dispatch a technician to assist in person. Good judgement was not being used to escalate calls proficiently and as a result, other callers were kept waiting. These and other issues were presented to our account manager and there was no improvement.

2.2 Proposed Improved Services

The objective is to create a centralized ITS help desk for faculty, staff and students that is aligned with our business processes, improves customer service and satisfaction, improves our reputation, and serves as a platform to identify new business initiatives.

2.2.1 Evening and Weekend Support by Dedicated, Professional Staff

Professional staff will be on hand to support evening classes. This had been a problem with an outsourced help desk because they were providing non-dedicated staff at the call center unfamiliar with our on campus events and procedures during those hours.

Our infrastructure team provided on-call support until 10 p.m. during the week and 8 a.m. to 10 p.m. on weekends and holidays for critical services. We needed to have a help desk with professional staff or student workers available to resolve or properly escalate issues during that time. This would result in cost savings in that area.

Insourced help desk technicians would be able to perform lower level tasks currently being done by other teams in ITS. It was previously noted that less than two hours per day was being spent on help desk calls. The other five hours can be used to improve productivity across all of ITS performing some of the tasks listed below.

Technology Support Services

- VoIP phone configuration and changes
- Updating and imaging the loaner laptop pool
- Creating support documents and how-to videos
- Enterprise Systems & Application Development
- Banner password resets
- File share permissions

Infrastructure

- Verifying backups
- Monitoring system up/down time

Providing faculty, staff and student support

- One support model for everyone, which will streamline processes and improve service
- Improving case management
- Conducting follow-up and satisfaction surveys

Providing classroom support

- Eliminating the need for a separate classroom support hotline
- Providing event support

- Centralized intake, which will force a workflow that saves time and provides immediate answers to important questions

Help for staff retirees and faculty emeriti

2.2.2 Staffing

Two new full-time help desk technicians would join the already established student help desk located on the third floor of Case-Geyer. The existing Service Desk Manager, Service Desk Assistant and student workers would combine resources to offer a more complete support solution. Interns from nearby Morrisville State College had been valuable to our team and would be able to provide additional support as part of the help desk.

The four existing Technology Support Coordinators (TSC) would continue to offer level 2 support while assisting the Service Desk personnel. Rotating shifts would be required by TSCs until a solid workflow is established. Vacations, sick days and any other absences by the help desk technicians will be covered by student workers, our current student help desk FTE's, and Technology Support Coordinators. A shift in resources would be required to accommodate a long-term disability.

2.2.3 Proposed Schedule

Call-in and Walk-up Service at the Service Desk:

Monday through Friday
7:30 a.m. until 11:00 p.m. (Shifts spread between two FTEs)

Saturday
11:00 a.m. until 4:00 p.m. (Shifts covered by student workers)

Sunday
11:00 a.m. until 11:00 p m. (Shifts covered by student workers)

2.2.4 Coverage

The Service Desk Assistant, interns, TSCs, and student workers will cover lunch breaks, vacations, and illness. Help Desk Technicians will be required to cover holidays. The outsourced Level One support provided one dedicated staff person on holidays.

TSS will continue to employ summer workers at the service desk in Case Library and Geyer Center for Technology.

Weekends and evenings have been a struggle to provide adequate support. With the proposed solution we will be able to provide dedicated professional staff during the hours that our outsourced helpdesk currently provides non-dedicated staff. This has been a huge concern since our labs and evening classes are not getting the support they need

Combining student workers and professional staff has proven successful at Hobart and William Smith, Hamilton College and St. Lawrence University. Data gathered from these help desks and others outside of the NY6 Consortium indicate that prime coverage days for professional staff are Sunday through Friday.

2.2.5 Required Skillset

Skills necessary to handle the current top five call types (password resets, voicemail setup, voicemail pin changes, spam, and printing issues) are at a very low technical level. Our main focus for these positions will be great customer service skills and entry-level technical skills. Interacting with our level 2 TSCs and the other teams within ITS will quickly grow their technical knowledge and their ability to handle a very broad range of problems. Colgate student workers will benefit from the same training as well as interns from local colleges.

2.2.6 Logistics: Where will we put them?

The two new Service Desk Technicians will occupy an office located directly behind the ITS Service Desk on the third floor of Case-Geyer. The optimal setup would be two cubicles with desk space for one professional staff and one student worker in each.

2.2.7 Startup Costs

- Two new full time help desk technicians
- Per HR - the total compensation needed for two positions would be approximately $112,280. This would result in an annual savings of $7,720.
- Continue one month to transition help desk ($9,995)
- Total startup equipment costs would be less than $15,000
- Cubicles and desks (<$5,000 total furniture cost)
- 2 Mac PCs ($2,500)
- 2 Windows PCs ($1,500)
- 2 Cisco VoIP desk phones (reuse phones in stock $0)

2.2.8 Marketing

ITS has been suffering from a damaged reputation for many years. Bringing the help desk back to Colgate offers the opportunity to launch a new support structure will remedy that damage. We will work with Colgate's Communication Department to develop a comprehensive plan to promote the new help desk and its offerings.

2.2.9 Summary

The overall action was to terminate our contract and hire two Help Desk Technicians. Repatriation of the Colgate Help Desk would improve support for faculty, staff and students by creating a single area of contact for technology services. Student workers currently staffing the student help desk would merge with the newly formed help desk. This new model shows a minimum annual cost savings of $7,720.00. The real savings will be evident when we see more value for the money we are spending.

3. ITS INSOURCED HELPDESK

3.1 Implementation of the Plan

3.1.1 Obstacles

Obstacles were everywhere. According to the plan we were going live on January 2, 2015.

The two positions were finally posted in early November. The search was very aggressive. The goal was to have two people hired by the beginning of December. Our new Help Desk Technicians started work on December 17, 2014. The scheduled kick-off date for our in house helpline was January 2, 2015 and the campus was shutting down December 22 through January 2 for holiday break.

In the midst of hiring we were presented with a petition signed by a number of faculty who were upset that we were getting rid of the helpline they loved. They were insisting that we take a step back and evaluate things once more before moving forward. Many complaints were made regarding the level of service they were receiving from our existing ITS staff. We also heard about things the outsourced helpline was doing that made our internal staff look very bad such as spending hours on the phone with the same person and supporting non-supported software. Several communications and meetings later, we convinced everyone that we were moving ahead with the plan. We contracted with Dean,

one of the technicians from the outsourced company, to assist with phones and to train and mentor our new technicians. Dean was very well liked by our faculty and staff; we hoped his participation would increase faculty buy-in.

On January 2 we went live with our two new Help Desk Technicians (Alex and Michael), Dean, Jon and Jen. We had three weeks before classes started. Everyone in ITS was asked to volunteer time answering the phones. This was an eye opening experience for many!

Jon and Jen created a rigorous training plan for Alex and Michael. Level 2 support technicians were given shifts on the phones with Michael and Alex shadowing them. The technicians met with each team within ITS (Technology Support Services, Infrastructure, Business Systems and Academic Technologies) to get a grasp of what each team supported. When classes began, Alex and Michael were answering the phones with Dean and Jon backing them up. Level 2 support was available via chat to assist Alex and Michael.

4. LESSONS LEARNED

4.1 Metrics

Average Ticket Lifecycle

Spring 2014 — 5 Days, 2 Hours
Spring 2015 — 3 Days, 0 Hours

Percent Resolved on First Contact

Spring 2014 — 4372 Calls
Fall 2014 — 5599 Calls
Spring 2015 — 5333 Calls

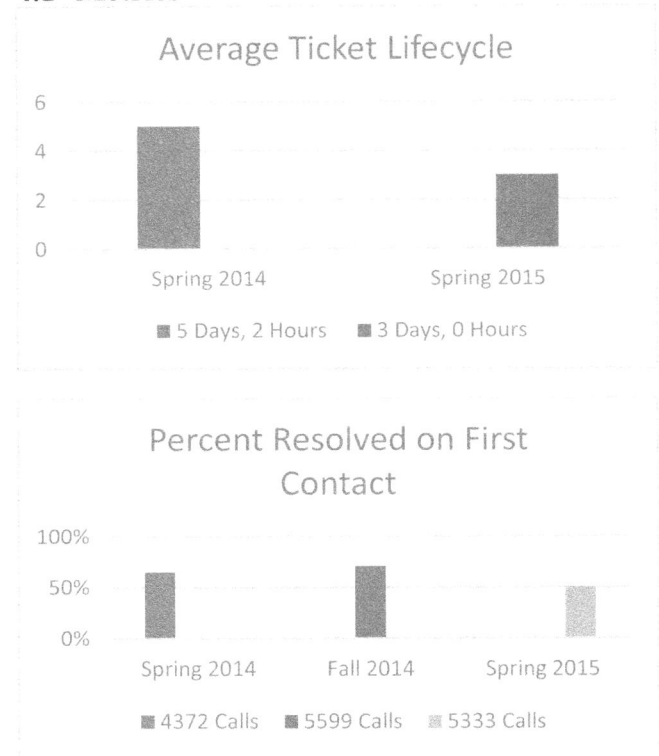

4.2 Looking Back

4.2.1 Support/Buy In

Gain the full support of the faculty and staff, including ITS staff. This may require better communications to the entire campus, to gain buy in, and to sell the idea.

4.2.2 Training

Be prepared for some rough moments. Two new technicians were unfamiliar with the culture, support structure, or the finer details of our infrastructure, equipment, and software. Training continues for our full time technicians as well as for our student staff.

4.2.3 Useful Data

We had limited data regarding call volume, time of day, peak periods, and first call resolution. This limited our ability to determine shift hours for our newly hired technicians.

4.2.4 Phone System

Our Cisco UCCX Call Center took a little getting used to. We experimented with Hunt Groups and other systems to determine what worked best for us and what was the best practice for holding or transferring calls.

4.3 Looking Ahead

4.3.1 Resolution Time

Resolution during first contact with the helpline was slightly higher due to inexperienced staff. They had the technical skills but had to build their confidence and learn the culture of Colgate. We anticipate this number to change in the fall 2015 semester.

4.3.2 Student Workforce

The spring 2015 semester was a test bed for our student workers. Our first real training of student helpline workers will occur prior to the fall 2015 semester. At that time our student workforce will increase by 50% from twenty to thirty. We hired additional students in the spring, and they have completed their first round of training and shadowing with our full time technicians. We hired additional students in the spring and they have completed their first round of training and shadowing with our full time technicians.

4.3.3 Constant Evaluation

We will continue to examine workflows, responsibilities, staffing, skillsets, metrics, customer service surveys and other tools to keep up with changing needs of the university, and make continual improvements where needed.

Patch Management:
The Importance of Implementing Central Patch Management and Our Experiences Doing So

Timothy Palumbo
Lehigh University
8B East Packer Avenue
Bethlehem, PA 18015
tip204@lehigh.edu

ABSTRACT

Lehigh University is implementing the Secunia CSI application to patch faculty/staff computers on campus. This paper will cover the patch management process from the beginning to end, including vendor identification, application testing, vendor selection, implementation, deployment, and interpreting the results. We will discuss the importance of using a patch management solution to guard against data breaches as well as how vulnerable computers are without one.

This paper will focus on why we chose Secunia over other products and why patch management is an increasingly necessary solution in all sectors. With breaches occurring daily, we must work on prevention. There are countless vulnerabilities across a variety of products on University computers, including: Adobe Flash, Java, and web browsers. Users often fall victim to viruses and malware as a result of these unpatched or outdated applications. Universities deal with sensitive and valuable data that needs to be protected. Patching software can help prevent breaches and therefore secure campus assets. No matter how you do it, the importance of patch management cannot be overstated.

Categories and Subject Descriptors
K.6.3 [Management of Computing and Information Systems]: Software Management – *software maintenance, software process, software selection.*

General Terms
Management, Security.

Keywords
Patching; security; patch management; Secunia.

SIGUCCS '15, November 09 - 13, 2015, St. Petersburg, FL, USA
Copyright is held by the owner/author(s). Publication rights licensed to ACM.
ACM 978-1-4503-3610-9/15/11…$15.00
DOI: http://dx.doi.org/10.1145/2815546.2815561

1. INTRODUCTION
Lehigh University is a small university located in Bethlehem, PA, and is well known for engineering and business. Technology support at Lehigh has historically taken a decentralized approach, with each college or administrative unit having separate computing consultants to manage their hardware, software, and other needs. While consultants share tools and information, they have typically not performed work outside their functional areas. Machine updating and patching was thus handled piecemeal, either done during routine visits or as a part of machine upgrades. This left large swathes of computers in terrible shape, as we relied on software automatic updates (which often prompted the user) to patch software for us. University applications many times would break as a result of automatic updates, making users wary of accepting any updates at all. Managing of patches was non-existent, leading to countless vulnerabilities on over 2,000 university systems. Patch management thus was key to fixing these problems.

Patch management is a part of systems management that involves patching, or updating, software on systems in an automated, remote fashion. This process includes retrieving the patch, testing it to ensure it works with university systems, and installing it on the desired target machines. Part of the entire process of patch management is vulnerability detection, wherein a system is scanned to see if it has the latest available patches. The results are used to create and deploy relevant packages.

2. PATCH MANAGEMENT
2.1 Choosing the Right Vendor
There are numerous vendors that offer patch management solutions, including Kaseya, Secunia, Kace, and Ninite. It is important that the product works with existing infrastructure. If it does not, it can be implemented without major changes that may delay deployment time.

Products such as Ninite [2] are low in cost, but also low in terms of features. One of the biggest needs we had as an organization was the ability to deploy completely custom packages, such as a custom version of Java. Multiple university systems, including Banner and Argos, rely on Java with special customizations. Ninite was unable to handle custom packages effectively, nor was it able to deploy to subsets of machines in a straightforward manner. Kace [4] is a powerful product that can deploy custom images and software packages, but relies heavily on internal staff to write custom packages, and does not offer vulnerability intelligence. The cost is also substantially higher than other products.

2.2 Why we Chose Secunia

Secunia [3] makes patching of most products as simple as a few clicks. Their package system automatically generates silent-install packages for the most common products on user systems, including Adobe Flash, Adobe Reader, Oracle Java, and Mozilla Firefox. For other packages, Secunia's underlying code makes it easy to deploy custom packages in a variety of formats. For example, a batch file can be inserted into a custom package that simply retrieves other custom scripts and files hosted internally. Secunia works by pushing updates through Window Server Update Services (WSUS), which was especially appealing to us. We wanted to eliminate update messages from our users' machines. Since updates are delivered through Windows Update, the user will no longer see update notifications for most products. This gives the user a clear set of expectations for updates.

3. TESTING THE ENVIRONMENT
3.1 Small Scale Implementation

Our environment, since it was previously completely decentralized, did not have an existing WSUS server. Thus, in order to fully test Secunia we needed to configure one. We set up a virtual WSUS using Windows Server 2008 (later upgraded to Server 2012) and applied the necessary policy changes to a set of local machines using local policy only. After testing packages successfully, we approached our Athletics department to pilot a larger test. Our Athletics department is housed in a separate Organizational Unit (OU) within Active Directory (AD), making it easy to apply a Group Policy Object (GPO) to a limited subset of systems. After testing out the GPO on our test machines successfully, we deployed the GPO to Athletics. The initial test only involved adding these machines to WSUS, adding the necessary certificates for third-party patching, and installing the Secunia agent to gather data.

3.2 Basic Package Tests

Initial testing involved creating and deploying packages for the standard products found on most machines. These included items such as Firefox, Thunderbird, Adobe Flash, and Adobe Reader. User rights were a large concern. Limited users currently cannot install software, thus their machines have seen the least updates. However, since Secunia updates are delivered through Windows Update, the users' rights are irrelevant, since the updates are run with the same rights as Windows Updates. Limited user machines will finally receive regular updates thanks to this deployment method.

Another large concern was how a package installation would be handled if the user was currently logged in and using the software being updated. Initial testing revealed that Secunia can update the majority of packages even if the program is currently in use. It appears that the program update is run and "finishes" once the program is restarted. We tested this for every program we could under a number of circumstances and found no deleterious effect as a result of updating in use programs –until Java was tested. A quirk of the Java installer is that it cannot proceed with open Internet browsers. Thus, the standard package from Secunia would fail if a browser was open. Worse, the standard package from Secunia was not customizable enough – some settings our systems required would not remain. While other programs could be customized right from the Secunia interface, Java required

special attention. Secunia by design allows the use of custom packages for these situations.

3.3 Custom Packages

There were a number of packages that Secunia either could not create easily or that required special attention due to university needs. Chrome, for example, required special install switches for the version we have historically installed on most machines (the "All Users" version instead of the Enterprise version.) Java was the single biggest hurdle for our organization. We have numerous applications that not only require the latest Java with customized settings, but some that also are dependent on older versions of Java. In order to update Java with minimal disruption to our users, we decided to create a custom Secunia package that would perform as follows:

1) Download our custom Java installer to the user's PC.
2) Add a registry entry to "RunOnce" that would invoke the installer at next boot.
3) Prompt the user for a restart after finishing.
4) Install during startup.

The benefit to this method was that Java could update at boot, which would not force the user to close browsers or interrupt their workflow. We simply inserted a batch file into a custom Secunia package to perform items 1 and 2, and used built-in features of Secunia to invoke the standard Windows Update restart dialog when finished. The use of these custom packages has resulted in Java staying current on University systems. To prevent Java from updating on systems that require older versions, we utilized an AD security group combined with a WSUS group in order to have a separate functional group for which we did not deploy the update. Secunia also allows us to specify which paths it will update. We can ignore Java 6 Update 35, for example, by unchecking the installation path for that version. Unfortunately this method will not work if the user logging in is not an administrator. Thus while it is effective in most cases, we still need to fine tune the installer to handle these exceptions.

4. DEPLOYMENT
4.1 Hardware Purchase

In order to scale our virtual WSUS to handle nearly 2,500 PCs when all areas are added, we needed to purchase physical hardware. The hardware requirements, per Microsoft, were quite low for a 500-3,000 client WSUS server [1]. These included a 1.5 GHz processor, 2 GB RAM, and a minimum 30 GB hard drive capacity for content. Unfortunately these requirements have not been updated for Server 2012, or included considerations for the addition of several supported products such as Windows 7, Windows 8, and newer versions of Office. Secunia also will work with a Microsoft System Center Configuration Manager (SCCM) deployment, so we decided to order hardware capable of handling an SCCM deployment should we change to this setup in the future. This included 16 GB of memory, 1.6 TB of space in RAID, and an Intel Xeon processor.

4.2 Using GPO to Deploy

Secunia and WSUS both have requirements as far as the necessary GPO to get the entire system operational. These include:

1) Tell systems where to find WSUS.

2) Set WSUS as the default update location.

3) Allow third-party updates via WSUS.

4) Install a self-signed certificate from WSUS to accept third-party signed updates.

5) Tell systems what WSUS group they belong to.

Other nonessential considerations included setting default installation times and disabling a user's ability to turn off updates. We chose 18:00 as the installation time, as the work day at Lehigh ends at 17:00 for most users. If they shut down before leaving, the updates would occur anyway. Leaving a machine on would not have a negative effect either, as it would get the updates and finish the process after the user restarts. In order to prevent complaints about too many restarts, most Secunia packages are not set with the flag that prompts for a restart: thus they occur without the user really noticing anything at all.

For managed labs we had a few special considerations, given these machines were in use until 23:00 weekday nights. The policy was modified to install updates at 00:00 and also force a reboot every Saturday to ensure the machines were regularly restarted. Before these changes, lab computers had to be restarted on a manual basis as students were not reliably restarting machines after updates.

4.3 Non-Managed Computer Issues

Unfortunately, multiple users at Lehigh are not in Active Directory for various reasons. We intend to add most of these users to AD, but some simply cannot be added. Secunia offers a customized "personal" version of the corporate agent to handle such cases. Non-AD machines cannot be managed by GPO at all. While local machine policy can be changed to point the machine to our WSUS server and retrieve the necessary certificate, it cannot be reliably updated in case of changes. Thus, if our server address or certificate were updated, each of these machines would manually need modification. The custom personal agent is basically their free Personal Software Inspector (PSI) agent available to consumers, but pointed to our instance of Secunia. Thus the results of scans are sent to our system, and approvals for certain applications can be handled by us instead of the user. Unfortunately custom packages cannot be created for these users, nor can program updates by modified in any way. It is still an effective way to retrieve data and monitor the health of non-AD machines.

4.4 Secunia Interface and Use

Secunia [5] uses a web interface for reporting, package management, and all other functions. In order to create and deploy packages, it relies on existing Microsoft APIs to communicate with WSUS. Since these APIs change based on the server OS, the OS of the machine used to deploy updates must match. With Server 2012 R2 installed, our deployment machine needed to have Server 2012 R2 or Windows 8.1. We created a virtual Windows 8.1 machine for this purpose, as we did not want to rely on physical hardware for patch management. If our server version was 2008 R3, we would need Windows 7 SP1 to deploy packages. To view reports and gather data, any operating system can be used.

5. RESULTS

5.1 Pre-deployment Data

Secunia rates system health using a simple scoring system that ranges from 0% to 100% secure. Secunia generates these scores based on simple criteria – the ratio of patched software from the total number of detected products installed. Thus five unpatched or end-of-life software items on a system with 100 installed programs would yield a 95% score. An institution can set threshold scores for their environment, wherein an e-mail or text is sent if a system falls below a certain score.

The range of system scores at Lehigh was initially very large, with the lowest scores in the 60% range and the highest scores at 99%. It's worth noting that in a deployment involving 1,704 total machines (as of this writing), not a single one had a perfect score at deployment time.

The average system score at deployment time combined across all functional areas was about 80%. Only one area had a starting score over 90% on average – that area being the OU being Library and Technology Services, where all IT personnel are housed. While this is strictly conjecture, it does seem to indicate that IT staff may be better at patching their machines manually than non-IT personnel.

5.2 Post-deployment Data

After creating over 90 software update packages and receiving updated stats, it was clear that Secunia was working. The average system score jumped all the way to 98% within a week. Below in Figure 1 is a graph generated by Secunia that shows "Extremely Critical" vulnerabilities across all systems over a five week period. Note that sudden peaks in the graph typically represent a new patch release by one of their supported vendors.

History of the number of "Extremely Critical" rated vulnerabilities relevant to your system. Data covers up to the last 5 weeks where possible. Mouse over data points to see exact values.

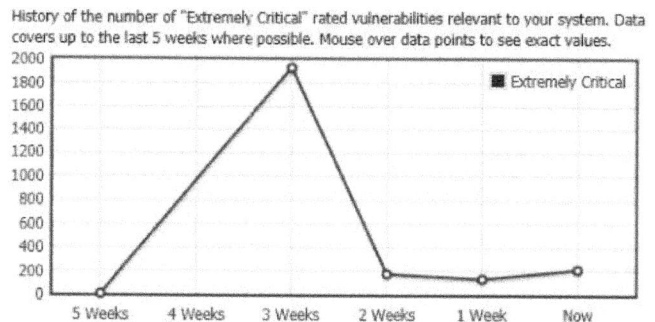

Figure 1. Extremely Critical Patches over 5 Weeks

As seen above, the number of vulnerabilities sharply drops after creating update packages that address them. Softer increases in the graph generally occur when a new group of computers is added that have not yet been patched.

5.3 Result Analysis

Secunia works by scanning all locations for out-of-date executables and library files. This has the added benefit of being able to detect programs that may have been installed in non-default locations by the user. However, this can cause problems if a program executable was saved in a backup, a temporary store, or other location but is not actually installed on a system. A small number of the detections were for programs that were clearly not installed (such as chrome.exe within C:\Backups\Old PC). Secunia allows for blacklisting of locations such as these, which removes them from the overall results. Packages, when created, can also be set to ignore unusual paths with a simple checkbox. The blacklist can be a powerful tool to ignore known locations where users backup data. For example, if all users at your institution store a backup at D:\Backup, this path can be ignored across all PCs, preventing inaccurate result data.

6. VULNERABILITY NOTES

Our experience with Secunia CSI has shown us just how important a patch management system is to maintaining the health of University systems. Across our systems, there were over 8,000 pieces of software installed that were out-of-date or end-of-life. That means we had over 8,000 points of failure well within our control. Secunia's analysis of the vulnerabilities included details about how the out-of-date software could be used by attackers to circumvent our security. A staggering 90+% of the known vulnerabilities found would allow an attacker to gain complete remote control of a system. Before implementing Secunia, almost 100% of our systems had at least one vulnerability that would allow remote access via a known channel. After a few months into deployment, almost half of our systems have a 100% system score, making our overall vulnerability to attack substantially lower. As we continue working on custom packages and updating or removal of software that is not needed, the number of attack vectors will continue to decline.

Patch management is certainly nothing new and many institutions have already adopted some form of it. But some have held off on it, either for budgetary or other reasons. We hope our experience will serve as a reminder that even in this day many programs still have little to no ability to automatically update themselves with certainty. Having a product in place to manage updates and assess system health is essential to any institution's health. With so much Personally Identifiable Information (PII) on systems, especially in colleges and universities, it is essential to do everything you can to mitigate a data breach.

7. REFERENCES

[1] Determine WSUS Capacity Requirements, Retrieved July 20, 2015, from Microsoft Corporation: https://technet.microsoft.com/en-us/library/cc708483%28v=ws.10%29.aspx

[2] Ninite Pro, Retrieved July 20, 2015, from Ninite: https://ninite.com/pro

[3] Patch Configuration, Retrieved July 20, 2015, from Secunia: http://secunia.com/?action=fetch&filename=ext_feature_description_Patch_Configuration.pdf

[4] Patch Management and Endpoint Security, Retrieved July 20, 2015 from Dell Kace: http://software.dell.com/products/kace-k1000-systems-management-appliance/patch-management-security.aspx

[5] Secunia CSI 7.0 – Technical User Guide, Retrieved July 20, 2015 from Secunia: https://secunia.com/?action=fetch&filename=Secunia_CSI7_Technical_User_Guide.pdf

Re-Inventing the Helpdesk. Again. In Five Weeks or Less.

R Kevin Chapman
Carleton College
One North College Street 3-ITS
Northfield MN 55057
507-222-4336
kchapman@carleton.edu

ABSTRACT

In the fall of 2013, following a change in management and departmental structure, the Carleton College's ITS Helpdesk was identified as "a problem." A triumvirate of previously disparate ITS staff were thrust together and tasked with putting it back on the right track, improving its reputation, streamlining processes, decreasing ticket turnaround time, and generally lifting spirits. With only a month before the start of the academic year, could they do it?

Categories and Subject Descriptors

K.7.0 The Computing Profession, General

General Terms

Management, Performance, Design, Human Factors, Standardization, Theory

Keywords

Carleton College; Helpdesk; Reputation; Call Center; Support model.

1. INTRODUCTION

In the fall of 2013, the Information Technology Services (ITS) department at Carleton College implemented a fairly aggressive reworking of their Helpdesk operation. The arrival of a new Chief Technology Officer earlier that year prompted a critical review of various departmental operations, and it quickly became apparent that the Helpdesk could and should be providing a more robust and reliable service to the community. Customers were unhappy at turnaround times for ticket resolution. They also felt that the level of experience across the student and professional staff varied too much when calling the Helpdesk, resulting in an inconsistent and frustrating experience.

The CTO decided to make changes to staffing, call handling and ticket resolution procedures. For strategic purposes, changes were also made to the hardware repair process, and tools were put in place to allow the department to better record and analyze data from our phone and ticketing systems.

SIGUCCS '15, November 09-13, 2015, St. Petersburg, FL, USA
© 2015 ACM. ISBN 978-1-4503-3610-9/15/11 $15.00
DOI: http://dx.doi.org/10.1145/2815546.2815571

Implementing these changes would be tough under any circumstances, but with a five week implementation window, changes had to be made quickly with little or no margin for error. This paper addresses some of the factors leading to this situation, details some of the changes we made, and attempts to summarize key outcomes.

2. A BRIEF HISTORY OF TECH SUPPORT AT CARLETON

ITS' front line technical support model has undergone a number of significant changes in the past ten years. Sometimes these were driven by the changing needs of our customers, sometimes by other factors drawing on ITS resources in new ways. In order to provide a frame of reference for the changes discussed in this paper, the following briefly reviews the changing face of this service.

For most of the 21st century, until 2007, ITS provided two distinct types of support. Faculty and staff were served by a liaison model, whereby a designated ITS staff member was assigned several departments to support. The liaisons were split into two teams: the academic computing coordinators supported faculty and other academic departmental staff, while the administrative computing coordinators supported the college's administrative departments.

The student community, on the other hand, was supported by a dedicated help desk: the Student Computing Information Center (SCIC). The SCIC was staffed by two ITS staff and approximately 40 student staff.

In 2007, following a departmental review, a new help desk (Rapid Response) was established specifically to serve faculty and staff. Rapid Response was managed by two ITS staff (formerly administrative coordinators) and approximately a dozen student staff. The purpose of Rapid Response was to provide more immediate break/fix support to both faculty and staff. This addressed the majority of issues faced by administrative departments, though liaisons did maintain contact for bigger picture items. The academic coordinators were then freed up to work more closely with faculty on pedagogical issues. The SCIC operation was left largely untouched, though staffing was reduced by one full time professional.

In 2011, a major new building opened on campus requiring the redistribution of ITS employees for support purposes. At that time it was decided to combine the two help desks into a single, combined resource for the entire campus. This was rebranded simply as the ITS Helpdesk. The two professional staff who had been responsible for managing Rapid Response were tasked with managing the combined help desk, effectively reducing the professional staff by one. The combined student staff numbered approximately fifty.

3. NOT QUITE ACCORDING TO PLAN

Unfortunately, the combined help desk struggled to reconcile what had been two very different support models and customer types. Rapid Response had already faced a similar dilemma when combining break/fix support for administrative departments, across which there was a consistency of tools and expectations much like a corporate environment, and academic departments, which were decidedly more fluid and distinct in their needs. Factoring in the student body, with an entirely different, residential support model, further complicated the balance of support needs.

Customers began to express frustration with the new operation. The turnaround time on ticket resolution increased significantly. The quality of phone support was inconsistent, as was the general approach to triage and troubleshooting. This inconsistency seemed to stem from varying levels of expertise among the student staff, itself a result of the rapid combination of two support groups who had been supporting very different audiences. Insufficient priority had been given to the documentation of new processes, or the development of new training for student staff in the lead up to the change.

When Carleton's new CTO arrived in the spring of 2013, the community's faith in the Helpdesk was low and it was clear that they were not receiving the support that they needed.

4. A SOLUTION IN MANY PARTS

After meeting with many departments across the campus, as well as key constituents, the CTO proposed several significant changes to the Helpdesk operations.

The plan was aggressive, and not without complicating factors. There were only five weeks until the start of the term, and the most significant changes had to be in place before that time. Summer projects, such as equipment replacements and lab maintenance, were still ongoing. Staff members would be required to transition to new roles while simultaneously completing said projects and implementing the proposed changes. Additionally, 40% of the Helpdesk student staff would be new that year, with little existing training material, let alone materials that matched the new processes.

Nevertheless, the key players agreed that the goals were achievable and the changes were implemented.

4.1 Professional Staff at the Helpdesk

Issue Addressed: Staffing levels and skillsets at the Helpdesk

Prior to their integration, the two help desks had been managed by three professional staff members. This dropped to two when they were combined. It was quickly decided that we should return to full strength by returning the number of staff to three. Some of the additional changes would also benefit from, if not require, an additional staff member in order to more reasonably distribute the load.

These three staff members had to be highly technical, with particularly strong customer skills. Ideally, they should have discrete strengths, such as hardware repair qualifications and supervisory experience, but also overlapping abilities so that they could comfortably back each other up, particularly when dealing with immediate customer support issues.

This all resulted in the re-allocation of staff. One of the existing Helpdesk staff remained in place, and two staff members were transitioned in from other teams within the department.

4.1.1 Outcomes of New Staff Structure

The three new staff quickly established their individual strengths and distributed responsibilities accordingly and amicably within the first few weeks of operations. The administrative and managerial work was evenly distributed across the triumvirate, as was general supervision of the student staff. The overlap in abilities allowed staff to balance the support load evenly between the three, and customer issues were being addressed and resolved in a timelier manner as a result.

4.2 Professionals Talk To Professionals (P2P)

Issue Addressed: Community concern regarding inconsistent troubleshooting over the phone

The notion of Professionals talking to Professionals (P2P) is that, when a faculty or staff member calls the Helpdesk, they will be routed to professional staff as opposed to student staff. The motivation behind this was to provide a higher and more consistent level of troubleshooting (or triage) to employees, in particular the faculty.

Student staff would then focus on support calls from their peers, the student body. They would also be freed up to work through open tickets, and make office visits as necessary.

If the professional staff are already on the phone, employee calls roll over to the student staff on duty, who then offer the options of a call back, the creation of a ticket for follow-up, or to troubleshoot themselves.

In order to achieve this P2P goal, two things needed to happen. The first was that each of the professional staff had to allocate approximately one third of their working week to take the primary role on the phones. Second, there needed to be a system in place to correctly route incoming calls.

4.2.1 Outcomes of P2P

The first and most obvious outcome was that faculty members in particular were much happier with the consistency of support when they called the Helpdesk. Our numbers for first call resolution were also much higher.

This also meant that professional staff members were able to get a better handle on support patterns when they arose.

However, an unexpected outcome of this approach was that, because our student staff was spending much less time on the phones, they were not getting anything like the amount of troubleshooting experience that they had in the past. We had always relied heavily on on-the-job training for our student staff, and the reduced exposure to support calls meant that, by the end of the first year, our student staff had not developed as much as both we and they had expected. This in turn meant that they were less confident when working on support issues, and less engaged in general. There was a clear need for a comprehensive and hands-on training program for our student staff, but there had been no time to develop due to the aggressive nature of the timeline.

Finally, with professional staff spending considerably more time answering phone calls, they had to develop new time management strategies in order to balance project work, offline support work and phone time.

4.3 Implementing a VOIP Call Center

Issue addressed: Professionals talking to Professionals; Data Collection

The existing campus phone system was not able to route calls as we required to achieve the P2P goals outlined above, so we needed to implement a system that would allow us to do so.

We decided to implement a VOIP based call center. This would allow us to implement a self-contained system without placing an additional burden on our Telecom department beyond establishing the initial connection to the campus PBX exchange.

The VOIP system allowed us to more easily and programmatically control how calls coming in to the Helpdesk were routed, e.g., all faculty calls are routed to the designated staff member.

This implementation had a three week window, which was certainly more aggressive than ideal. Our vendor confirmed that it was possible, though clearly implied that it was inadvisable. However, the Helpdesk staff determined that the advantages outweighed the risk. It was necessary to meet the P2P goals, which were the highest priority. The alternate implementation date – Winter Break 2014 – would require training on both an interim and then the final solution in the space of three months, and it was agreed that training staff just once was preferable.

There were other features that we hoped to take advantage of, such as integration with our ticketing system and the ability to listen in on or coach student staff during support calls. However, these were deemed future goals due to the extremely short implementation window.

4.3.1 Outcomes of Call Center
Call routing worked exactly as we had hoped and the feedback from faculty and staff was overwhelmingly positive. Integration with the campus PBX proved simple, and we have maintained a single analog line in case of a network outage that affects the VOIP system.

An additional benefit is that we now have access to a great deal of data, which allows us to analyze call volume, call patterns, success or failure of the P2P implementation, and more.

We have not, however, been able to implement some of the additional features that we had hoped to bring online during the course of the 2013-14 academic year. In particular, the ability to monitor and join in on calls being taken by our student staff has lost us what we now realize would have been a particularly valuable training tool. We have since worked with our vendor to reconfigure our implementation to allow us to activate these and other features.

4.4 Hardware Repair
Issues addressed: The need to reallocate an FTE within the department; duplication of effort on printer maintenance.

Within the department, there was a need to create a new leadership position focused on Academic Technologies. We decided that we could further reduce the workload around hardware repairs which would then be coordinated by the Helpdesk, and subsequently reallocate the corresponding FTE.

4.4.1 Printers
In the past, ITS staff would triage printer problems, and attempt minor repairs which might require ordering and waiting on the delivery of replacement parts. If this attempt was unsuccessful, or the problem required a qualified technician, we would place a service request with our vendor. Their technician would then have to assess the problem for themselves, which in turn might require a second visit to effect repair. This was a cumbersome process, often with duplication of effort and slow resolution.

Under the new model, we contract with our vendors for all services. When a customer calls to report a problem, we simply log a call with the vendor who is typically able to resolve problems within four to eight business hours.

4.4.2 Apple Hardware
We were maintaining Apple hardware in-house, and decided that this model was working particularly well. Rather than outsource this, we formalized our implementation of Apple GSX and two of our professional staff became certified Apple technicians.

As a result, we are able to run Apple's hardware diagnostics, expedite shipment of replacement parts, whether under warranty or not, and effect all repairs in a particularly timely manner.

4.4.3 Windows Hardware
As there is not a comparable program with our vendors for Windows equipment, we make use of the individual manufacturers' warranty repair services. Helpdesk staff is required to perform triage and diagnostics on malfunctioning Windows hardware to determine if the repair will fall under warranty. If it is, it is immediately shipped to the manufacturer. Otherwise, our Hardware Asset Manager will assess the cost of a repair versus the replacement of the equipment and proceed accordingly.

4.4.4 Outcome
With the formalization of the repair process for the three major categories of hardware, repairs are handled in a consistent and more streamlined manner. This has reduced the turnaround time on repairs across the board. It also set clear boundaries on the troubleshooting expectations, allowing Helpdesk staff to process repairs more efficiently.

4.5 Ticket Response and Resolution Times: A Goal
Issue Addressed: Slow resolution times on tickets.

While it was not publicly announced until the following academic year, there were specific goals in mind for processing and resolving issues that were logged by customers via our ticketing system (as opposed to over the phone.) The goals were to acknowledge and/or respond to a ticket within four business hours, and to resolve 85% of new tickets within two business days. It was not expected that we would achieve this right up front, but we did work towards that outcome throughout the first year of operations.

4.5.1 Outcome and Assessment of Goal
It was interesting to note that these goals were generally easier to achieve on tickets logged by staff than those logged by faculty. This was in large part due to a general difference in audience behavior. Staff were more likely to respond to requests for additional details, appointment times, and other information, and dialog with Helpdesk staff as necessary to resolve the problem. Faculty tended to be less responsive, opting more to log a problem and move on, often resulting in lengthy delays between communications and therefore resolutions.

5. END OF YEAR ONE
To summarize the outcomes already noted above, by the end of our first year operating under the new model, we had seen the following outcomes:

- A very positive reception from our customers;
- Faster and more accurate resolution of phone calls;
- Faster turnaround on support tickets;

- Printer issues were resolved much faster, and almost eliminated from Helpdesk operations, freeing up staff time;
- Hardware repair was more streamlined and consistent, also freeing up staff time;
- A loss in overall student experience and engagement;
- An inability to implement advanced call center features, further contributing to degradation of student staff experience.

While problems existed, their effect was purely internal and did not adversely affect the customer experience, which was overwhelmingly improved.

6. YEAR TWO: A PERFECT(LY AWFUL) STORM

Year two started with the loss of one of the three professional staff members, who took a position on a different team within ITS. The timing was such that the department was unable to hire a replacement before the start of the academic year, which ultimately delayed the hiring until Winter Break. This proved to be somewhat disastrous for the Helpdesk as a series of unfortunate events subsequently combined with an overall increase in support calls overwhelmed our operation.

6.1 We Got Knocked Down...

During the summer of 2014, Carleton opted to move the hosting of our email system from in-house to a well-established third party provider. The transition did not go as smoothly as expected, and we experienced frequent outages during Fall Term. During this same timeframe, we experienced unexpected problems with various infrastructure systems. Like many schools, we found ourselves struggling to resolve wireless issues with consumer electronics, in particular iOS and Mac OS devices. We also saw unexplained outages on our shared network resources.

At the same time, we recorded a significant increase in the number of calls at the Helpdesk. While some of these were inevitably related to the various system outages noted above, we observed an overall increase in general support calls. We have since chosen to view this positively, as a sign that our community was regaining confidence in our service. However, the net result of this was that the Helpdesk was being overwhelmed. With a continued focus on P2P support, the two remaining professional staff began to lose ground on their tickets.

By way of a measure, consider the following numbers from the 2013-14 academic year. Thirty assigned open tickets were considered normal for each of the professional staff. If that count reached the mid-thirties, a concerted effort was made to catch up. If the count came close to forty, staff hunkered down and put in extra hours and effort in order to reduce the count. By halfway through Fall Term 2014, both staff were sitting on approximately one hundred and thirty tickets each, and were unable to make significant headway on reducing those numbers.

Inevitably, the service and our reputation began to take a hit once again.

6.2 ... But We Got Up Again

The first step to resolving this situation was to fill the open FTE, which we did in December 2014. For the first six months, this new employee's focus was to develop and implement a strategy for reducing the overall ticket count.

The strategy that we implemented made significant use of our underutilized student staff. In essence, the student staff would tackle the oldest tickets, following up with clients to determine the status and then either close tickets that had in fact been resolved but not updated, or work through solutions if the issue persisted. The professional staff meanwhile focused on the newest tickets, with a view to faster initial response and resolution times. If all went according to plan, the two groups would meet in the middle.

The strategy proved successful, and over the course of the next six months our simultaneous open ticket count dropped from 434 to 132. More importantly, our customers acknowledged our efforts in a very positive manner and we have maintained generally good relations with the community throughout the process.

7. CONCLUSIONS

Despite the aggressive timeframe, ITS was able to implement a significant and positive change in help desk operations prior to the start of the 2013-14 academic year, and throughout Fall Term 2013. The VOIP call center was successfully implemented and routed calls exactly as intended, allowing us to achieve the goal of P2P which played heavily into repairing relations with our clients (in particular, faculty.) Moving printer maintenance and repair to dedicated third parties has reduced down time and been greeted positively by our community. Our hardware triage and repair operations are much more manageable, requiring less time and effort on the part of Helpdesk professional staff.

It was also made clear that our staffing level is a fine balance and that we cannot afford to drop below that level for a prolonged period of time. The loss of a single professional staff member had a significantly negative impact on our service levels, albeit in part due to an unfortunate confluence of events and increase in overall support volume. In the future, when a member of our team moves on, we will give utmost priority to hiring a replacement. Additionally, in lieu of hands-on training in the form of fielding calls from faculty and staff, our student staff require a properly structured and engaging training program.

8. LOOKING AHEAD

As we stand at the start of our third year, we intend to continue along the same trajectory, with a view to continual improvements. This year, our specific focus will be on three areas.

First, and considered most important by all three professional staff, is the development of a comprehensive training program for our student staff. We rely on them to run the Helpdesk outside of our core working hours and to increase our support capabilities all round. They also deserve a better and more engaging work study experience.

Second, we will be looking to implement additional features in our call center. This will partly help with the student training effort noted above. We also hope to integrate it more closely with our ticketing system.

Third, we intend to increase our use of metrics in order to measure our own performance.

Assuming that we are able to accomplish these improvements and maintain the current service levels, we believe that the ITS Helpdesk will re-establish itself as a trusted service on Carleton's campus.

Instructional Technology Communication and Outreach

Trevor M. Murphy
Williams College
56 Hopkins Hall Drive
Williamstown, MA 01267
1-413-597-2231
tmurphy@williams.edu

Randy Matusky
Lyndon College
1001 College Road
Lyndonville, VT 05851
1-802-626-6374
randolph.matusky@lyndonstate.edu

ABSTRACT
Instructional designers and technologists use a variety of means for communicating with faculty. There are IT Newsletters, brown bag lunches, visiting speakers, listening tours, department meetings, lightning talks, email blasts, one-on-one meetings, hallway conversations, and the list goes on. The authors from Lyndon College and Williams College consider and compare the various paths available for communicating with faculty about technology projects and opportunities at small institutions. Best practices of the various outreach efforts will be shared.

Categories and Subject Descriptors
K.7.0 [**The Computing Profession**]: General.

General Terms
Management, Human Factors.

Keywords
Communication, Listening, Outreach.

1. INTRODUCTION
1.1 Institutional Context
Williams College is a private, residential, liberal arts college located in the northwestern corner of Massachusetts in the town of Williamstown. The college has 2,000 students and 300 faculty members. The Office for Information Technology at Williams College consists of four groups including Networks and Systems, Desktop Systems, Administrative Information Systems, and Instructional Technology. The Instructional Technology group provides faculty with pedagogically informed technology support.

Lyndon State College is a public liberal arts college in northeastern Vermont. The college has 1,450 students and 57 faculty. The Office of Information Technology at Lyndon College consists of nine staff members including a Chief Technology Officer, a LAN/System Administrator, and a Coordinator of Instructional Technology.

The communication and outreach efforts of the Instructional Technologist at Lyndon College and Instructional Technology at Williams College are the focus of this paper.

SIGUCCS '15, November 09-13, 2015, St. Petersburg, FL, USA
© 2015 ACM. ISBN 978-1-4503-3610-9/15/11...$15.00
DOI: http://dx.doi.org/10.1145/2815546.2815576

1.2 Goals for Communication and Outreach
The goals for information technology communication and outreach relate to the mission of the college, which stipulate that not only is the technology available, but it is used well.

The Williams College Office for Information Technology supports the College's mission of offering the best liberal arts education by helping faculty and students to develop effective uses for technology in teaching, learning, and research. Lyndon College's Office of Information Technology supports the Lyndon College mission of success for each and every individual student.

The IT groups at Williams College and Lyndon College make decisions on the IT services and technologies to support on campus. Ideally, these services and technologies are chosen to best meet the needs of the faculty, staff, and students. Without input from stakeholders there can be a misunderstanding of what the IT needs of the campus. In addition, there can be a lack of campus awareness of the IT services and technologies available.

One of the challenges for IT organizations is the frequent change in technology services. The basic functions of a course management system, email, and electronic classrooms may remain the same, but the vendors, versions, and interfaces often change.

In addition, faculty, staff, and students change over time. IT usage differs between first year students and graduating seniors. New faculty have very different IT habits than senior faculty. It is tempting to assume that faculty, staff, and students are the same year after year because they share many traits in common. However, differences in technology use can be captured in surveys [1]. Conversations with campus technology users often reveal insights and can help in determining the content and format of outreach efforts.

To truly support the mission of the college, not only do faculty, staff, and students need to know how to use technology, but they also need to be aware of best practices. Communication and outreach needs to be geared towards meeting these challenges.

2. LISTENING
Knowing your audience can help with crafting communication outreach efforts. Williams College conducted a listening tour where Instructional Technology Specialists and Reference and Instruction Librarians reached out to faculty to talk with them about the services they use and how they prefer to communicate with IT and the Library.

Goals were set for how many faculty members to connect with. The focus of these meetings was collecting information about the services faculty use, the services they would like to see offered, and how they would prefer to communicate with the IT and the Library. To keep the meetings on topic, the Library and IT representatives had to refrain from addressing technical issues brought up during the meeting, advertising services that may be of interest, and conducting on the spot training to correct misconceptions. Follow up emails would be used to address concerns from the meetings. Notes from the meeting were taken, shared with faculty, and then stored for analysis.

A range of questions were asked:

- What Library and IT services do you use?

- Of these services, what works great and what doesn't work as well as it could?

- What services would you like to use that we don't currently offer?

- What trends do you see in the classroom with your students?

- What are you working on in terms of current projects and research?

- How do you want to hear from the Library and IT?

The information that comes out of these conversations shows how some faculty are well served by IT services and how others struggle. Meetings have happened with 21 faculty to date. Some faculty arrive on campus, find out what resources are available, and adapt to those resources. Other faculty purchase their own software rather than using a tool or software that has the same functions and is supported by the college. There are still passionate advocates for overhead projectors and chalkboards. The Keynote vs. PowerPoint argument has not been settled. Some faculty need training, but will not attend training.

When it comes to communication, most faculty embrace email, although when it comes to communicating with students, they find that texting sometimes works better. While they read email regularly, they do not want email abused. One faculty member said she would like one email from IT a year. At Williams College there is a curated custom mass email called Daily Messages that goes out to all faculty, staff, or students. Messages submitted the previous day are presented in a single email in digest form. Almost all faculty said they peruse Daily Messages for information. Some felt that Librarians and IT staff attending an occasional department meeting would be useful. Communication methods not recommended included printed newsletters, Google Calendar, phone messages, and posters. Not mentioned were technology lunches and workshops.

Another benefit of having these conversations is the direct feedback on the needs of faculty and the utility of the IT and Library services currently provided. Sometimes there are misconceptions and a common tool already exists that can solve their problem. In our outreach, we can try to make sure faculty are aware of the tools we provide. Other times there are suggestions that clearly would benefit the college such as adding a flashcard app to the content management system. Much of the output of these meetings are the everyday challenges that faculty are facing. As an IT organization we can start looking at ways to confront the common complaints. The less common issues may be addressed one by one.

Finally, listening to faculty is an act of goodwill that is a clear part of fulfilling the mission to help faculty and students to develop effective uses for technology in teaching, learning, and research.

3. LEARNING FROM OTHER SOURCES
3.1 Peer Institutions
Peer institutions likely have similar communication goals and needs. Establishing a connection with a peer institution is a good way to compare notes on communication strategies. If the needs are similar, resources such as documentation, promotional materials, and communication utilities can be shared.

3.2 SIGUCCS Communication Awards
The SIGUCCS Communication Awards are annually given to IT staff members at colleges and universities that submit their best communication and outreach efforts. Many format categories are considered including websites, printed and electronic newsletters, classroom documentation, printed and electronic how-to guides, quick reference guides, general service promotional materials, campaign materials, student created promotional materials, and short and long promotional audio and video. Judges recognize the best submissions in each category.

Award winning submissions are creative and make effective use of best practices for each format. Browsing the winners of any category will reveal striking graphic design and clever use of visual cues, solid content, and good storytelling. There are comics, IT themed t-shirts, calendars packed with IT information, hand bags, videos of student worker interviews, annual reports, engaging websites, and strong technical writing accompanied by wonderful graphics.

SIGUCCS Communication Award winning submissions are useful to provide inspiration and ideas on how to craft excellent communication and outreach materials. SIGUCCS Communication Awards can be found at: http://www.siguccs.org/communication_awards.shtml.

4. COMMUNICATION AND OUTREACH EFFORTS
A variety of outreach initiatives are important. In listening to faculty it becomes evident that there isn't one outreach method that will connect with all faculty. Some faculty will not attend workshops. Others do not read or respond to email. There are early adopters and there are also IT users who wait until a service stops to learn about the new alternative.

In 2001, the Office for Information Technology at Williams College scraped the IT website for information and published it as a book called the "Tech Reference Guide." A faculty member remarked, "This is fantastic, but why did you wait so long to share all this information?" Sharing information is insufficient if the information is not noticed.

Choosing opportunities for communication can be done strategically and can be informed by talking with the audience you are trying to reach.

4.1 Department Meetings
At Williams College, an Instructional Technology Specialist will often team up with a Librarian to be part of a department meeting agenda. IT and Library topics of interest can be discussed with the faculty. Often, unresolved issues and questions will come up that need to be addressed. These meetings are an opportunity to share any changes to IT and Library services as well as get feedback on areas that need attention.

Not all departments are open to having outside members attend a department meeting. Sometimes confidential information is discussed. Some departments meet every week while others hold department meetings infrequently making the meeting agenda too full to include informational content. In making a pitch to attend a department meeting it is good to have a time estimate and an agenda ready. The agenda might be shaped by the sponsoring department.

At Lyndon State College part of the role of a department head is to ensure that all the faculty under them have access to appropriate training. The Coordinator of Instructional Technology meets individually with every department head during the initial two weeks of every semester. During these meetings, discussions center on new projects for the semester, and if any specific training events are needed. It is also a way to remind the department heads of existing training resources, such as the two day online learning best practices class and the 1-on-1 Moodle gradebook lessons.

4.2 Technology Committees
A standing technology committee can serve as a sounding board for changes to technology services. The Information Technology Committee at Williams College is composed of four faculty, five administrators, and three students.

The Committee on Information Technology monitors and recommends policies for faculty, staff, and student use of information technology throughout the college. It meets regularly to review and provide feedback to the college on plans for developing technology-related policies and resources. The committee is chaired by a faculty member.

One of the benefits of having such a committee is that there is already a pool of informed faculty advocates on hand when a big decision is made that will entail a campus wide technology service change.

4.3 Workshops
4.3.1 Traditional Workshops
At Williams College, a new course management system (CMS) presented an opportunity to reach many faculty with needed information. It was quickly found that several different workshop types were needed to accommodate the different needs of the faculty. A quick-start session focused on the minimum knowledge necessary to get a course created making use of very few course management tools. Topic specific workshops helped advanced CMS users make sense of new interfaces to use specific tools like quizzes or the grade book. Drop in sessions had no agenda and attendees could count on bringing their own materials and being assured of help. General information sessions appealed to faculty who wanted to know a little bit about how everything worked so they would know what was possible. Many faculty wanted to have one on one time with an IT specialist to help them import content from the old CMS to the new CMS.

The key was creating a variety of workshop options with published agendas and then encouraging faculty to attend the workshop that best fit their needs. Sometimes a one-on-one visit was necessary to help the faculty member adjust to the new CMS.

The same opportunity came with the transition from a Williams College managed email system to Google mail. The workshops were well attended and carefully scripted.

Workshops used to be offered at Williams College for Adobe applications or for web development. These workshops gradually had fewer and fewer attendees. Another difficulty was scheduling training so all interested parties could attend. Sometimes a workshop attendee wanted to know how to put error bars on a graph in Microsoft Excel, and would attend an entire training only to find that the presenter did not cover error bars on a graph. For numerous reasons, the workshop model seemed in need of replacement. A subscription to Lynda.com is now offered to meet most application specific questions. However, the need for training remains. Lynda com does not offer coverage of all topics where training is required.

At Lyndon State College, such as at Williams College, a variety of different workshops were also needed in order to encourage greater use of the college's learning management system. Core concept or quick-start workshops were developed to focus on best practices for teaching a hybrid or online class and on how to create a Moodle class from scratch. Specialized workshops were created for particular training issues, such as how to run a discussion forum, or how to setup a gradebook within Moodle. Finally, department specific workshops were created in order to meet the individual needs of every department, such as using Mahara for the creation of electronic portfolios, which was needed for the department of Education at Lyndon State College.

4.3.2 Faculty Talks
Sometimes a different set of constituents will attend if the workshop is more of a demonstration by a colleague. When a colleague presents, the content tends more toward pedagogical use of the tools. If a faculty member in the sciences is talking about how they use a content management system in their teaching, for example, the talk will be of interest by other science faculty who are interested perhaps picking up some new techniques or best practices. Instead of learning how to use the course management system, they learn why. The IT department at Williams College seeks out faculty to give talks about how they use technology in their teaching.

Workshops seem to work when the new information being presented is needed by a large campus group. If the changes affect the campus as a whole, then a series of workshops can be helpful.

4.4 Tech Talks
Tech Talks are monthly held discussion groups at Lyndon State College. They cover a wide-range of issues in the world of educational technology and teaching pedagogy. The general format for these discussions includes a brief review of any news in educational technology, a 20-30 minute presentation on a particular topic (such as teaching strategies for online learning and project management apps), and an opened conversation among the presenters, guest speakers and attending faculty and staff. All Tech Talk presentations will be uploaded onto the Office of Information Technology training website. They are held during the second week of every month, from 12:00 to 1:00 pm. It has been a great way to generate discussion among the Lyndon State faculty and staff.

At Lyndon College, the attendance average for the Tech Talks has been 17 people, a majority of which are faculty members. In order to reach a greater audience, there are plans to record future Tech Talks and host the videos on the OIT training website. Since attendees often miss important information during the discussion, these videos will provide them the opportunity to revisit the event. It will also be a good way for adjunct faculty members that live far from the college to view the discussions. Future plans will include the use of a synchronous video conferencing tool by faculty members situated off-campus. Video conferencing will allow all faculty members the opportunity to fully participate in the Tech Talks. The tool we will use will either be Adobe Connect or Citrix GoToMeeting.

4.5 Tech Lunches

Scheduling times to meet can be challenging. Occasionally a lunch is an opportunity gather around a particular topic. Providing lunch for all attendees can be expensive, but it can be a good way to get attendance by all interested parties. At Williams College, a tech lunch is less scripted than a workshop. They can be discussions or demonstrations. A recent tech lunch was held to gather the interested people who make use of the college's high performance computing cluster.

4.6 Tech News

At Lyndon State College, the Coordinator of Instructional Technology has initiated a monthly newsletter called Tech News. This newsletter focuses on current changes in the field of educational technology, specifically on issues affecting higher education. A further focus has been placed on changes within the area of New England, since Lyndon State College is located in the state of Vermont. Every issue is two-to-four pages in length and is sent to the entire faculty and staff via email. The newsletters are also uploaded onto the Office of Information Technology website: http://oit-training.lsc.vsc.edu/?page_id=37.

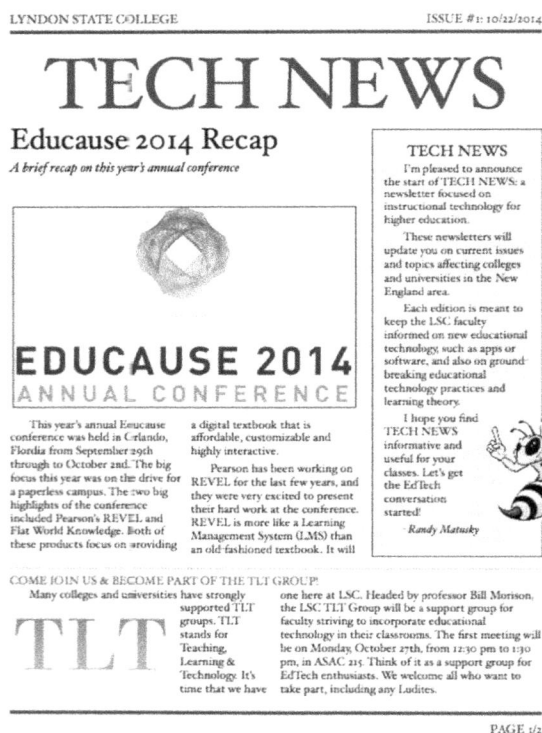

Figure 1: Tech News from Lyndon State College.

4.7 OIT Training Website

The Office of Information Technology, led by the Coordinator of Instructional Technology, created a training website, which launched during September, 2014. The website is used to host training videos, manuals and other training documents. The site has been used by the entire Lyndon State College, including students, staff and faculty. A focus has been placed on Moodle, the learning management system used by the college. One of the site's main goals is to provide the faculty with the technical competence to successfully create and run a Moodle course. Faculty are encouraged to submit training video or manual requests to the Coordinator of Instructional Technology.

4.8 Documentation

Documentation plays a key role in supporting training. It makes it easy for the trainer to correctly explain each component of the system. Training documentation is essential for promoting effective communication between the technical trainers and instructional designers and the faculty and staff of the college. At Lyndon State College, a wide-variety of training documents is used for each project. Examples include training manuals, PowerPoint slides, recorded presentations, webinars, newsletters and online guides. The Coordinator of Instructional Technology builds all of these training documents. They are all hosted on the OIT training website for 24/7 full access by all faculty and staff. This allows for on-the-job training and troubleshooting.

For documentation to be useful, it needs to be organized, searchable, and up to date. It is helpful if help desk staff refer users to the documentation so they can find it on their own the next time they have a problem.

5. CONCLUSION

A variety of different communication media types help ensure both transfer of knowledge and successful application of the new skills learned by the faculty and staff. The Office of Information Technology at both Williams College and Lyndon State College communicate using IT newsletters, brown bag lunches, visiting speakers, guided tours, department meetings, newsletters, webinars and one-on-one meetings. Each of these different forms of communication plays a vital role in disseminating IT information, documentation and technical training knowledge to both faculty and staff at each respected college.

At the same time the implementation of these communication efforts are different at Williams College and Lyndon State College. These differences reflect differences in culture, institution, and in IT needs of the faculty. Learning about what information the constituents at your institution need and how they want to receive IT information will shape the way your institution will assemble its communication plans.

6. ACKNOWLEDGMENTS

Thanks to Jonathan Morgan-Leamon, Director of Instructional Technology at Williams College, who supports the author's professional development.

7. REFERENCES

[1] Warren, Chris. 2013. Technology Use Survey. http://oit.williams.edu/itech/faculty-mailings/technology-use-survey/

Signed, Sealed, Delivered:
Improving Your Messages to the Community

Elizabeth Cornell
Fordham IT
Fordham University
718-817-0398
cornellgoldw@fordham.edu

ABSTRACT

Whether it's an outage, scheduled maintenance or an announcement about a new technology resource, the pressure is on you to create effective and readable messages.

Henry David Thoreau once said that he had received no more than one or two letters in his life that were worth the postage. To be sure, most of your communications don't require postage and won't be cherished forever. However, they should be worth the time it takes to read them.

University faculty, staff, and students are bombarded with hundreds of messages every day, from multiple sources. They appreciate it when your communications are organized, concise, and understandable.

This paper discusses ways to improve written content for emails, blogs, and other communication channels. It concentrates on how to cut the flab from writing and strategies for organizing information. It also covers how to choose the best words for promoting an organization's resources and services.
DOI: http://dx.doi.org/10.1145/2815546.2815565

Categories and Subject Descriptors

I.7.2 [**Document and Text Processing**]: Document Preparation

General Terms

Documentation, Human Factors

Keywords

SIGUCCS 2015, communication, writing

1. INTRODUCTION

Writing is difficult. Even the most seasoned writers, including Nobel Prize winners, feel that way. Of course, most of the time, no one writing emails and blog posts for their IT department is out to win a prize. But writing concisely, so the message can be heard by the target audience, is challenging. This paper will discuss how communicators working on behalf of an IT department can improve their written messages to a college or university community.

My background includes talking to people—both students and colleagues—about their writing and easy strategies for improving it. Talking about writing happens to be one of the things I've missed since giving up my teaching job for the English Department at Fordham University. If my students learned one thing from me, it was how to make sure they chose the right words and content so that their message is organized and not full of unnecessary words. That's one of my most important strategies for creating messages in my current job, which is director of IT communications at Fordham University.

The overall goal of this paper is to offer some strategies for improving the written content for emails, blogs, and other communication channels used by an IT department. This paper has three main objectives:

1. Content matters: How much information does one need to include in a particular message? What are ideal lengths for different kinds of messages? What's the best way to organize information?

2. Cut the Flab: In writing, unnecessary words and phrases sneak into messages. This paper discusses how to detect them and what to do with them.

3. Selling and Spinning: Find the right words so the target audience will understand that the message is relevant to them. This is crucial for drawing attention to the message and getting heard. It's also important to choose the right words for your message and not say too much in delicate situations.

2. IT COMMUNICATIONS IN HIGHER ED

First, some background about my organization: Fordham University has over 17,000 members and just under 100 people working for the IT department. My position of director of communications was created because the VP/CIO and the senior leadership team felt the IT department needed a unified voice and public face: it was too challenging to do that if mass communications came from different people and parts of the IT organization. When I arrived, IT's primary tool for communicating with the university community was email. Email remains an important channel for us, though its effectiveness at reaching people is debatable. Even so, we continue to rely on it (but not exclusively) because a survey of faculty, staff, and incoming students indicated that their preferred method of communication is email regarding outages, maintenance, trainings, and events However, unless it's an emergency situation, we do not send the community more than one email a day; the fewer we can send in a week, the better.

My job, since I assumed the position two years ago, has been to improve the quality of email communications, strengthen our use of existing communication channels, and create new ones: These main channels include our pages on Fordham's website, Twitter, the Fordham IT blog, digital signage, promotional handouts, and an internal newsletter for IT staff. They are used, as appropriate, for communicating about outages, maintenance, workshops, talks, events, and news about new or existing resources and services. We use most of these channels every day. Currently I'm developing a strategic plan for using the channels in a more integrated way.

The techniques for writing covered in this paper can apply to most any type of writing. Since many communications I prepare are first composed for emails and then recycled for other outlets, writing for email will be used the starting point for this discussion about writing messages that get read.

2.1 Content Matters

For years, marketers have said that people spend, on average, 15 seconds reading an email. These days, it's very likely an email—or a tweet, blog post, most anything online—will be read on a mobile platform. One source says 65% of all email is read on a mobile device [2]. No doubt that percentage will continue to grow and that people will spend even less time per message. What these numbers mean to IT communicators is that messages must be tailored so they use the fewest words to say everything the reader needs to know. This is especially true when communicating a message about some routine maintenance or an outage.

The following is an example for a scheduled maintenance with Blackboard. This is the draft, sent by an IT staff member (with the request to send it out immediately, before the end of the day, which was in 20 minutes):

Dear Colleagues,

Please be advised that there will be some maintenance performed on the Advancement, Human Resource, Finance and Student Information Systems (Banner) and they will be unavailable on Saturday May 8th 2015 to May 9th from 10:00PM through 9:00AM.

Please note that during this time both Self-Service Banner (SSB) and Internet Native Banner (INB) will be unavailable. This would include final faculty grading, student registration, class schedules, transcript requests, available courses, on-line payments, Advancement, Finance, HR and Banner reporting, etc.

Please be aware that the University portal, My.Fordham.edu will be available during this time, as will all non-Banner services accessible via the portal, such as E-mail, Degreeworks, Blackboard, etc.

We thank you for your patience, cooperation, and understanding and apologize for any inconvenience this may cause.

If you have any questions or concerns, please feel free to contact the IT Customer Care by phone at (718) 222-2222 or via email to: helpit@university.edu.

Here are some issues with the email.

- Not organized.
- Hard to read.
- Content not presented clearly.
- Too wordy.

How do you revise this email so someone will want to read it?

2.1.1 Better organization

Organize information according to importance.

Primary information:

- Summary of systems affected and the date.

Secondary information:

- More details about what in particular is affected.

Tertiary information:

- Many people don't know what INB and SSB are: define the terms, after the important information is given.
- IT contact information

2.1.2 Make it easier to read

- Put space between the paragraphs.
- Avoid lists of words in a sentence, avoid clustering them together.
- Avoid repeating words.

Content and how it's arranged—the order in which the information is placed and the white spaces between the facts--are important. But also important is the number of words per paragraph, even per line, in some cases.

2.2 Cut the Flab

According to an infographic published by *AdWeek*, the ideal length for a single line in a paragraph is 40-55 characters [1]. Everyone has a different rule of thumb, and a good one is to keep the number of lines per paragraph from two to at most three. A few techniques for good paragraphs:

- Be alert for unnecessary and repeated words.
- Don't apologize for routine maintenance.
- Avoid flab that sneaks in to writing:
    - to be able to
    - to try to
    - to have to
- Start sentences with strong nouns: "Banner will undergo maintenance..." as opposed to "There will be some maintenance performed on Banner..."
- Don't overuse the passive voice: "We are improving the WiFi" (Alternative: "Students now enjoy even faster WiFi...")
- Avoid the conditional voice: "This would include final faculty grading..."
- Avoid "Please note," "Please be advised," "Be aware."

Here is the revised email:

Dear Colleagues,

Self-Service Banner (SSB) and Internet Native Banner (INB) will undergo maintenance from Friday, May 8, 10:00 p.m. through Saturday, May 9, 9:00 a.m.

During this time, final faculty grading, student registration, class schedules, transcript requests, available courses, and online payments cannot be accessed. Also, human resources, finance and student information systems modules and reporting will not be available.

My.university.edu, the University portal, will be available, as will all other services accessed via the portal, such as Gmail, Degreeworks, and Blackboard.

What are SSB and INB?

Self-Service Banner (SSB) is accessed via my.fordham.edu. You use it to get information about pay stubs, taxes, grades, courses, and so on.

Internet Native Banner (INB) is mainly for administrators. This is where work occurs that is related to finance, human resources, and other administrative functions.

Questions? *Contact IT Customer Care: 718-222-2222 | HelpIT@university.edu*

2.3 Sell IT

Another part of an IT communicator's job is to promote events. In my case, very often the staff member leading the event sends me a draft of an email. Often that content gets expanded into a blog post or condensed into a tweet. Here is an example of a recent communication someone asked me to send out about 3D printing:

Subject: 3D printers

Hello All,

3D Printing is one of the newest Tech Trends on Campus! Faculty Technology Services will be hosting a Round Table to discuss how the university can best use the technology on Tuesday 4/21 at 11:00 on both campuses:

FTC at Campus 1, Room B-27
FTC at Campus 2, Room 416

For more information about 3D Printing, please visit the Tech Trends in Education Wiki or stop by either FTC.

This promotion for a roundtable on 3D printing needs to be improved in the following ways:

- 3D printing should be sold to a skeptical audience.
- Better organization of information.
- More clarity in the details and avoid abbreviations.
- Carefully choose keywords to attract faculty attention.
- Reduce capitalizations of regular nouns.

Elements of the revised email:

- Addressed email to faculty
- Added examples of 3D printing in use at the university to show that the printer not some whimsical, trendy tool, but useful to faculty and their students. Use bullets to separate information.
- Gave time and place without the introductory information "Time: April 21, 11:00 a.m." and "Place" etc.
- Used words relevant to a higher ed setting. When communicating with faculty, choose the words that define and reflect what they do. Use words such as research and pedagogy, and related terms that they strongly identify with. You'll attract their attention because what's being stated or advertised will seem relevant to their teaching and research.

Revision:

Subject: Find out how 3D printing can engage your students

Dear Faculty,

3D printing is transforming student engagement at the University, across the liberal arts curriculum.

For example,

- *Physics students no longer have to study 2D models of catapults in a book because they design and print their own*
- *History students print out historic artifacts for closer study*
- *Art and design students print out models of their work*

Join us! We'll demonstrate 3D printing and discuss how 3D printers can support teaching and research at the University. Here's our working agenda.

Tuesday, April 21, 11:00 a.m.
The Faculty Technology Centers
Campus 1, Room B-27
Campus 2, Room 416
RSVP on Eventbrite

For more information about 3D printing, please visit Faculty Technology Service's Tech Trends Wiki.

2.4 Spin IT

Damage control: We all have to do it at some point in our careers as IT communicators, if not at least once a semester. Sometimes it's even the kind of situation when the IT department may have a legitimate reason to apologize. Here's an example of a draft created for a troublesome situation related to a university website.

To the Community:

Over the past three days, our website, University.edu, has experienced catastrophic infrastructure issues related to its databases. Efforts to restore the site, including a content freeze, have only been intermittently successful, and this morning you may be waking to pages that read "Access Denied."

No content or links has been lost. We have built a new database on a new server and will be populating it with our current content. After testing and validation, we will point our site to the new location which will restore service worldwide and full functionality. This process will take a few hours, however, and we ask you for your patience.

We apologize for this inconvenience and assure you that we are doing everything possible to get our site up and running again.

What about this email needs to be changed and improved?

- Too long and detailed
- Too much information
- Sounds too dire.
- No levity.

Revision:

Dear Colleagues and Students,

Over the past three days, our new website, University.edu, has experienced infrastructure issues related to its databases.

We restored full functionality to the site today. However, you may encounter some pages that read "Access Denied," due to geographic location, browser settings, and other individual variances. This will clear up over the next few hours while the site propagates worldwide.

Apologies, and thanks for your patience.

Best wishes for a good break.

Elements of this revision:

- Two short paragraphs. One states the issue. The other begins with positive news that the problem has been corrected.

- Removed negative adjectives.

- Removed parts about what was done that didn't work.

- Left out details about how the site will get back online.

- Apologized and said thanks—errors were made.

- Left the email on a positive note: Let's think about spring break, instead!

3. CONCLUSION

The people on the receiving end of communications from an IT department expect clarity, precision, and details—but not so many details that the message becomes information overload. When composing a message, whether it's an email or blog post or tweet, choose the words carefully. Anyone who writes, no matter what's being written and for whom, should ask him or herself the following questions: Am I using the words that will resonate with my audience? How much information can I leave out and still get the message fully across? And, if I can say my message in five syllables, can I say it in four syllables? Can I say it in three? In two? One?

When using a minimum number of words, it is crucial to pay attention to how the information is organized: Place the most important information first. That way, the reader can tell instantly if the message is relevant. And, select the right words and examples—words and concepts your reader can identify with and the words that present the IT organization in the best way possible.

Follow these basic writing strategies and your audience will thank you for not taking up too much of their valuable time with a message that's hard to read and for giving them all the information they need, and no more.

4. REFERENCES

[1] Nudd, Tim. "Infographic: The Ideal Length of Everything Online, From Tweets to YouTube Videos Is your brand going on too long?" AdWeek. Oct. 14, 2014. AdWeek.com.

[2] O'Dell, J. "65% of All Email Gets Opened First on a Mobile Device." VB News. Jan. 22, 2014. Venturebeat.com.

Implementation and Experience of Learning Support Application for Students in Classes

Naomi Fujimura
Kyushu University
4-9-1, Shiobaru
Minami-ku, Fukuoka, Japan
+81 92 553 4434
fujimura.naomi.274@m.kyushu-u.ac.jp

Kazuyuki Kusunoki
Kyushu University
4-9-1, Shiobaru
Minami-ku, Fukuoka, Japan
+81 92 553 4434
kusunoki.kazuyuki.777@s.kyushu-u.ac.jp

Shuhei Endo
Big Ban System Corporation
1-10-11, Shiba-Daimon
Minato-ku, Tokyo, Japan
+81 3 5777 2801
sendou@bbsystem.co.jp

ABSTRACT

ICT (Information and Communication Technology) is now widely used in the education area. Many teachers provide educational material as files of Word, PowerPoint, or especially pdf files in their classes. It is very convenient and useful for students to keep them on their own PCs. However, it is difficult for students to add some notes onto such files.

On the other hand, many students hesitate to ask questions and to express their own opinions in classes in Japan. We know that some facilities like BBS (Bulletin Board System) encourage students to ask their questions and to express opinions in classes.

In Kyushu University, all students are expected to have their own PCs according to the policy of "Bring Your Own PCs (BYOPCs)." We want to promote the paperless learning for classes. We implemented the new learning support application that provides the following facilities with the facility of SharePoint and Yammer in Microsoft Office 365:

1) To add the note to the educational material provided by teachers via SharePoint in classes.

2) To make it possible for students to share the questions, comments, and opinions via Yammer with their own PCs among the attendees in the class.

We implemented the application software in Windows 8.1 to realize the above facilities. Then, Big Ban System Corporation and Microsoft Japan commercialize it as an application based on our original application. We report the design and experience of the learning support application to our university.

Categories and Subject Descriptors

K.3.1 [**COMPUTERS AND EDUCATION**]: Computer Uses in Education - *Collaborative learning, Computer-assisted instruction (CAI)*

SIGUCCS '15, November 09-13, 2015, St. Petersburg, FL, USA
© 2015 ACM. ISBN 978-1-4503-3610-9/15/11...$15.00
DOI: http://dx.doi.org/10.1145/2815546.2815582

General Terms

Management, Documentation, Design, Experimentation, Human Factors, Verification.

Keywords

Windows 8.1, Office 365, SharePoint, Yammer, Learning support, BYOD, SNS

1. INTRODUCTION

ICT (Information and Communication Technology) is now widely used in the education area. We adopted the new policy of "Bring Your Own PCs (BYOPCs)" since 2013 in Kyushu University [1]. It is to introduce the ICT environment for all students to learn at anytime, anywhere, and at their own paces. We want to promote the paperless learning for classes.

Teachers are supposed to provide as many educational materials as possible online. Students are also expected to bring their own PCs in classes required. The target students of BYOPCs have been increasing every year. Three out of four undergraduate students have their own PCs and are using them in 2015.

Many teachers provide educational material as files in Word, Excel, PowerPoint, or especially pdf files in their classes now. It is very convenient for teachers to prepare and distribute them and useful for students to keep them on their own PCs. However, students have difficulty in adding notes on such files. It is necessary for students to be able to write some notes on the online materials.

On the other hand, many students hesitate to ask questions and to express their own opinions in classes in Japan. We know that some facilities like BBS (Bulletin Board System) and SNS (Social Network Service) encourage students to ask their questions and to express opinions in classes. We think it is necessary for us to implement the application to encourage students to express their own opinions in classes.

2. BACKGROUND AND REQUIREMENT

We have classes that include over one hundred students. We also have classes with distance learning systems on several campuses [2]. In those cases, it is convenient for teachers to provide educational materials with pdf files for students. It is also convenient for students to keep them on their own PCs. However, students have difficulty in reading educational materials and listen to the teacher simultaneously. Teachers lack the interactive feeling too. Web learning system is not good for such purposes.

We need the application that supports the following:

- To reduce the time to distribute educational materials in a class.

- To support the interactive relationship between a teacher and students.
- To support the large class with a distance learning system.

3. SYSTEM SPECIFICATION

3.1 Facility

We implemented the new learning support application that provides the following facilities with SharePoint [3] and Yammer [4] of Microsoft Office 365 [5] in Windows 8.1.

- Students can add the note, free lines, and stamp to the educational material provided by teachers in the class, and save them.
- Students can share the questions, comments, and opinions through their own PCs among the attendees in the class.
- Students can synchronize the educational materials to the teacher's PC by hand or automatically.
- Teachers can manage the educational materials for every class separately

Microsoft Japan recognized that it is a good tool for education in a class and for meeting not only in university, but also companies. Then, Big Ban System Corporation (BBS) [6] and Microsoft Japan commercialized it as an application based on our original application. We named it ClassLook.

3.2 PC Environment

We adopted Windows 8.1 for our learning support application because of the following:

- Almost 87% of students have Windows PCs in our university in total according to the policy of "Bring Your Own PCs."
- Windows 8.1 is the latest OS and has a better ability for multi-tasking than before.
- Our university has had a Campus Agreement with Microsoft since 2007 [7]. Therefore, students do not have to pay any additional charge to upgrade OS to Windows 8.1.
- Students can use Windows in Boot Camp or a virtual machine such as VMware in Mac OS X. Students can install Windows 8.1 without any additional charge because of Microsoft Campus Agreement.
- Windows 8.1 provides a good handling facility for touch panels and easy finger input.

We used the facilities of SharePoint and Yammer of Office 365 as the basic infrastructure in our learning support application. We made the contract for Office 365 as Faculty of Design in Kyushu University at first. Kyushu University made the contract for the whole university recently and is now preparing to provide Office 365 to all staff members and students.

3.3 System Appearance

Figure 1 shows the relationship between a teacher and students. The teacher shows the educational material to students with ClassLook based on SharePoint. Students can see the educational materials in their own PCs. They can share the opinion with the chat facility based on Yammer between a teacher and students.

3.4 Setup and Authentication

Figure 2 shows the initial screen with the setup menu on the right side of the screen when ClassLook starts. Figure 3 shows the setup screen for SharePoint and Yammer. Users are expected to set up the URL for educational materials and client ID and secret to identify the Yammer channel. The teacher is supposed to ar-

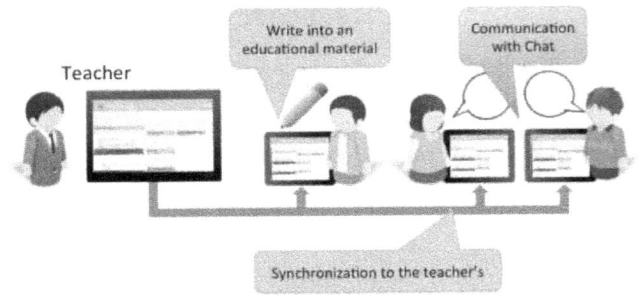

Figure 1 Image in a class with ClassLook

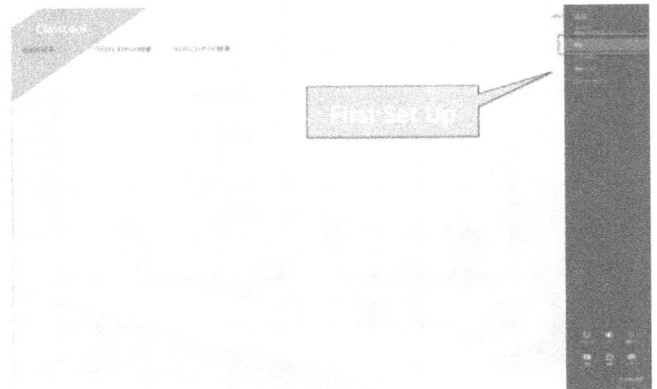

Figure 2 Initial screen with setup menu

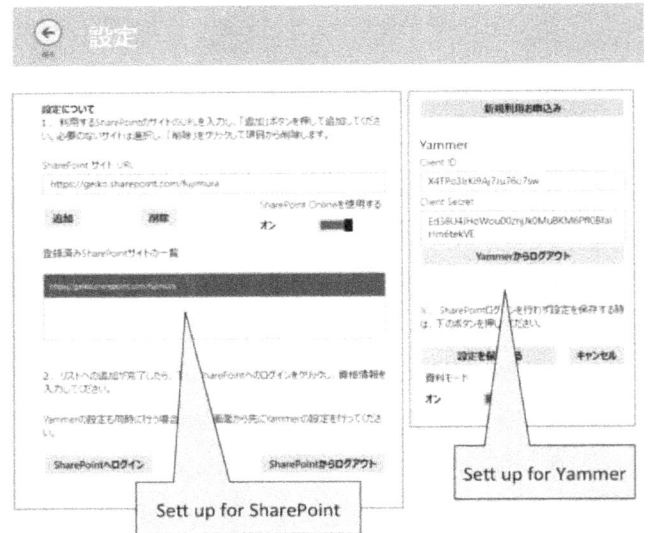

Figure 3 Setup for SharePoint and Yammer

range the URL and get the client ID and secret for each class before the class begins.

4. USER INTERFACE

4.1 Screen Appearance in ClassLook

When students start ClassLook, they can see the screen as shown in Figure 4. Each square corresponds to a class. After students click the icon of e.g. "SIGUCCS," a screen is displayed as in Figure 5 is displayed. It contains several documents for one lecture. Figure 6 is a sample screen for the educational material of pdf file.

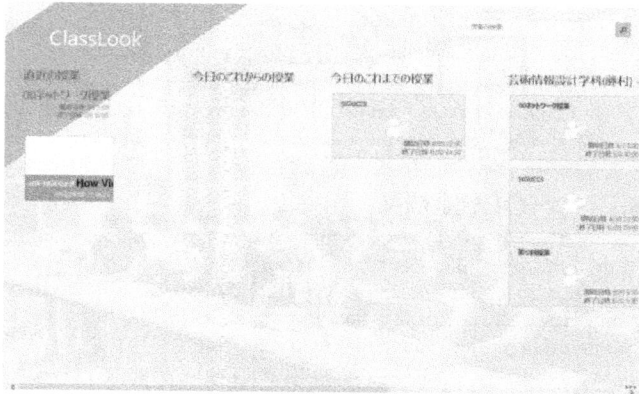
Figure 4 Usual top screen

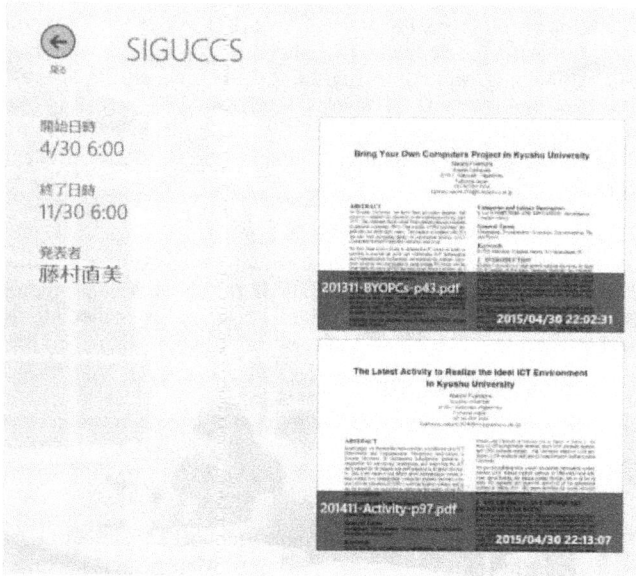
Figure 5 Screen for a class contents

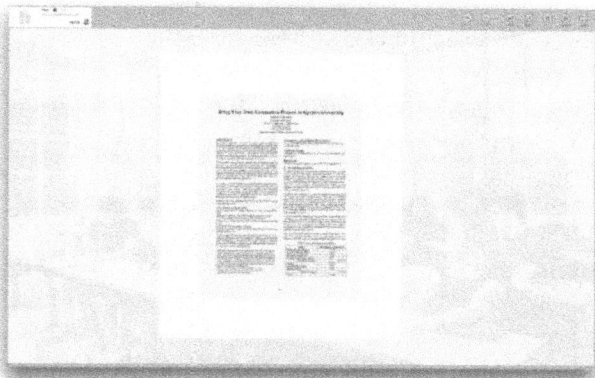
Figure 6 Screen of educational material

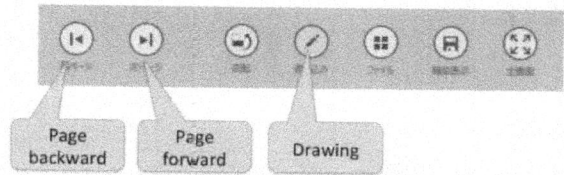
Figure 7 Menu for page control, drawing, and so on

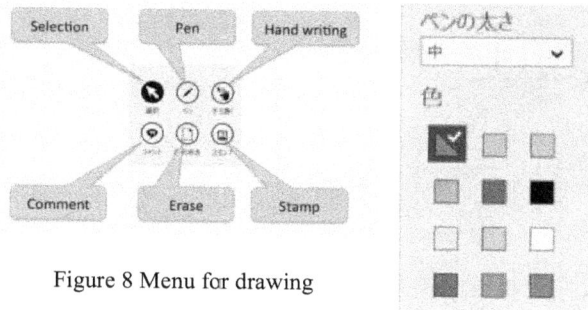
Figure 8 Menu for drawing

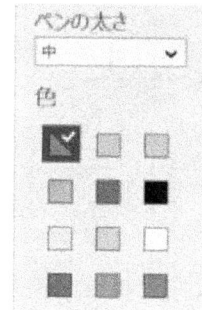
Figure 9 Colors for Pen

Figure 10 Screen of draw material

Figure 11 Screen for Synchronization

4.2 Page Control
Figure 7 is the menu for functions such as page control. Users can move a page forward and backward.

4.3 Drawing and Erase
When users click the icon of "Drawing" in Figure 7, Figure 8 is displayed. Users click "Pen", then they can select the color of pens as shown in Figure 9. Figure 10 is a sample screen of hand-writing, comment, and stamp. It is possible for users to use mouse, finger or touch pen to draw lines. Comments can be inserted through the keyboard. Those lines, comment, and stamp can be erased by drag after selecting "Erase".

4.4 SYNCRONIZATION TO TEACHER
Students can move the position of their contents to that of teacher's by clicking the "Sync" icon on the left top of the screen as shown in Figure 11.

4.5 CHAT BY YAMMER
It is not enough for students to see the educational materials and add lines, comments, and stamp. It is better for students to communicate with a teacher and other students during the class. We implemented the chat function with Yammer in Office365. Teacher is expected to prepare client ID and secret for Yammer before beginning the class. Students are expected to set them up as described before.

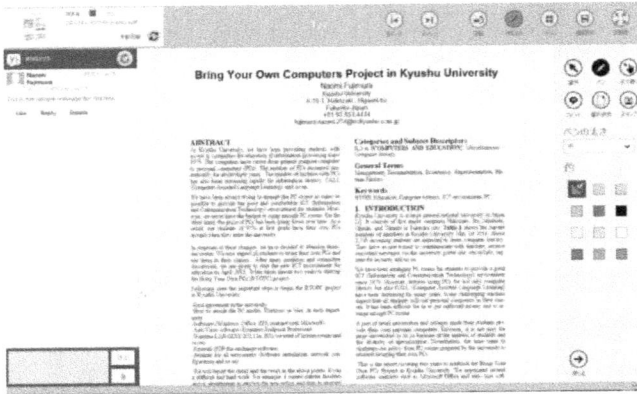

Figure 12 Screen of material with chat window

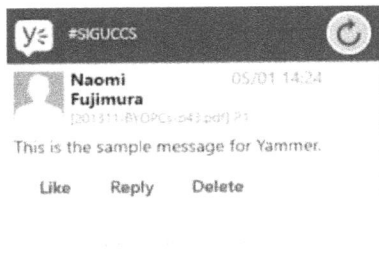

Figure 13 Screen for Chat by Yammer

Figure 12 shows a sample screen with full function for ClassLook. This is the screen that students watch during the class. Figure 13 shows the zoomed chat screen, which contains a sample message that appears on the left side of the screen.

5. Questionnaire

We used this application in our laboratory seminar and the class in the second semester of 2014.

We got the following points in our laboratory seminar. We prepared the necessary PCs in advance.

- Memo facility is simple and easy to write memo without any stress.
- It is interesting to see the message in real time.
- Chat function is useful for easy minutes in a meeting.
- It is easy to understand the usage of ClassLook.

Our department specifies the PC model to Mac. Students can use Windows even on Mac, but they are forced to install Windows. They installed Windows 8 when they entered our university. However, ClassLook requires the Windows 8.1 environment. We asked students to upgrade Windows from 8 to 8.1. Many students accepted our request, but not all.

We also got the following comment in our class.

- It is difficult for students to install ClassLook and setup it on Mac.
- In Windows, students can use ClassLook without any stress. However, it is not so good in Mac OS than in Windows from

the viewpoint of response

- It is useful to know the other's opinions during the class.
- Students feel happy when they send their opinion online because they hesitate to speak their opinion in voice during the class. They can ask the questions without any hesitation at once.

6. CONCLUSION

Teachers are trying to prepare many educational materials online in their classes and students can concentrate to listen to the teachers and explanation under the "Bring Your Own PCs" environment. However, one of the most important issues is to write some comment in online education materials freely. Our application makes it possible to write comments, lines, and stamps in pdf files. It also makes possible to encourage students to share and say their opinions and remarks,

The Information Infrastructure Initiative (III), where Dr. Fujimura (first author) is the director of III and is responsible for introducing, maintaining, and improving the ICT environment for all staff members and students of Kyushu University, is preparing the usage for Office365 by July 2015. We hope many teachers and students use this application and embrace the good and efficient learning in classes.

7. ACKNOWLEDGMENTS

We appreciate the students who were willing to use our learning support application in the seminar and in the class. We also appreciate Mr. Satoru Nakagawa of Microsoft Japan for connecting us to Big Ban System Corporation to realize this application.

8. REFERENCES

[1] Naomi Fujimura. 2013. Bring your own computers project in Kyushu University. In *Proceedings* of ACM SIGUCCS 2013, (Chicago, USA, November 5 -8, 2013). ACM SIGUCCS, 43 - 50, DOI=http://dl.acm.org/citation.cfm? id= 2504789

[2] Takahiro Tagawa, Naomi Fujimura, Satoshi Hashikura, and Hitoshi Inoue. 2009. Introduction and Management of Inter-Campus Learning Assistant System for Distributed Campus, In *Proceedings* of SIGUCCS 2009 (Saint Louis, MO, USA, October 11 - 14 2009), ACM SIGUCCS, 253-256, DOI= http://dx.doi.org/10.1145/1629501.1629547

[3] SharePoint: https://products.office.com/en-us/SharePoint/collaboration

[4] Yammer: https://about.yammer.com/

[5] Office 365: http://products.office.com/en-us/?WT.mc_id=OAN_en-us_MSCOM-SRCH1-IMG

[6] BBS, Big Ban System Corporation: http://www.bbsystem.co.jp/

[7] Naomi Fujimura, Itsuo Omagari, Masatsugu Ueda, and Keiichi Irie. Experience with Software Blanket Contract in Kyushu University, In *Proceedings* of SIGUCCS 2008 (Portland, OR, USA, October 19 – 22 2008), ACM SIGUCCS, 307 – 310, DOI=http://dx.doi.org/10.1145/1449956.1450046.

Implementation and Experience of

the Online Peer Grading System for Our Real Class

Shunsuke Noguchi
Graduate School of Design, Kyushu University
4-9-1, Shiobaru, Minami-ku
Fukuoka, Japan
+81-92-553-4434
noguchi.s.006@s.kyushu-u.ac.jp

Naomi Fujimura
Faculty of Design, Kyushu University
4-9-1, Shiobaru, Minami-ku
Fukuoka, Japan
+81-92-553-4434
fujimura.naomi.274@m.kyushu-u.ac.jp

ABSTRACT

In an online learning course like MOOC (Massive Open Online Course), peer grading is useful for scaling the grades of assignments to the large number of students. Peer grading is also attractive because it reduces the burden of teachers and gives rich feedback to learners. In Kyushu University, we have a demand for using peer grading in some classes that include a large number of students. However, the discussion about operating peer grading in our university has not been discussed sufficiently.

We developed the online peer grading system to cope with the large number of students in the class. Students can upload their assignments, grade others, and receive feedback from other students via the system. We operated it in our university's class in order to verify whether peer grading works well and return accurate scores.

In this paper, we verify it with an analysis of the data of user behavior, and also comparison between peer and teacher grading scores. We show questionnaire results. As a result, although there are still issues to improve, we find the validity in peer grading to some extent.

Categories and Subject Descriptors

K.3.1 [**Computer Uses in Education**]: Computer-managed instruction (CMI)

General Terms

Measurement, Performance, Design, Reliability, Experimentation, Human Factors, Verification.

Keywords

Peer grading, Peer assessment, MOOC

SIGUCCS '15, November 09-13, 2015, St. Petersburg, FL, USA
© 2015 ACM. ISBN 978-1-4503-3610-9/15/11...$15.00
DOI: http://dx.doi.org/10.1145/2815546.2815581

1. INTRODUCTION

Students are graded by their attendance, report submission, and written examinations in university classes. Report submission is particularly an important index to know how well students understand its course contents. In this paper, we focus on "peer grading," in which students grade other students' reports, and describe the result of development and implementation of the peer grading system.

These days, there is much research studying on peer grading. Sadler and Good (2006) showed usability of peer grading by the statistical method [1]. Due to a progress of ICT (Information and Communication Technology), peer grading is important and attractive to evaluate assignment in MOOC (Massive Open Online Course). Besides OCW (OpenCourseWare), MOOC in which students can obtain a degree by submitting the report on online, spread widely and rapidly. Coursera by Stanford University [2] and edX by MIT [3] are famous as a successful MOOC in the world. Peer grading serves as a critical tool for grading complex reports with hundreds/thousand of students in MOOC. This is because it is almost impossible for teachers to grade a large number of reports every week. Chris (2006) proposed algorithms for improving accuracy of peer grading [4].

We have been providing a large number of video content in classes on platforms such as YouTube [5] and iTunes U [6] for many years in Kyushu University. We introduced Blackboard Learn [7] as a LMS (Learning Management System) in early stage. We adopted the new policy of "Bring Your Own PCs" in our university since 2013 [8]. In this situation, students can download teaching materials and submit reports by their own PCs anytime, anywhere. Teachers can grade students' reports on this system by themselves.

The class named "Network as a Social Infrastructure" began in April 2015. This class is open in multiple campuses by using the distance learning system [9]. Approximately 300 students attend the class. It is difficult for the teacher to grade a large number of reports by themselves every week. Therefore, we decided to introduce peer grading in this class. Before introducing it formally, we had to examine how well peer grading works in our real class.

2. SYSTEM OVERVIEW

Figure 1 shows an overview of our peer grading system. We used an Apache server, PHP, and MySQL for the server.

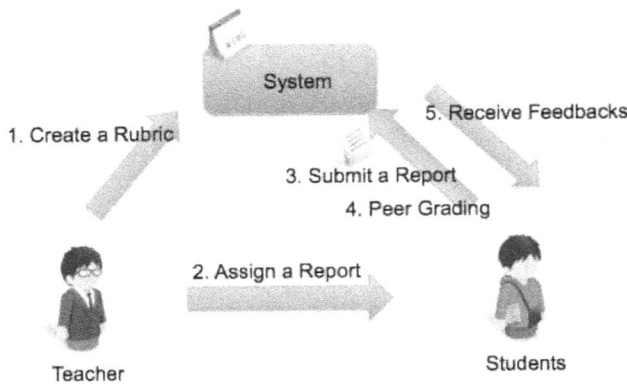

Figure 1. Peer Grading System Overview

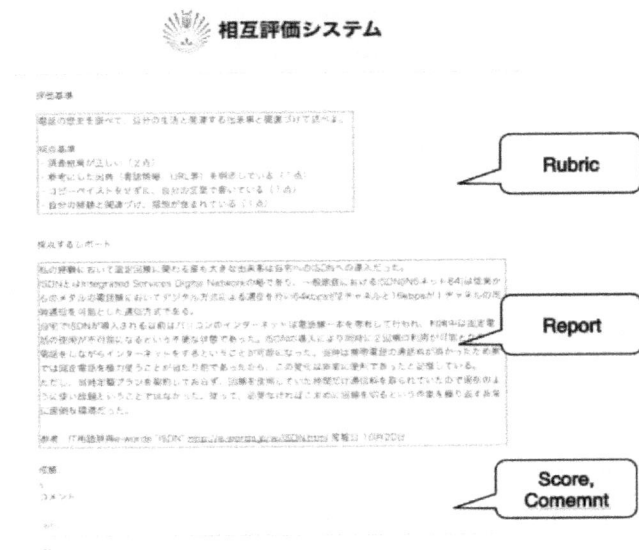

Figure 2. Schedule for Peer Grading

1. Create a Rubric (Teachers)

Teachers use the system in their real classes. A teacher uploads the content of an assignment and a rubric into the system. This rubric is crucial because students grade their peers' report with it.

2. Assign a Report (Teachers)

Teachers explain the content of assignments, the rubric, and deadline in their real class.

3. Submit a Report (Students)

Students upload their reports before the deadline. They can modify their report as many as they want until the deadline. The server stores the uploaded reports. Students can do "self-grading" after they submitted their reports. In a word, they can grade their own reports according to the rubric. Self-grading is optional.

4. Peer Grading (Students)

Figure 2 shows the schedule for peer grading. A teacher assigns homework in the class. Students submitted their reports by the deadline (usually one week). After the deadline of submission, students grade their peers' reports.

5. Receive Feedback (Students)

Students can browse feedback graded by their peers. It means to give students educational effects. They can refer to the comments when they write their next report, or gain motivation.

6. Extra Functions

This system includes extra functions as follows besides the above.

- Conduct a questionnaire.
- Output results of peer grading in CSV format.
- Teacher Grading

3. EXPERIENCE
3.1 Class
We operated the system for the "*Network Service Design*" class in the second semester 2014. The Main participant were the 2nd grade students of the department of art and information, School of Design. The class aims to give fundamental knowledge of communication system such as telephones, mobile phones, the Internet, and social fundamentals. The member of students in the class was 66. The number of assignments was 11, and the number of submitted reports was 601.

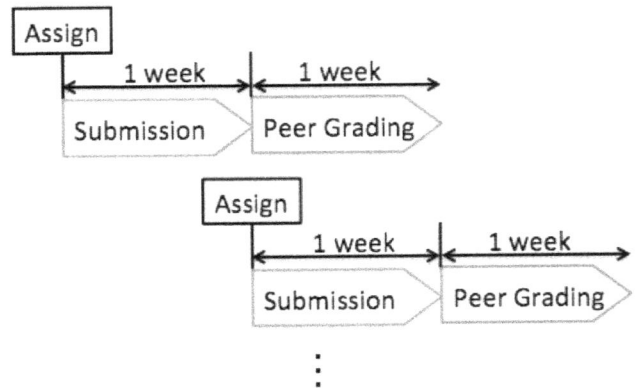

Figure 3 Peer Grading Screen

3.2 Peer Grading
Students grade their peers' report during the peer grading period as shown in Figure 2. Figure 3 shows the peer grading screen. They can input not only the score but also comments. Report to grade is assigned by the system randomly. Students grade other's report anonymously in order to prevent the invasion of irrelevant factors such as human relations.

Table 1 shows a number of submission and peer grading. "Report Submission" is the number of report submitted for each assignment. "Peer Grading" is the sum of peer grading which grade submitted report for the assignment.

3.3 Questionnaire
We carried out a questionnaire when half of the semester had elapsed. Table 2 shows the result (N = 33). We adopt a 5 point scale. "Positive" means a percent of "strongly agree" or "agree." We gained the following comments from students besides Table 2,

- Request for the improvement of User Interface
- Positive opinion. For example, "*I'm grad to receive feedback and motivated*".

Table 1. Results of Peer Grading

No.	Report Submission	Peer Grading	No.	Report Submission	Peer Grading
1st	60	250	7th	54	214
2nd	58	177	8th	52	162
3rd	58	241	9th	49	139
4th	58	197	10th	57	173
5th	57	200	11th	44	106
6th	54	194			

Table 2 Results of questionnaire (N = 33)

	strongly agree	agree	neutral	disagree	strongly disagree	positive (%)
Q1. I find it easy to use the system.	11	21	0	0	0	**100**
Q2. Layout or expression of reports is good.	8	17	5	3	0	**76**
Q3. I feel the peer graded score valid.	9	17	5	2	0	**79**
Q4. I am motivated on account of peer grading.	5	13	11	4	0	**55**
Q5. Peer grading allow me to review the contents of the class.	8	17	6	1	1	**76**
Q6. I feel that my ability to grade improved.	5	9	11	8	0	**42**
Q7. I find comments meaningful.	4	7	12	7	3	**33**

- Negative opinion. For example, "*I feel unpleasant because I received inscrutable feedbacks*".

3.4 Time to grade

The system keeps time when students grade. Figure 4 shows the histogram. The blue bar shows the frequency. Interval is 10 seconds. The red line shows the cumulative total of frequency. The system keeps time when students grade other's report.

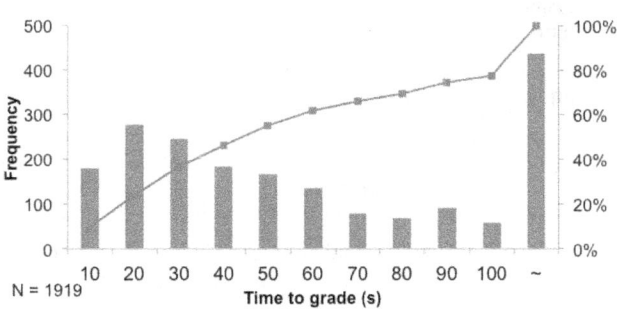

Figure 4. Time to Grade

4. DISCUSSION

4.1 Peer Grading

The number of submissions is 50 - 60. Most of the students submit reports. The number of peer grading is approximately 200. A student grades 3 or 4 reports. It is because the teacher told students to grade more than 3 reports in the class for each assignment. We think the number of peer grading is sufficient.

When we look at the time to grade (Figure 4), we think it is not good enough. About 40 % of peer grading is done in less than 30 seconds. It would be doubtful in grading with too short time. We reflect on our past conduct not to teach how to grade or show the samples of peer grading.

4.2 Questionnaire

We asked the students to get the information about user interface and the effect and benefit of peer grading with the questionnaire. The number of answers is 33.

Q1 and Q2 are the questions about usability or the design of the Web page in the system. The answer was largely positive. We will use the comments about user interface as a reference to improve the system.

Q3 – Q7 are about educational benefits of peer grading. The answers for "Q3. I feel the peer graded score valid." and "Q5. Peer grading allow me to review the contents of the class" are positive. According to the result of Q3, it seems students accept peer grading. We also find out that peer grading is a good opportunity to review through the result of Q5,.

On the other hand, there are a very few positive answers for "Q6. I feel that my ability to grade improved." We reflect on our conduct not to coach how to grade. Furthermore, only 33 % of students answered positively on "Q7. I find comments meaningful." When we look over the comments, there are some comments that seem doubtful. In contrast, there are some students who say "I am glad to see my report was graded properly." We have to incentivize students to grade in the future work.

127

4.3 Comparison between self and peer grading

We compare the self-grading with peer grading score. We adopt the average as peer grading score and computed Pearson product-moment correlation coefficient as the correlation coefficient. We get the result of r = 0.10.

We also compare self-grading score with teacher grade score. We get the result of r = 0.09.

As a result, we found out that self-grading is totally useless. We think that it is difficult for students to grade their own reports objectively.

4.4 Comparison between peer and teacher grading

We compare peer grading score with teacher grading score. Figure 5 shows the result of comparison between peer and teacher grading. We get the result 0.60 of correlation ratio. We can say that it has positive correlation. When we look at Figure 5, we can find that teacher scores tend to be lower than peer scores by students. We browse reports and its comments to find the reason. We find out that the teacher deflates the score severely because poor quality and quantity of reports. However, students grade the higher score because the report satisfies the rubric.

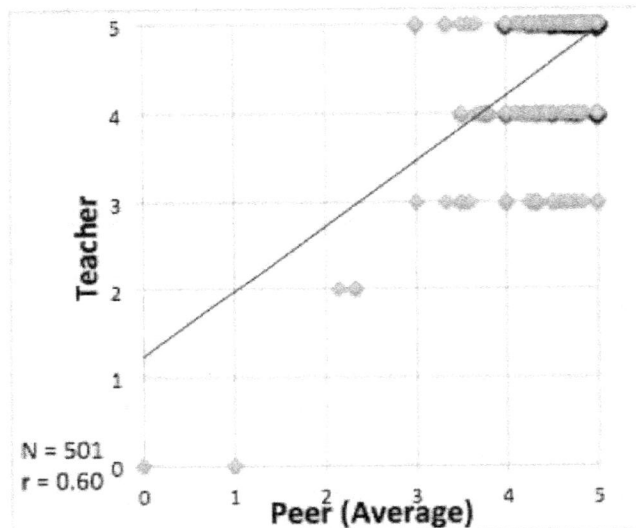

Figure 5. Comparison between peer and teacher grading

5. FUTURE WORK

The system is now operated in the class named *"Network as Social Infrastructure"* in the first semester 2015. The number of students is about 300 in 5 rooms of three campuses in total. The number of students is so many that we never experienced before. Therefore we hope the peer grading system works well.

According to the findings in our research, we will improve the system as follows:

- To improve the user interface according to the result of questionnaire.
- To implement the mechanism to motivate the students to do peer grading by giving incentive such as bonus mark points.
- To find the way to get rid of the doubtful grades.

We also want to examine data in a different point of view as follows.

- The number of peer grading for each report to guarantee a valid peer grading score.
- The relation of the student's score and their ability to grade.
- The relation of the time and the ability to grade.
- Develop algorithm to improve accuracy of peer grading.

6. CONCLUSION

We decided to introduce peer grading in our university's class. The reason is the large number of students due to the class being open by using the distant learning system in many campuses. Before introducing it formally, we had to examine how well peer grading works. So we developed peer grading system and operated it in the real class. As a result, we found the validity in peer grading to some extent. The system is now being operated in our university's class with many participants. We expect we can use our peer grading system in MOOC courses in the future.

7. REFERENCES

[1] P. M. Sadler and E. Good. 2006. The impact of self-and peer-grading on student learning. Educational assessment, 11 (1): 1-31. DOI=10.1207/s15326977ea1101_1

[2] Coursera : https://www.coursera.org/

[3] edX : https://www.edx.org/

[4] Chris Piech. 2013. Tuned models of peer assessment in MOOCs. In Proceedings of The 6th International Conference on Educational Data Mining (EDM 2013), (Memphis, Tennessee, USA, July 6 – 9, 2013), http://arxiv.org/pdf/1307.2579v1

[5] YouTube Kyushu University : https://www.youtube.com/user/ KyushuUniv

[6] iTunes U Kyushu University : http://itunes.icer.kyushu-u.ac.jp/

[7] e-Learning System Kyushu University : https://bb9.iii.kyushu-u.ac.jp/

[8] Naomi Fujimura. 2013. Bring your own computers project in Kyushu University. In *Proceedings* of ACM SIGUCCS 2013, (Chicago, USA, November 5 -8, 2013). ACM SIGUCCS, 43 - 50, DOI=http://dl.acm.org/citation.cfm? id= 2504789

[9] Takahiro Tagawa, Naomi Fujimura, Satoshi Hashikura, and Hitoshi Inoue, Introduction and Management of Inter-Campus Learning Assistant System for Distributed Campus, In *Proceedings* of ACM SIGUCCS 2009, (St. Louis, MO, USA, October 11 – 14, 2009), ACM SIGUCCS, 253 - 256, DOI=http://dx.doi.org/10.1145/1629501.1629547

Open Source Platform for Teaching Administration of Unix-like Systems

Dmitri Danilov, Artjom Lind, Eero Vainikko
Institute of Computer Science, University of Tartu
J. Liivi 2, Tartu, Estonia
{dmitri.danilov, artjom.lind, eero.vainikko}@ut.ee

ABSTRACT

Unix-like operating systems are time-proven leaders of the server-side software and have cumulative share of ~60%. At least 10% of Unix-like systems are used on personal computers. Popularity of cloud based on-demand infrastructure (SaaS) has simplified the process of obtaining the hosting platforms for the developers. As a result, the demand for qualified administrators of Unix-like systems is growing rapidly. Education of Unix-like system administrators is a complicated and uncertain task due to diversity and large amount of different Unix-like platforms. The vendors of commercial distributions offer training courses and certifications. However, a significant number of open source distributions are remaining uncovered by structured and defined training routines. Considering these facts, we organized an open e-course relying on Debian Linux. In this paper, we will share our experience of the course development and teaching. Our main contributions are a scalable, secured and automatic task verification system; and a supplementary infrastructure solution that allows performing the course tasks at any location with internet access. Powering the course with these two developed components resulted in improvement of time resource and course quality. In addition, we will describe our developed solution in detail and analyze qualitative feedback of the students gathered during three years of teaching.

Categories and Subject Descriptors

K.3.1 [**Computers and Education**]: Computer Uses in Education - *Computer-managed instruction.*

Keywords

System administration; teaching; automatic evaluation

1. INTRODUCTION

The evolution of the web during the last few decades has resulted in a huge demand on skilled system administrators.

SIGUCCS'2015, November 09-13, 2015, St. Petersburg, FL, USA
© 2015 ACM. ISBN 978-1-4503-3610-9/15/11 $15.00
DOI: http://dx.doi.org/10.1145/2815546.2815583

Free and open source Unix-like operating systems became the most used platform for many services available through the internet.

However, this kind of software requires certain skills and experience to be effectively used. Universities are often criticized for imbalance between theory and practice in the education process. Quite often fresh system administrators have a good understanding of Unix-like operating system architecture, but have a little or no practical experience in service configuration on a such platform. In order to be successful in the labor market, system administrators need to go through many configuration tasks with instructor guidance before they get enough experience for independent education and work. That process requires a lot of university human resources to be effective.

In the University of Tartu[1] we have organized system administration courses for five years. During the last three years, we constantly developed the infrastructure of the course and as a result we were able to manage high amount of students with limited human resources. However, what is more important, we managed to increase the quality of the course according to the students' feedback. In this paper, we will describe in detail the problems encountered during the course management and the solution developed to solve these problems along with students' feedback.

2. CLASSIC APPROACH: PROBLEMS

Universities can hardly compete with the private IT sector in providing a better job offer, which leads to lack of qualified teaching staff. Because of this fact, the Universities tend to employ the master or phd students part-time to teach the practical part of the courses. Even if the system administration course has one or two experienced professionals in the teaching staff, the amount of 100+ students (in our case) is hardly manageable as each student requires personal guidance discovering his own way to prevent the operating system from booting. Personal guidance, searching for the configuration mistakes and student operating system recovery in same cases takes hours of work for one student.

Another problem is often related to the equipment availability. In our case, we had a computer class with 15 available machines resulting in 9 lab groups and ~9 students per machine. Taking into account that this class is also used for other courses, the access to the machines for students is quite limited. As the course is positioned as the basics of system administration on Unix-like operating systems, the

---

[1]Official page at: http://www.ut.ee/

material of the practical part is quite broad and most of the students are not able to progress fast enough having access to the machines only during the labs. Making mistakes and troubleshooting the reasons is a significant and important part of system administration. Unfortunately, it is hardly predictable in time estimations due to different initial skills and personalities of the students.

One of the most complicated problems is related to the evaluation process. Impartial and correct evaluation is an important part of the overall motivation and success measure for the self-rating. Evaluation of the configured services in theory is not complicated as it can be automated with shell scripts. However, the problem resides in a constant requirement of the feedback for the students during their configuration tasks. Running the evaluation scripts just once at the end of the semester will lead to unsatisfied results and frustration from the students' side. Running evaluation scripts for each lab multiple times requires more dedication from the teaching staff in providing feedback and guidance in troubleshooting configuration for nearly each student. Limited lab time, large amount of students asking for evaluation and guidance results in a high amount of pressure on the lab instructor.

When we joined the teaching staff and were assigned to the system administration course, it had all the problems described above. It was quite nervous to give labs and listed problems were mostly solved with the human resources. Each lab had 2 instructors and in order to decrease the pressure on the teaching staff each instructor mostly had only one lab during the week. Around 12 lab instructors were assigned to the course to run it successfully. Despite the number of lab instructors, many of them were not experienced enough. As a result, the students' feedback to the course was sometimes quite low. The situation became more complicated when university administration standardized the amount of human resources assigned to courses and limited the amount of lab instructors for the lab to one instructor. This was the point, where we started to redesign the course in order to handle the challenges it provided.

3. SOLVED PROBLEMS

During the course redesign, we defined and focused on the three main problems: system recovery, class infrastructure access flexibility and evaluation. Infrastructure flexibility and system recovery was solved by virtualization software. Instead of PC-based Linux instances, students used individual virtual machines (VMs) which could be easily ported (from class to home, from Windows to Mac, etc.). Moreover, as the virtual hard drives of the VMs were just VDI files on the host platforms they could also be easily backed up. However, with hard disks becoming files it complicated the lab evaluation, as files are easier to exchange. As a part of motivation, we demanded completion of the lab tasks as a requirement for the final examination. Digital signatures solved this smaller problem. Digital signature represents an encrypted student data automatically written to the random unpartitioned hard disk space. This step allowed us to personalize initial distribution installation hard disk files. Making a system backup and restoring became a trivial task of hard disk file copying. It also removed a requirement to restore students' instances by lab instructors.

The class infrastructure access flexibility was a more complex problem. Thanks to the *Network Technology* course

running in the same class, we had an access to the server with 8 TB space and *iSCSI* to the class network. By utilizing this server, we built an infrastructure schematically illustrated in Figure 1.

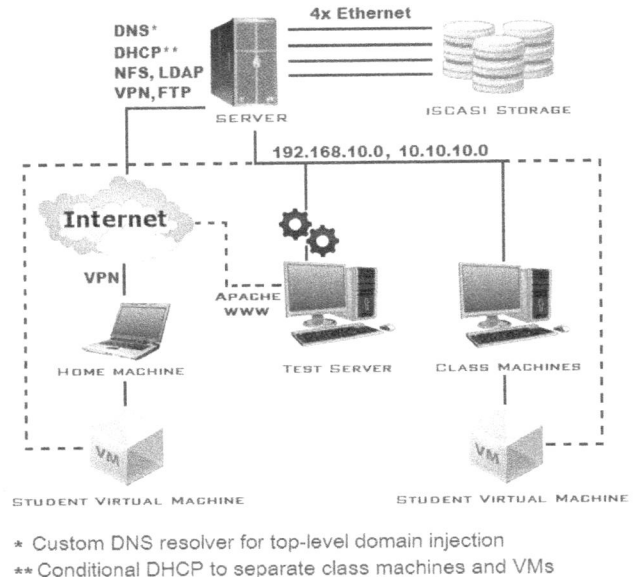

* Custom DNS resolver for top-level domain injection
** Conditional DHCP to separate class machines and VMs

Figure 1: Course infrastructure

Student accounts and access to the file system are managed with an *LDAP* server. Each student gets access to their personal home directory with initial signed Debian Linux instance files hosted by the server via *iSCASI*. Class machines are just client machines with mounted disks over *NFS* and pre-installed virtualization software. In practice, students come to the class and are able to pick any available machine to get into their personalized environment. At start, student credentials are the student's name and an initial password similar to all accounts. After the first login, students are supposed to change their passwords and start working with lab instructions. Virtual machines are bridged to the network adapter of the class machine and utilize the same network but with different IP range (10.10.10.0).

The next step is access to the class infrastructure from home. The left bottom corner in Figure 1 illustrates a student's personal computer connected to the infrastructure through the *VPN* tunnel. During the first lab at class, students generate their personal private keys and send certificate requests. During the second week students receive signed certificates and are able to establish a *VPN* connection to the class server. With the signed certificate students can access their personal folder through *FTP*, download their hard disk file and run the virtual machine bridged to the *VPN* tunnel. This allows the virtual machine to be attached to the class network. In the course infrastructure setup, we used a L2-level tunnel with TAP-adapter devices. The actual class DHCP service was used to assign the IPs. This decision guaranteed transparency between the class and students' personal machines. In practice, this means that after the first lab, students can work on labs from home at any time. This solution also allows us to automatically set and prioritize our internal *DNS* server for student's home machine. This is needed for one of the labs, where students configure their own *DNS* server in order to allow the custom top-level domains like *one. two. three.* dependent on the class group name. We solve this by using the typical domain injection technique intercepting all domain request with our custom DNS resolver. Our internal *DNS* server just forwards *DNS* requests to the student's virtual machine for lab specific domains.

As the last step, we designed and developed the test server. It consists of two parts: a visual part and the test service part (See Figure 2). The visual part is used to provide feedback to the students. It is a *PHP* application served by *Apache HTTP Server*. The test service part represents a complex python application that executes tests locally on the test server and remotely on the student's virtual machine according to the test type. Test service is responsible for monitoring the class network and constantly run tests for available machines. Student instances are tested in parallel and there is no significant difference in execution time if amount of online machines grows. This application is also easily scalable as it is possible to run multiple application instances on different IP ranges without conflicts.

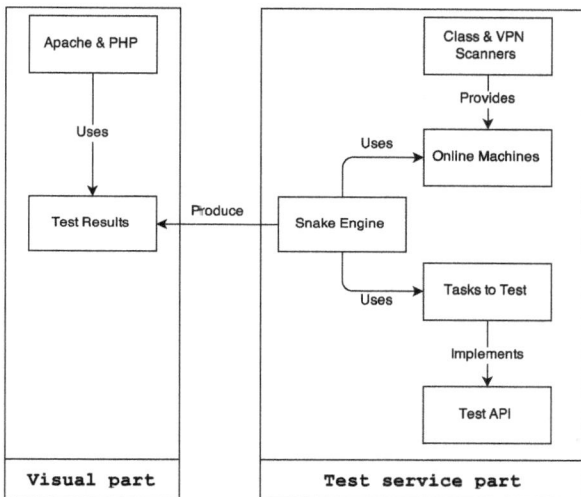

Figure 2: Test server components

At the moment of writing this paper there are 153 tests covering 9 labs with an average 2-3 topics per lab. Test types vary from simple service status checks to rather complicated folder share mounts. The visual part reflects test results produced by the test service. Students can monitor the list of lab tests with description, test time and test success status with a web browser. Each student has an access only to his personal test results. This is achieved using client certificate authentication over HTTPS; students use the same certificate and private key as for the VPN server to access the web page of the testing server.

Each test is a small python script executed by the parent application. For example, one of the local tests tries to mount specific folders over *NFS* that students are supposed to configure. One of the remote tests checks if a student instance received an email and it was redirected to the correct mailbox without errors. Remote tests are sent and executed remotely using *SSH* in a way that do not leave execution his-

tory. During the labs, we encouraged students to find any security vulnerabilities and get an "A" grade for labs as a reward for finding them. During the three years of teaching students did not find any security vulnerabilities. According to one feedback of an experienced student: "*it was easier to do labs than cheat the system*". Quote

During the labs, instructors have a full picture of the student's progress monitoring test summary list called "progress monitor". Progress monitor allows it to filter test summaries by test time, online status, location, group number and other parameters. Summaries include student name and machine number allowing the lab instructor to easily address their guidance to the students who need it the most.

At the end of the labs, students have practical examination in class that counts for 50% of the final grade. During the examination, students get their configured instance with plenty of artificial errors introduced. During two tries with the best result selected, students troubleshoot their instance configuration and try to fix the problems. Students have a limit in time and an aid of the test server that constantly checks instances for selected services availability and their configuration correctness.

4. COURSE FEEDBACK

In the University of Tartu, students register for the courses using a university internal *Study Information System*. After the end of each course, students are providing feedback regarding the course quality and teaching staff competence. During the three years of redesigned course teaching and its infrastructure development, the overall course grade given by students increased by around 15% from C+ to B+. At least 50% of the registered students provided their feedback to the course each year. There were 100+ students in average divided into lab groups of 15 students. Each lab group was successfully managed by one lab instructor. According to the lab instructors' feedback, the new course infrastructure solution allowed them to optimize their time resources and dedicate more time to actual guidance of the students. Evaluation tests made lab instructions more clear for understanding. Lab instructor progress monitor provided a valuable aid and allowed to focus on students with the lowest progress in a more personalized manner. Access from home allowed students to progress on labs with a comfortable tempo and removed a significant amount of stress during the labs.

After the new infrastructure introduction, we received many positive comments in the students' feedback:

- "*A very good course. Some labs in the beginning may seem tough, but you can easily pass the final exam as long as you understand the principles of those tough labs.*"

- "*This course is practical and I would recommend it to all the students if you need not just theory.*"

- "*The labs are very helpful, I learned a lot from them as the student is forced to do extensive hands-on jobs throughout the whole semester which gets them used to linux.*"

- "*I would like to say to future students about this course is that this course is worth taking. If you are new to linux or want to go through a proper learning process of what system administrator do, do not miss this course. This course team is highly motivated to teach you something."*

- *"good practicing opportunity"*
- *"I have learned so many things from this course. Theory and practical both were very good."*

As an experiment, this course was also given completely remote for students from other universities with the only obligation to be physically present during the examination. Previously recorded lectures were published online. Most of the students liked this approach because they did not need to travel between different cities to visit lectures or labs (3 hours one way). Despite the online availability of the video lectures, we received interesting feedback like this: *"One of the best classes I've ever taken. I know the guys are very busy but I would prefer to combine the labs with a 90 minutes weekly or every other week lecture."*. From this feedback, we concluded that there is a group of students that also require motivation on watching lectures if they are given online. However, most of the feedback was positive like this: *"Though the teaching was done entirely through a course blog, both teachers were extremely responsive and helpful. This was my first class like this and I was impressed."*.

5. RELATED WORK

At the time we joined the teaching staff we had a good overview of the corresponding course in UT, however we lacked an overview of teaching experience in the other universities. When we prepared the course and designed the lab infrastructure we tried to also take into account best practices shared by other researchers in that area. When choosing the Debian operation system (and open source in general) we also relied on the experience reported in [4]. Our decision towards usage of VMs were mostly obvious, nevertheless we referred to the work reported in [2]. In addition the reports on applying Linux [1] and virtualized environments [3] in teaching of the *System Administration* were used to adjust and optimize the topics we covered in our course. Finally, the decision towards automatic validation scripts was influenced by teaching emulators like in [5] and also proprietary emulators used in CISCO systems for teaching the *Network Administration*.

6. CONCLUSIONS AND FUTURE WORK

In this paper, we described an infrastructure solution for the *System Administration* course developed and used in the University of Tartu. We believe that initial problems we described in section 2 are quite common for the Unix-like *System Administration* courses due to the complexity and variety of the available services and operating system components. Thanks to the developed infrastructure components described in section 3 we achieved positive results in overall course management.

Although we improved the course infrastructure to manage high amount of students with limited human resources, we still see a lot of space for further improvement. The weakest part is the initial infrastructure setup. It requires plenty of time to configure all components: main server, test server and class machines for the course at each semester start. We seek for opportunities to simplify the infrastructure by utilizing cloud technology. Having students' virtual instances

on the server side will increase overall control and speed up an initial setup of the course.

7. ACKNOWLEDGEMENTS

This research was supported by the Estonian Doctoral School in Information and Communication Technology and Estonian Science Foundation.

8. REFERENCES

[1] ADAMS, D. R., AND ERICKSON, C. Linux in education: Teaching system administration with linux. *Linux J. 2001*, 82es (Feb. 2001).

[2] BEGNUM, K., KOYMANS, K., KRAP, A., AND SECHREST, J. Using virtual machines in system administration education. In *Proceedings of 4th International System Administration and Network Engineering Conference. System and Network Engineering* (2004).

[3] FEYRER, H. System administration training in the virtual unix lab. *preprint* (2008).

[4] HÖPFNER, H. Open source software in education: a report of experience. *Informatics in Education-An International Journal*, Vol 2_1 (2003), 15–20.

[5] SKEITH, R., AND THORNTON, M. Unix and high-level language education using windows operating systems.

Student Driven Digital Signage

Raymond Scott Lawyer
Siena College
515 Loudon Road
Loudonville, NY 12211-1462
1-518-783-2463
rlawyer@siena.edu

ABSTRACT

Digital Signage has been used Siena College since 2004, in the Financial Trading Lab. Expansion was initially limited to a single display in the Lobby of the college's signature building.

The purpose was a medium for Academic affairs to disseminate academic events to the community. While the value of digital signage was known by a limited group at the institution, there was no movement to increase the presence of digital signs around campus. This changed in 2013 when the Student Senate championed a pilot project by providing funding for the hardware. Information Technology Services, ITS, provided support and the free to use, Rise Vision Content Management platform. We will present the lessons learned and continue to learn through this pilot implementation. We will discuss the hardware used as well as the use of the Rise Vision Platform.

Categories and Subject Descriptors

H.5.1 [**Multimedia Information Systems, Animations**]

General Terms

Management; Design; Economics; Experimentation

Keywords

Content Management; Cloud; Digital Signage; Google Apps for Education; Raspberry Pi; Rise Vision

1. ABOUT SIENA COLLEGE

Siena College is a private, Catholic liberal arts college located on 174 acres in suburban Loudonville, NY, two miles north of New York's capital city of Albany. Founded in 1937 by the Order of Friars Minor, Franciscan Friars.

SIGUCCS '15, November 09-13, 2015, St. Petersburg, FL, USA
© 2015 ACM. ISBN 978-1-4503-3610-9/15/11$15.00
DOI: http://dx.doi.org/10.1145/2815546.2815579

Siena offers 27 undergraduate degrees, plus 50 m inor and certificate programs through three schools, School of Business, School of Liberal Arts, and School of Science. One graduate degree, an M.S. in Accounting first is offered with an average 40 students enrolled each semester since the program was first offered in the fall of 2009.

Siena employs 229 full-time faculty, 119 adjunct faculty and 567 full and part-time staff and administrators.

2. DIGITAL SIGNAGE

Digital Signage [1] describes the display of information using multiple types of digital media on displays that most commonly use Light Emitting Diode (LED) or Liquid Crystal Display (LCD) technology, but also using projectors and screens. Digital signage system components include a display, media player (some sort of computer) or distribution system, and a content management system.

Digital signs can be seen at educational institutions, fast food restaurants, transportation hubs, museums, hotels, malls, and along highways. Their content can be updated easily and much more frequently than their static counterparts.

2.1 DIGITAL SIGNAGE AT SIENA

The Hickey Financial Technology Center (HFTC) was constructed in 2004 as part of a major renovation to the signature building on campus, Siena Hall. The center, at that time contained two LCD displays, a 3-color LED Ticker, and two 3-color LED Data Displays, and included one LCD display in the hallway outside the center. The ticker and data displays primary purpose was to display financial information and news from the financial markets; Only the ticker could display graphics.

The LCD display in the hallway became Siena's first digital sign using a PC based application, Rise Vision Enterprise. The application was powerful but also complex making it difficult to use for the average user. Content was created and stored on the same PC creating a single point of failure.

Rise introduced a new platform sometime around 2008, which was comprised of a client installed on a Windows PC (player) and a content management system hosted by Rise. This system was much easier to manage and use than the previous system, and it was shortly after this new platform was introduced that the first digital sign outside of the HFTC was installed. Content was managed by Academic Affairs while the hardware was supported by Information Technology Services (ITS).

Sometime in 2010, the Student Senate first approached Siena College's Chief Information Officer (CIO) about the possibility of installing additional digital signage across campus. They wanted an alternative to the traditional messy bulletin board.

Around the same time there were discussions held with the Public Safety department, cable provider, and campus TV station about a possible solution using the campus cable plant to distribute content, in particular emergency notifications. While ITS was able to obtain funding for the distribution, we were unable to secure funding for the displays at that time and with change in the student senate the project was put on hold.

Fast forward to March 2013 when the student senate contacted ITS about the possibility of installing digital signage. The Student Senate had proposed using the Raspberry Pi devices for the media players and WordPress for content management. ITS had internally evaluated three digital signage platforms Xibo, Concerto and the newly designed Rise Vision platform back in 2012. ITS determined that the new Rise Vision platform best met our needs and recommended it as the platform for this pilot project.

3. RISE VISION PLATFORM

Rise Vision is a cloud hosted digital signage platform hosted on the Google Cloud. The platform is free to use and is accessed via any web browser but Google Chrome is recommended. HTML5 presentations can be created using the included visual editor or any editor you choose.

Presentation content can include the same types of content that you would see on any web site including images and video. Many widgets are available to use so that you don't have to know how to code the HTML yourself, although you are able to customize the presentations in any way that you see fit. Presentations are stored on the platform but content included in the presentations use cloud storage. You can subscribe for unlimited storage from Rise Vision for a $10 a month fee or provide your own storage, for example Google Drive. The content needs to be accessible via a URL.

In order to receive the content from the platform you need a player, hardware that connects to the physical display(s) and runs the Rise Vision Chrome App Player. This player communicates with the platform, receives the content and displays the content on the displays. The player hardware can be a PC or laptop running Windows or Linux, a Raspberry Pi2, or an Android device (see Figure 1).

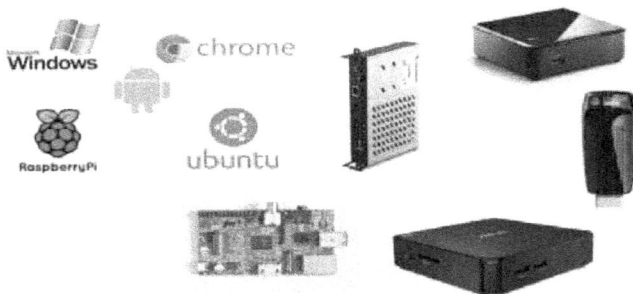

Figure 1 Rise Vision supported operating systems and hardware © Rise Vision

The presentations, displays (players) and users are all managed via the platform. Presentations are scheduled to be played where and when you choose. Users are added and their roles defined via the platform. The platform uses Google accounts for authentication so users are required to have a Google account.

The platform also allows the creation of sub-companies. These sub companies can have their own users, displays, presentations. Users in the sub-company can only access to those items within their sub-company. Content can be shared among sub companies using presentations, but only the users within the sub-company where the presentation resides can modify the content of the presentation.

4. STUDENT DRIVEN PILOT

The Student Senate was able to fund 6 consumer grade Sharp LCD TVs and 6 Raspberry Pi's to be used as the player hardware for the Rise Vision platform. The locations selected were a Student lounge in the Science Center, outside the post office, inside the sub shop, outside the campus store, and one in each of the two campus dining halls. The displays and Raspberry Pi's were ordered by the students and a work order generated for Facilities to install the necessary data and power outlets at the chosen display locations.

We met with the Student Senate and gave them a demonstration of the Rise Vision platform. Two student senators were tasked with the lead and were given access to the platform to begin learning the system and to create presentations.

Around the same time ITS began testing a first generation Raspberry Pi. ITS staff had no prior experience with them and they were not officially supported by Rise Vision. There was, and still is, much interest within the user community to find a low cost player solution. A member of the Rise Vision community modified the Rise Vision Linux player application to work with the Raspbian Linux distribution that runs on the Raspberry Pi. I configured the Raspberry Pi as described which included installation of the Rise Vision Player, Unclutter, and the configuration of screen saver and display settings.

We tried to run presentations that had multiple content areas including a photo album, images, ticker crawl, weather, and news information. We discovered the player would work well for a time, but would then crash. We found that for other than very basic presentations that the Raspberry Pi didn't work for us. Luckily the investment was not large.

We needed to find an alternate player solution as the official dedication of the displays was quickly approaching. We were able to use a combination of older laptops running Windows and Linux as well as several Chrome Boxes provided by Rise Vision as part of a pilot project with Google.

Several student senators became familiar enough with the platform and began to create presentations. At first content was limited to announcements and events from student organizations and the Office of Student Life. These presentations were created and managed entirely under the direction of the Student Senate without interference from professional staff.

The presentations were hard to read at times. Text was too small or voluminous to read, fonts and or the font color prevented the text from standing out from the background.

The digital signs were noticed by many on campus. Other departments expressed interest in using digital signage and comments were made about the difficulty in reading the presentations displayed on the existing signs. Text was too small or voluminous to read, fonts and or the font color prevented the text from standing out from the background.

Enrollment developed a presentation for its living room, the School of Science developed presentations for the Science Center, and Public Safety developed a presentation to provide its officers with information about campus events and other notices.

The students managing the digital signs realized that they had to make their presentations easier to read and that they needed to standardize on a template that was both attractive and functional. They asked for and were given permission to use the Enrollment template as the basis for a revised template. This updated template contains three content areas two of which they are using and one that will be deprecated.

The two content areas currently contain a calendar of events and an area for announcements. Presently the calendar of events information is fed from a shared Google Calendar that is maintained by a number of constituents in a number of campus departments. The announcements content area is maintained by the Office of Student Life.

5. POST PILOT

The pilot increased the awareness of digital signage and also demonstrated the value over the traditional bulletin board (see Figure 2). The students managing the signs told me they have seen an increase in attendance at student sponsored events since the installation of the digital signs.

Many departments have started to think about productive ways that they may wish to use digital signs. Many departments have already created content to be displayed on the student managed signs while others have shown interest in creating their own content, and others have made plans to install their own digital signs. Currently, twenty people from eleven different departments contribute content to the student managed signs.

With the increased usage of digital signs comes increased reliance. The hardware needs to be reliable, the content needs to be kept current, and presentations need to follow some defined best practices.

While we continue to investigate new types of player hardware and use a mix of Chrome Boxes and laptops running Windows and Linux, we have standardized on a preconfigured Linux player from Rise Vision. We have chosen to use Sharp consumer grade displays for most installations because of their low cost, compared to commercial grade displays, and their performance and reliability.

We have a good number of content contributors and awareness of digital signs continues to increase, but we need to continue to find ways to reach out to those departments that are not actively using digital signage. We also need to make sure that the content creators follow best practices so that the content is optimized for display on digital signs.

Making sure that there is continuity when it comes to managing content is especially important with students who are only here for four years. With presentation content stored in the cloud and the potential for this content to be stored in personal cloud storage (Google Drive) we need to make sure that all content is stored where others can access it when students and employees separate from the college.

We learned much from this student driven project. Letting the students have independence to create the presentations without interference from Student Life and others led to some of the growing pains that we discussed, but was also useful in exposing issues that we had not previously thought about. We currently provide informal, ad-hoc training on the use of the Rise Vision platform but realize in order to better leverage the platform and our displays that we need to formalize this training with a focus on industry and Siena best practices.

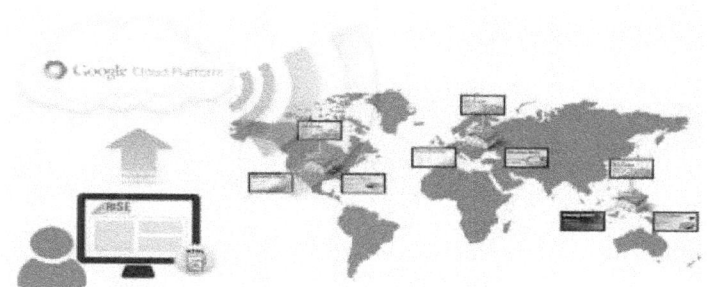

Figure 2. Rise Vision Platform. © Rise Vision

6. ACKNOWLEDGMENTS
Thanks to Rise Vision for the use of the Chrome Boxes and for permission to use their images. Thanks to Patrick Madden for his conversation with me.

7. REFERENCES
[1] "Digital Signage Glossary of Terms." Digital Signage Federation. Digital Signage Federation. Web. 05 April 2015. <http://www.digitalsignagefederation.org/glossary>.

Student Employee Attendance Point System

Carla Hoskins
Purdue University
150 N. University Street
West Lafayette, IN 47907
765-496-8334
hoskinsc@purdue.edu

Theresa Morgan
Purdue University
150 N. University Street
West Lafayette, IN 47907
765-494-1597
theresa@purdue.edu

Anders Johansson
Purdue University
150 N. University Street
West Lafayette, IN 47907
765-494-1597
jjohanss@purdue.edu

ABSTRACT

Are your student employees reliable? Do they show up for their shifts? Through attending SIGUCCS conferences we have learned that many other institutions are struggling with developing attendance policies that get their students into work. We have developed a point system that is working very well that we would like to share. We started with a 3 strikes you're out base and built on that. A no-call, no-show is worth 5 points and at 15 points we terminate. We have a point structure for late and sick shifts to complete the system. All of this information is covered during new Lab Assistant orientation and is published online where the students can review it. Each time a student accrues points we send them an email telling them how many points were added and what their total is for the semester. We meet with them when they reach 10 points to go over their points so far and to make sure they understand that they will be terminated if they reach 15 points. We reset their points at the beginning of finals week. Points accrued during finals week carry over to the next semester. We typically run with between 100 and 110 students and we terminate between 1 and 6 students each semester for attendance reasons. We feel that these numbers are great and thus demonstrate the effectiveness of our system.

Categories and Subject Descriptors

K.6.1 [Project and People Management]: Staffing

General Terms

Management, Documentation, Performance, Human Factors.

Keywords

Student Employment, Attendance.

SIGUCCS '15, November 09-13, 2015, St. Petersburg, FL, USA
© 2015 ACM. ISBN 978-1-4503-3610-9/15/11…$15.00
PDOI: http://dx.doi.org/10.1145/2815546.2815580

1. THE SYSTEM

Our Lab team at Purdue University employs approximately 110 student employees during the academic year. They work in 14 labs that are staffed either all day or in the evening. We have devised an attendance point system that allows us to make sure our student employees are accountable for their shifts and that we are treating everyone equally. The basis of our system is rooted in a 3 strikes and you're out model. Each student starts at 0 at the beginning of each semester, or for returning students, their counter is reset to zero the first day of finals week of the preceding semester. If a student has 3 no-call no-show shifts they are terminated for reaching 15 points. Hence the 3 strikes. Students are given lesser point values for being late, calling before their shift starts, or subbing out a shift less than 48 hours in advance. The points system is covered during orientation and the point assignment table is shared with them on their Wiki to be reviewed at any time during the semester.

Table 1. Point Assignments

Event	Points
05:01-10:00 minutes late	1
10:01-20:00 minutes late*	2
20:01-30:00 minutes late*	3
More than 30 minutes late*	4
Time-Off Request or Tradeboard post (24-48 hours in advance)	3
Time-Off Request or Tradeboard post (Less than 24 hours in advance)	4
No call, no show	5
Unexcused sick shift	4

* If you call in before the scheduled start of your shift to notify us that you will be late, one fewer point will be assigned (to a minimum of 1 point).

After a student has an incident that earns them any points they receive an email from the Administrative and Scheduling Coordinators, hereto referred to and known by the students as the Admins. After a student reaches or crosses the 10 point threshold they are sent an email advising that they must meet with a member of the Admin team before they will be permitted to work again. In this meeting the Admins go over each time the student earned points and why. The student are then reminded that they will be terminated if they reach 15 points. These meetings generally take less than 10 minutes. We believe that the communication with the students via the point emails and required Admin meeting are a big part of the success of this system. Sample emails can be seen in Section 5.

2. COMPANION POLICIES

2.1 Sick Shift Policy

There are couple companion policies that help make our attendance policy successful. Our sick shift policy states that the student must call in before the start Pof their shift in order for the shift to qualify as a sick shift. If they do call in before the start of their shift they must visit the free Purdue student clinic or a doctor of their choice within 2 weeks of the sick shift and provide the Admin team with a doctor's note for the shift to be excused. If they fail to do this they will be assigned 4 points, which is the same as the number of points assigned if someone calls in right before their shift for no reason. Before this year unexcused sick shifts were only assigned 2 points. About 50 percent of our sick shifts were unexcused at that point. After this adjustment unexcused sick shifts dropped to 30 percent.

2.2 Minimum Hours Per Week

We require all of our students to work a minimum of 11 hours per week. If they do not work 11 hours 3 times during the semester they are terminated. After not working 11 hours the first time, the student receives an email. After the second time, they are required to meet with the Admins. At this meeting we go over the two times they didn't meet the requirement and make sure that they understand they will be terminated if it happens again. A follow-up email is sent after the meeting. Having a sick shift during a week does not excuse a student from the 11 hour requirement. Students are not required to work 11 hours during weeks that contain holidays as most labs are closed during those weeks. They are required to work 11 hours during finals week.

3. SCHEDULING SYSTEM

We use a scheduling system called When To Work (W2W). This system has a tradeboard that we allow our students to use and it allows our students to submit time-off request. Time-off request must be submitted more than 48 hours before the start of their shift to avoid points. We picked this amount of time because Admin staff do not work on the weekend so this allows most requests for the weekend to be handled on Friday. Higher level student employees are given access to W2W to handle last minute weekend requests. The tradeboard is only used if a student can work but doesn't want to and they make this decision less than 48 hours before the shift starts. They can place their shift on the tradeboard and if someone else takes it they don't have to work and they don't receive any points. If no one takes the shift they must work the shift or call in if they can't work, otherwise it is considered a no-call no-show.

4. WRAP UP

When considering the number of student employees we employ during the academic year, and the demands we make regarding the number of hours they must work each week, we feel that this system is serving us well and might be beneficial to other institutions.

5. SAMPLE EMAILS

5.1 Late

John,

Because you were 21 minutes late for your shift in BCC, this will count as 3 points. You have a total of 5 points for the semester.

If you wish to appeal this, you must do so by responding to this email within 7 days.

5.2 Late-Called Ahead

Jane,

Because you were 11 minutes late for your shift in STEW but called ahead, this will count as 1 point. You have a total of 3 points for the semester.

If you wish to appeal this, you must do so by responding to this email within 7 days.

5.3 Tradeboard-Less than 24 Hours

Jeff,

Because you added this shift to the Tradeboard less than 24 hours in advance and were unable to work the shift or have another LA take the hours, you have been assigned 4 Attendance Points. You have a total of 6 Points this semester.

If you wish to appeal this, you must do so by responding to this email within 7 days. If you have any questions please contact us.

5.4 Tradeboard-24-48 Hours

Julie,

Because you added this shift to the Tradeboard 24-48 hours in advance and were unable to work the shift or have another LA take the hours, you have been assigned 3 Attendance Points. You have a total of 3 Points this semester.

If you wish to appeal this, you must do so by responding to this email within 7 days.

If you have any questions please contact us.

5.5 No-Call No-Show

Jim,

Because you missed your shift in BRES without notifying Operations, you have been assigned 5 attendance points. You have a total of 9 points this semester.

If you wish to appeal this, you must do so by responding to this email within 7 days. If you have any questions please contact us.

5.6 10 Point Meeting Required

Jasmine,

Because you were 15 minutes late for your shift in WTHR but called ahead, this will count as 1 point. You have a total of 10 points for the semester.

You are not allowed to work until you meet with a member of the Admin Team. If you cannot arrange a time to meet with one of us before your next shift at 9:30 on Wednesday, 5/6, the shift will be removed from your schedule.

Please reply to this email with dates and times you are available to meet with one of us to discuss your attendance.

If you wish to appeal this, you must do so within 7 days.

If you have any questions please contact us.

5.7 10 Point Meeting Confirmation

Joshua,

This email is to confirm that you and I met to discuss your attendance points today. You currently have 10 points for the semester, and if you attain 15 points we will terminate your employment. Please be sure to be on time for your shifts, and follow proper excusal procedures for the rest of the semester.

If you have any questions please contact us.

5.8 11 Hour Minimum (First Time)

Jerry,

Lab Assistants are required to work a minimum of 11 hours each week, you only worked 9.5 hours during the week of May 4th.

If you continue to work less than 11 hours we may terminate your employment.

If you have any questions please contact us.

5.9 11 Hour Minimum (Second Time)

Jack,

Lab Assistants are required to work a minimum of 11 hours each week, you only worked 8 hours during the week of May 4th and 10 hours during the week of May 11th.

You need to set up a time to come in and meet with one of us this week to discuss this. Please reply to this mail and let us know when you are available to meet.

If you continue to work less than 11 hours we may terminate your employment.

If you have any questions please contact us.

6. ACKNOWLEDGMENTS

Our thanks to Robby Crain, Jim Myers, Larry French and the many other predecessors that developed the foundation of the system we use today

Introduction of Unchanging Student User ID for Intra-Institutional Information Service

Yoshiaki Kasahara
Kyushu University
6-10-1 Hakozaki, Higashi-ku
Fukuoka 812-8581, Japan
+81 92 642 2297
kasahara.yoshiaki.820@m.kyushu-u.ac.jp

Naomi Fujimura
Kyushu University
4-9-1 Shiobaru, Minami-ku
Fukuoka, Japan
+81 92 553 4434
fujimura.naomi.274@m.kyushu-u.ac.jp

Eisuke Ito
Kyushu University
6-10-1 Hakozaki, Higashi-ku
Fukuoka 812-8581, Japan
+81 92 642 4037
ito.eisuke.523@m.kyushu-u.ac.jp

Masahiro Obana
Kyushu University
6-10-1 Hakozaki, Higashi-ku
Fukuoka 812-8581, Japan
+81 92 642 7654
obana.masahiro.049@m.kyushu-u.ac.jp

ABSTRACT

In Kyushu University, a traditional "Student ID" based on student number assigned by Student Affairs Department had been used as the user ID of various IT services for a long time. There were some security and usability concerns using Student ID as a user ID. Since Student ID was used as the e-mail address of the student, it was easy to leak outside. Student ID is constructed based on a department code and a serial number, so guessing other ID strings from one ID is easy. Student ID is issued at the day of the entrance ceremony, so it is not usable for pre-entrance education. Student ID will change when the student moves to another department or proceeds from undergraduate to graduate school, so he/she loses personal data when Student ID changes. To solve these problems, Kyushu University decided to introduce another unchanging user ID independent from Student ID. This paper reports the design of new user ID, ID management system we are using, and the effect of introduction of new user ID.

Categories and Subject Descriptors

K.6.5 [**Management of Computing and Information Systems**]: Security and Protection – *Authentication*

Keywords

Identity Management System; Service Continuity

1. INTRODUCTION

Universities provide various kinds of IT services such as e-mail, online course registration, e-learning and so on, to support students' learning, studying, and campus life. Usually a kind of "user identifier" is issued per user, and password authentication is used to identify and authenticate users for these services. For users' convenience, many organizations provide a unified identifier per user which can be used for various internal services instead of assigning different credentials per service [1][2].

Kyushu University also has various IT services for students. Most of them used user ID called "Student ID", derived from student number since 1995. Initially the authentication infrastructure using "Student ID" had been provided by the Educational Center for Information Processing as a part of IT education system (including Unix and Windows servers, PC terminals, e-learning system, etc to use during IT-related lecture courses). Now it is operated by the Information Infrastructure Initiative where we belong to. The use of Student ID has been expanded to other IT services operated by other departments such as course and record management system, syllabus system, library system, student portal etc.

Such ID has several advantages. Every student has one unique student number, so it is easy to uniquely identify a student by his/her Student ID. IT services operated by various departments don't need to maintain their own set of user IDs. The student number in Kyushu University includes a department code the student belongs to, and enrollment year. That information can be used for sorting/filtering a student list without additional metadata.

On the other hand, we gradually realized that using student number as user ID had some security risks. The student number isn't considered a secret, so it is weak against ID harvesting and brute force attack. For example, Student ID has been used as a local part (before the "@") of e-mail address due to historical reasons. Student number contains a serial number within a department, so it is easy to guess other possible ID strings from a Student ID and it can be used for reverse brute force attack (trying a trivial password against a large set of user IDs).

Also there were some difficulties providing services using student number. Student numbers are only finalized after finishing admission procedures, and a student receives the number with his/her ID card at an orientation course just after the entrance ceremony. Some departments wanted to allow successful candidates of our university to use a part of IT education system and e-learning system for pre-entrance education, but it wasn't possible to use student number as a user ID. Another problem was the discontinuity of user accounts between undergraduate and graduate school students. Because a student number will change after proceeding to a graduate school, the same student was treated as a different user in various services such as e-mail, library, and storage services. These students had to migrate their data by themselves, and using the new Student ID as a graduate school student is not possible until receiving a new ID card.

To solve these problems, we decided to introduce a new user ID scheme specialized for intra-institutional IT services beginning in 2014. In this paper, we describe the design of new user ID scheme, its implementation and deployment, and the effect after the introduction of new user ID.

2. IDENTIFIER IN KYUSHU UNIVERSITY

First of all, we describe a brief history of user identifiers in Kyushu University.

2.1 Student ID based on Student Number

The Educational Center for Information Processing started to issue a unified user identifier for students since 1995. At that time, to provide education of the Internet and IT literacy, accounts for all the students were needed on their IT education system.

Student ID was introduced based on student number. A student number in Kyushu University consists of 9 characters shown in Figure 1. Due to the limitation of operating system at that time, user ID had to start from an alphabet and the maximum length allowed was 8 characters, so a student ID was generated by shuffling some parts of the corresponding student number, which caused confusion among new students.

Student Number → Student ID

| 1 | A | B | 0 | 8 | 0 | 0 | 1 | X | ⇒ | a | b | 1 | 0 | 8 | 0 | 0 | 1 |

Figure 1 Student ID until 2008

This conversion had been used until 2008, even after such a limitation had become obsolete in modern operating systems. Since 2009, student numbers has been used as-is for Student IDs.

2.2 ID for Staff Members

For staff members, the Information Infrastructure Initiative started to provide a unified user ID starting in 2007. We discussed the design of the ID scheme considering attack tolerance, usability, maintainability, and the number of users [3]. Finally we decided to assign a unique 10-digit pseudorandom number to each user as a user ID, and named "SSO-KID" (roughly meant Single Sign On - Kyushu University ID).

2.3 Identity Management System

As we mentioned in Section 2.1 and 2.2, Kyushu University had introduced an identity management system (IDM) for students first. The IDM for students was implemented as a part of the IT education system. After that, IDM for staff members was introduced separately by another company in 2007. We had to maintain and interconnect both IDMs, which complicated the

entire system and repeatedly caused inconsistencies of user account data between them.

Upon replacement of the IT education system in the end of 2013 fiscal year, we decided to introduce a new, unified IDM containing data of both students and staff members, because IDM for students would also retire with the old education system. We considered it as an opportunity to introduce the new ID scheme for students similar to SSO-KID in order to solve problems with using "Student ID" derived from a student number.

3. REASONS FOR NEW ID SCHEME

In this section, we describe more details of issues using "Student ID" derived from a student number as a user ID and expected outcome by introducing new user ID scheme. The new scheme was similar to SSO-KID (for staff members), and called "Student SSO-KID".

3.1 Security Risk

We started to consider that security risks of using student numbers as user ID wasn't negligible. "Student ID" is (almost) the same as student number, and student numbers are not considered a secret. It is clearly printed on a student ID card, and commercial services offering discounts to students often make a copy of the face of the card or note the student number of a customer.

Historically, Kyushu University used "Student ID" as the local part of e-mail address of the student. For example, a student whose student number is "1AB14001X" is assigned an e-mail address "1AB14001X@s.kyushu-u.ac.jp". Recently we started to provide a service to create an alias of the e-mail address derived from the user's real name [4][5], but e-mail addresses based on student numbers are still actively used internally. As mentioned in Section 1, student numbers contains a sequence number, so it is easy to generate possibly valid IDs from one real ID obtained from outgoing e-mail messages.

If valid IDs are known, it is easier to intrude into an IT system by brute force attack. There were some incidents of e-mail account hijacking recently. We don't know the real cause of hijacking, but we decided to separate student number and user ID to mitigate some risks.

3.2 Service for Pre-entrance Candidates

In Kyushu University, a student number is issued when a candidate has finished the admission procedure after receiving an acceptance letter. The list of newly enrolled students is finalized at 17:00 on March 31st every year, so their student numbers can be finalized on April 1st or later. Actually the number will be available to these students on receipt of their student ID cards in the entrance orientation class after the entrance ceremony around April 7th.

As far as using Student ID, other university events which need to use IT systems have to be scheduled after giving student ID cards, but there were demands to offer services for pre-entrance candidates. For example, the information department wanted to provide an e-learning course to let them self-study about the basic knowledge of the university IT services. Also, the student affairs department wanted to allow early course registration for popular classes. To enable these services, we needed a new user ID scheme independent from student numbers.

To solve the problem, we decided to assign student SSO-KID to successful candidates and provide information about how to activate the account with an acceptance letter. The available space of 10-digit SSO-KID is one billion, so assigning unique SSO-KID to candidates is not a problem. If a candidate declines, we just deactivate the SSO-KID and never use it again.

3.3 Health Checkup and PC Tutorial

In Kyushu University, all the undergraduate students must get a health checkup in the year of entrance and graduation. About 5,000 students get a checkup, so an efficient method is needed to identify who finished a checkup. Kyushu University requires all the students bring their own PC for learning [6], and a similar method is also needed in a Bring Your Own Device (BYOD) orientation class for newly enrolled students (around 2,700 participants).

Usually a student can be identified quickly by a barcode of the student number printed on his/her student ID card. But newly enrolled students need to get a health checkup and a BYOD orientation class before they receive their ID card, so we had to identify them manually. By providing the student's SSO-KID printed on an acceptance letter (with barcode), student identification should be far easier and efficient.

3.4 Continuity of User Accounts

As mentioned in Section 1, discontinuity of user accounts between undergraduate and graduate school students was also a problem. A student number changes after proceeding to a graduate school or moving to a different department. Due to that, the same student was treated as a different user in various services such as e-mail, library, and storage service. Such students had to migrate their data by themselves, or their data would be erased. The previous IDs are valid for one month after graduation for convenience, but that implies another security risk because students can use university's IT services for a while even after graduation.

By introducing student SSO-KID and assigning one unchanging unique ID to each student, students can use IT services without interruption and do not need to perform data migration. To do that, we need to track change of each student's student number appropriately.

4. DEPLOYMENT AND EFFECTS

In this section, we describe our strategy to introduce and deploy student SSO-KID, and effects observed after the deployment.

4.1 Deploy Strategy

As mentioned in Section 3, making a user ID independent from a student number should have many benefits. On the other hand, sudden change of the user ID scheme must be confusing from the users' perspective, and it is almost impossible to adopt the change to all the IT system in our university at once.

To allow easier and smoother transition of the user ID scheme, we decided on two deployment strategies. First, only new students enrolled in 2014 or later will use student SSO-KID as their primary user ID. Actually a student SSO-KID will be assigned to every student, but existing students will continue to use Student ID as their user ID until graduation or proceeding to graduate school. Second, to support IT systems which cannot adopt student SSO-KID by administrative or technical reasons, we will continue to provide a Lightweight Directory Access Protocol (LDAP) server which can authenticate users by Student ID.

4.2 LDAP Server Configuration

Kyushu University authentication infrastructure provides LDAP servers for intra-institutional IT services [7]. These LDAP servers provide user ID information in "cn" and "uid" attributes. Before introducing student SSO-KID, both cn and uid hold Student ID. To deploy student SSO-KID, we decided to provide two kind of LDAP servers as shown in (A) and (B) of Table 1. LDAP (A) is provided for services which cannot adopt student SSO-KID immediately. We encourage using LDAP (B) to gradually migrate from Student ID to student SSO-KID. We decided to keep Student ID in cn, because in some cases a system needs to search students by a Student ID or student number. Also by using a custom LDAP search filter, a system can authenticate students by both Student ID and student SSO-KID. We expect that LDAP (B) will become LDAP (C) within several years.

Table 1 User ID information in LDAP servers

	(A)	(B)		(C)
	Legacy	Enrolled before 2014	Enrolled in 2014 or later	Student SSO-KID only
uid	Student ID	Student ID	Student SSO-KID	Student SSO-KID
cn	Student ID	Student ID	Student ID	Student ID

Upon introducing student SSO-KID, administrators of the e-mail system and campus cloud systems decided to use student SSO-KID for all the students. These systems implemented their own LDAP (C) server and populated the database by using data provided from the IDM system. Both systems happened to be replaced/upgraded at almost the same time as the IDM replacement, and it was decided to fully adopt student SSO-KID from the beginning.

4.3 Acceptance Letter

As mentioned in Section 3.2 and 3.3, student SSO-KID is included in an acceptance letter as shown in Figure 2.

The letter includes student SSO-KID, an activation code, and a

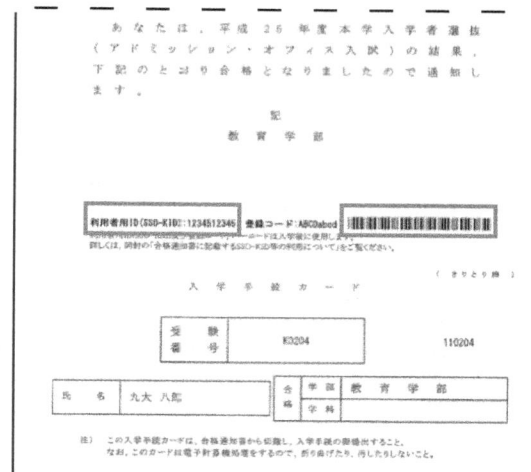

Figure 2. An Example of Acceptance Letter

barcode of student SSO-KID. The activation code is required to activate the account using an online activation site, and after activation the student can use a part of IT education system and e-learning system in Kyushu University before entrance. The barcode is used to efficiently identify students in a health checkup and BYOD orientation.

4.4 Student ID Card

From 2014, student SSO-KID is printed on the back side of student ID card as shown in Figure 3. It was difficult to replace all the existing ID cards at once, and it was another reason we didn't deprecate Student ID immediately after introducing student SSO-KID. For compatibility with existing equipment, the barcode denotes student number, not student SSO-KID.

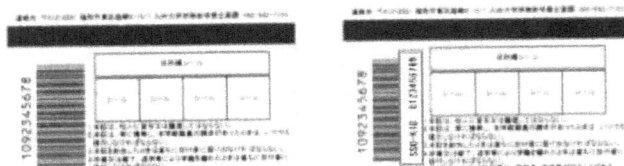

Figure 3 Backside of student ID Card (Old / New)

4.5 Effects

Until now, overall effects of introducing student SSO-KID have been favorable. For example, we reduced the reception process of a BYOD orientation class from 30 minutes to 5 minutes. Staff of health checkup also welcomed barcode of student SSO-KID printed on an acceptance letter because it simplified the process of new student identification greatly.

As mentioned in Section 3, introducing student SSO-KID has some benefits including lower security risks by reducing unnecessary exposure of user ID, providing pre-entrance services, and account continuity.

In 2014, pre-entrance learning materials were not fully prepared, but online learning classes were partially provided to some pre-entrance candidates, which was not possible before introducing student SSO-KID.

Because student SSO-KID was introduced in the end of 2013, almost all students still need to change their user ID from Student ID to SSO-KID when proceeding from undergraduate to graduate school, so the effect of account continuity wasn't notable. For the e-mail service, we designed the system that these students could change their user ID from Student ID to SSO-KID without service interruption. It was mostly successful in 2014, but partially broken in 2015 due to slight modification of the e-mail service and mismatching of account handling policy between IDM and the e-mail service. We had already sorted out the root cause of the problem, and are now discussing how to implement a solution.

5. CONCLUSION

In this paper, we described the design and deployment of a new student user ID for intra-institutional IT service in Kyushu University. Previously we used "Student ID" derived from student number as a user ID, but there were some security and usability concerns.

Beginning fiscal year 2014, we started to assign a student SSO-KID to every student which was a unique 10-digit pseudorandom value, and used it as a user ID for various IT services. By introducing student SSO-KID, several issues caused by using student number were solved. Especially the observed effect of a more efficient student verification process during new student's health checkup and BYOD orientation class.

We have to refine and improve account management and IDM operation continuously. For better support of account continuity, each IT system needs some modification, and legacy systems must be replaced. Many IT systems in Kyushu University are not under our direct control, and we need to encourage the use of student SSO-KID. Also, we will cooperate to implement better pre-entrance services for students.

6. ACKNOWLEDGMENTS

Our thanks to all the users using our IT services, and staff members of the authentication infrastructure working group to develop and maintain these systems in Information Infrastructure Initiative of Kyushu University.

7. REFERENCES

[1] Ito, E., Kasahara, Y., and Fujimura, N. 2013. Implementation and operation of the Kyushu university authentication system. In *Proceedings of the SIGUCCS 2013*(Chicago, IL, November 3 - 8, 2013). ACM, New York, NY, 137-142. DOI=http://dx.doi.org/10.1145/2504776.2504788.

[2] Ohta, Y., Kajita, S., Tajima, Y., Tajima, H., Hirano, Y., Naito, H., and Mase, K. 2010. Name Identification Method for Lifelong ID in Higher Educational Institutions. Journal of IPSJ, Vol. 51, No.3, 965-973. (In Japanese)

[3] Nogita, M., Kasahara, Y., Ito. E., and Suzuki, T. 2006. A Study of Identifier Naming Conventions Suitable for User Authentication. Technical report of IEICE. ISEC Vol.106, No. 411 (20061206), 67-72.

[4] Fujimura, N., Togawa, T., Kasahara, Y., and Ito, E. 2011. Primary Mail Service for students based on their names. *IPSJ SIG Technical Report*, Vol. 2011-IOT-14, No. 10, 1-6.

[5] Fujimura, N., Togawa, T., Kasahara, Y., and Ito, E. 2012. Introduction and experience with the Primary Mail Service based on their names for students. In *Proceedings of the SIGUCCS 2012* (Memphis, TN, October 17 - 19, 2012). ACM, New York, NY, 11-14. DOI= http://dx.doi.org/10.1145/2382456.2382460.

[6] Fujimura, N. 2013. Bring your own computers project in Kyushu University. In *Proceedings of the SIGUCCS 2013*(Chicago, IL, November 3 – 8, 2013). ACM, New York, NY, 43-50. DOI= http://dx.doi.org/10.1145/2504776.2504789

[7] Ito, E., Kasahara. Y., and Fujimura, N. 2012. A study of LDAP load balancing for University ICT services. *IPSJ SIG Technical Report*, Vol. 2012-CSEC-57/2012-IOT-17, No. 11, 51-56.

Five Things I Have Learned From My Travel Adventures That Have Made Me a Better Employee

R. Eddie Vinyaratn
University of Southern California
School of Social Work
669 West 34Th Street
Los Angeles, CA 90089-0411
011-213-821-6752
vinyarat@usc.edu

ABSTRACT

There have been many studies done supporting the importance of work-life balance. There are many benefits to taking time off from work, not the least of which are reducing stress and improving mental health. Taking time off from work will also make you a better employee. I love to travel and I love technology. The five things that I have learned from my travel adventures that have made me a better employee are organization skills, problem solving, multicultural sensitivity, communication, and how to breach my comfort zone.

Categories and Subject Descriptors

K.6.1 [**Management of Computing and Information Systems**]: Project and People Management – *management techniques, systems analysis and design.*

General Terms

Management, Performance, Experimentation, Human Factors.

Keywords

Work-life balance, organization, problem solving, tolerance, communication.

1. INTRODUCTION

We spend many hours of our days at work. In today's connected society, work does not stop except for sleep. Even then, work can impinge. With smart phones, one can be at work almost 24/7. However, this can lead to a stressed out employee and a decrease in morale. One of the many things that an employer can do to increase morale and reduce burnout is to encourage a better work-life balance. One way to achieve a better work-life balance is to take time off from work to travel.

One thing that is constant when you travel is change. Change causes a person to look at new ideas and innovations. I have had the opportunities to take time off from work to travel to different parts of the world. From these travel adventures, and through the change process, the five things that I have learned that have made me a better employee are organization skills, problem solving,

SIGUCCS '15, November 09-13, 2015, St. Petersburg, FL, USA
ACM 978-1-4503-3610-9/15/11.
http://dx.doi.org/10.1145/2815546.2815553

multicultural sensitivity, communication, and how to breach my comfort zone.

2. FIVE THINGS I HAVE LEARNED

2.1 Organization

With limited vacation time (compared to seemingly unlimited work time), a successful travel adventure requires research and planning. Going to a new travel destination without knowing what types of activities are available at the site can add a degree of chaos, which will have the opposite of the desired de-stressing results. My planning includes researching the activities that the destination has to offer and creating a To-Do Activities list. For example, some of the available options from one of my recent trips included rafting, hiking, bungee jumping, and riding a zip line. Since one of the goals of taking time off is to relax, I try to have no more than one major activity planned in a day while I travel.

I use an app on my smart phone to keep track of all the activities in my To-Do Activities list. I may have found more potential activities for a destination than available days. My To-Do list lets me adjust my priorities during my trip, depending on how tired I am after the day before or the weather.

Similarly, I also use To-do lists to organize and prioritize my work. I find this to be the simplest way to keep up with all my projects and responsibilities. I usually have more than one major goal a day to complete. To keep track of all my responsibilities, I use my Office 365 Tasks as my To-Do list.

2.2 Problem Solving

Travel to foreign lands can frequently involve getting lost and dealing with chaos, somewhat like your typical day at work. With all the planning and research prior to a trip, something unexpected always occurs. My biggest problem when I am travelling is I always get lost. I am proud to say that I have no problem asking for directions – a quick fix to the problem of being lost. Over the years I have found that the local people give the best directions, even when there is a language barrier. Local residents also give the best advice on places to eat and things to do. Their suggestions may end up making it onto my To-Do Activities list!

Work problems can also be like getting lost when I travel. In this case, I get lost trying to find a solution to a problem. When I need help at work, I research for solutions from online resources. This can give me too many options or solutions. The most valuable resource is my colleague. By having the courage to ask them for help, I am able to deal with challenges new and old.

2.3 Multicultural Sensitivity

I have been able to learn about cultural diversity and different traditions during my travel. I have gained invaluable experience from being able to interact with the people in their country. One example was while travelling through the northern part of Thailand. I was born in Thailand and speak Thai. However, when I interacted with the hill tribes people I discovered they speak their own dialect and live their lives much differently than other Thais.

To get along well with your colleagues, it is important to be respectful of their cultures. The faculty and staff at USC School of Social Work are diverse and come from many backgrounds. Working in Information Technology has given me the opportunity to interact with most of the faculty and staff in the School. In addition to remembering all of their names, I try to connect with them on a more personal level. By getting to know them more on a personal level, I have been able to be more sensitive to their culture.

2.4 Communication

I have been to countries where English is not the primary language. When I was travelling through France, the only words I knew in French were *bonjour, si'l vous plait* and *merci*. The only sentence I knew in French was *"Parlez-vous anglais?"* But I was able to travel through France with my limited French because I made the effort to speak their language (and very likely because they speak English as well—but only if you ask them in French).

In Information Technology, there exists a lot of "tech speak" that may as well be French to the faculty and staff. I try to eliminate technical jargon when explaining problems and solutions to non-technical Social Workers. Combined with knowing a little bit about their background, I can gauge their technical level. However, I still keep all of my explanation as simple as possible unless they ask for technical descriptions.

2.5 Breach your comfort zone

The most exciting thing about travelling is the opportunity to try new things. From eating unfamiliar food in Jamaica to bungee jumping in New Zealand, travelling has given me an opportunity to experience change. One of the most memorable adventures was rappelling off Morning Glory Arch in Moab, Utah with my wife as the counter weight. This was a change of activity and scenery from my most exciting day at the office.

Similarly, technology changes constantly and we must embrace change. The faculty and staff may not adapt to change as rapidly as the IT staff. We try to provide as much support as possible when we implement new software or platforms. We provide one on one training, as well as online resources to help them succeed. We try to help them breach their comfort zone and allow them to embrace change.

I must also admit that there are some faculty and staff in the School I would rather not have to work with. I suspect that this is true of everyone. But I still must find a way to assist these people, just as I found a way to try some strange food in Jamaica. It is something that we all must do. When faced with one of these people, thinking about looking over a cliff edge and bungee jumping helps me dive into working with them.

3. CONCLUSIONS

Taking time off from work is important to achieve a work-life balance. Travelling and experiencing change will broaden your perspective in life. I have become better at organizing my responsibilities and solving problems and prioritizing my tasks. I learned how to be more culturally sensitive and better communicate with my colleagues in IT as well as with the school's faculty and staff. Lastly, change encourages innovations and new ideas that can lead to increase activity and efficiency.

From my past adventures, I am a better employee by applying all the new experiences to provide better customer service for the faculty, staff, and students at my School.

4. ACKNOWLEDGMENTS

Thank you to my wife, Susan, for being my travel partner. Many thanks to Terry Wolff for allowing me to take time off from work to be able to achieve work-life balance. And many thanks to SIGUCCS family for reviewing and making this paper possible.

Just Another Day at the Shop: From Small Business to College IT

Travis Freudenberg
Carleton College
1 North College Street
Northfield, MN 55057
1-507-222-4074
tfreudenberg@carleton.edu

ABSTRACT

In the fall of 2012, I closed the doors of my computer service and repair shop and started working for Carleton College as a Computing Support Specialist stationed in the help desk. Though the client base I supported increased tremendously and my title and responsibilities changed, at the end of the day my goal was still the same: provide end users with the best technical support in town. In this paper I will examine how the skills gained and lessons learned running a small IT business (interrupt driven time management, customer service as a way of life, and Murphy's Law as a constant) can be applied to the unique demands of IT in higher education.

Categories and Subject Descriptors

K.6.1 [**MANAGEMENT OF COMPUTING AND INFORMATION SYSTEMS**]: Project and People Management – *management techniques, staffing, systems analysis and design, systems development*

General Terms

Management, Performance, Human Factors.

Keywords

Helpdesk, time management, customer service.

1. INTRODUCTION

While most entrepreneurs take the sensible path and start their own business after acquiring years of experience and building a well thought out business plan, my promotion from Field Service Technician at Next Level Cafe to Company President of Reboot Computers took place in less than 24 hours, as the company decided to close the office I was working in, and I made the decision to buy it from them and rebrand it as my own business. In the two years that I was the sole employee of Reboot, I had to learn (often the hard way) how to manage my time and deal with the unexpected, all while striving for a high level of customer service. When I started working at Carleton, I started applying these skills and experiences to my new career at the helpdesk.

1.1 About Reboot Computers

Reboot Computers provided residential and small business IT support from a retail storefront in Northfield, Minnesota from 2010-2012, focusing on virus removal, data recovery, hardware repair, and data backup.

1.2 About Carleton College

Carleton College is a private undergraduate liberal arts college in Northfield, Minnesota. The college currently enrolls 1,991 students and employs 220 full time faculty, and has a professional IT staff of 40 with an additional 50 student staff at the helpdesk.

1.3 About the ITS Helpdesk

Carleton College's ITS Helpdesk is a combined service point that provides support to faculty, staff, and students. Three full time staff supervise the 50 student staff at two service points, and provide primary phone support during business hours to faculty and staff.

2. Lessons Learned

2.1 Interrupt Driven Time Management

The majority of literature devoted to time management focuses on the idea of eliminating interruptions in order to complete projects and tasks [1]. In both a retail service and college helpdesk environment, interruptions are the rule, not the exception. In a retail environment, a walk-in customer or a phone call were not so much interruptions as they were business opportunities, and I quickly had to learn to incorporate these interruptions into my workday. As the only employee of my shop, I could be replacing a logic board, only to be interrupted by a customer walking in with a virus infected laptop, a phone call from a business client with an Outlook problem, and a text message from my Google Voice number. I had to develop a way to manage these interruptions, and I've been able to apply this to my work at the Carleton ITS Helpdesk, which has a significantly higher service volume. The obvious difference between working as a sole proprietor and working as a member of a team is the depth of support available in a team environment. As such, I was able to expand from simple triage style management (based on urgency of the issue and service level agreements) to a delegation-based model.

The Rules of Interrupt Driven Time Management

2.1.1 It is not sustainable.

Interruptions generate work in the form of service tickets. You will need a block of uninterruptable time to focus on resolving these tickets, either through delegation to the appropriate team member or by working on them yourself.

SIGUCCS'15, November 09–13, 2015, St. Petersburg, FL., USA
ACM 978-1-4503-3610-9/15/11.
http://dx.doi.org/10.1145/2815546.2815552

2.1.2 You must remain open for interruption.

At Carleton's helpdesk, the expectation is that the majority of faculty and staff phone calls will be answered by professional staff. While first call resolution is important, issues that will require extended phone support time are ideally resolved by scheduling a service call with the end user, or delegating the ticket to the appropriate team member for resolution, keeping you free to continue taking calls and answering questions from the student staff.

2.1.3 You will need a support network.

It is crucial to have available student staff, or additional professional staff, available to assist in times of high call volume or for the delegation of in depth support issues.

2.2 Customer Service As A Way Of Life

The most valuable asset a service company has is its reputation, and it is earned slowly through excellent customer service. Unfortunately, a thoroughly dissatisfied customer, a poor Yelp or Google review, or a "I wouldn't bring my laptop to that guy" comment down at the local coffee shop can quickly affect the bottom line of a retail service company, as customers will simply go someplace else for service. While working for NLC, our CEO encouraged us to create "Raving Fans" – to provide a level of customer service that created happy, and returning, clients [2]. When I went into business for myself, I maintained that same philosophy. My chief competition was Geek Squad, and my goal was to have the flexibility to compete with them on price, but more importantly, in customer satisfaction. This meant the occasional free repair or home visit. The idea was that the good will gained would be worth more to my reputation than a diagnostic fee. When I transitioned to Carleton, I was relieved to not have to worry about the financial aspects of a particular service call; I could focus on providing customer support. There are other considerations that come into play in the world of academic IT, however. While IT departments in higher education have the benefit of having a captive audience (we're effectively the only shop in town), it is just as important to focus on how we are interacting with our customers, and equally important, the importance of timely and efficient service. Our CTO recently tasked our department with following Disney's "Plus One" approach to customer service; the idea that "you should solve your client's problem and then go one step further in providing value to them" [3]. Though we don't see the same immediate financial benefits, we now have a shared departmental philosophy, a focus on service metrics to judge our own performance, and a renewed importance of training our own professional and student staff.

2.3 Murphy's Law As A Constant

IT in general, and the helpdesk in particular, can be very stressful places to work. Just as nobody goes to the auto shop to say "my car's running great!", when clients walked into the front door of my shop or call the helpdesk, it is because they have a problem, and are usually frustrated because of it. It is therefore crucial as an IT professional to expect, and accept, the chaotic nature of our profession. Within the first six months of opening my shop, I had dissolved my business partnership, lost one-third of my shop space to a remodel, experienced weeks of construction that left my server room covered in concrete dust, lost access to my front door for a week, and had the wrong number and address placed in the phone book. Learning to stay positive and focus on providing great customer service, despite the slings and arrows of outrageous fortune, is the key to a successful IT business or department.

When I joined the staff at Carleton, it was during a time when ITS was in transition. The helpdesk was entering the third year of providing support to both faculty/staff and students (having previously been separated into two different divisions), and we had just begun the search for a CTO. After various changes in professional staff at the helpdesk, the start of fall term 2014 found us down one full time staff member at the helpdesk, and with a student staff that consisted of nearly 50% brand new, untrained student workers. Naturally, this was the month that we would experience the highest call volume we'd seen since switching to a Voice over IP (VoIP) system the previous fall (see Figure 1).

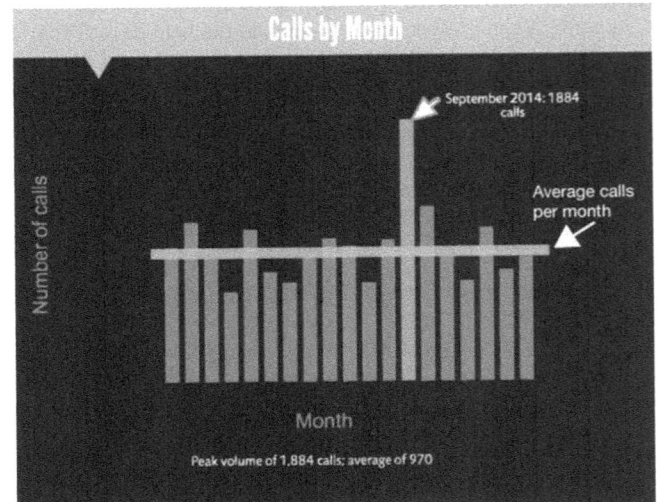

Figure 1. Help desk call volume, per month.

The adage "hope for the best but expect the worst" is a helpful training tool, and at a spring all-staff ITS meeting at Carleton, we role-played through various "Perfect Storm" scenarios to test our IT incident response strategy. The training proved very useful, as on May 13th, 2015, in the process of installing a backup fiber line, our primary fiber line was damaged and we lost all external network access, including email (as it was outsourced through a third party provider), for approximately six hours.

3. Conclusion

Though the day-to-day operations are different, the core values of an IT business and a college helpdesk are essentially the same: Provide the best possible technical support to enable the end user (be it business client or college community) to do their job.

4. REFERENCES

[1] Morgenstern, Julie. *Time Management from the Inside Out.* 2nd ed. New York: St. Martin's Griffin, 2004. Print.

[2] Blanchard, Kenneth H, and Sheldon M. Bowles. *Raving Fans: A Revolutionary Approach to Customer Service.* New York: Morrow, 1993. Print.

[3] Scannell, Janet. "From The CTO." *ITS Update Newsletter;* (Apr. 2015), https://apps.carleton.edu/campus/its/about/update/?story_id=1262944&issue_id=1262939

A Wearable LED Matrix Sign System Which Shows a Tweet of Twitter and Its Application to Campus Guiding and Emergency Evacuation

Takashi Yamanoue

Fukuyama University
Fukuyama, Hiroshima
729-0292, Japan
+81-84-936-2111
yamanoue@fuip.fukuyama-u.ac.jp

Keiichiro Yoshimura

Kagoshima University
Korimoto, Kagoshima
890-0065, Japan
+81-99-285-7187
k7290946@kadai.jp

Kentaro Oda

Kagoshima University
Korimoto, Kagoshima
890-0065, Japan
+81-99-285-7187
odaken@cc.kagoshima-u.ac.jp

Koichi Shimozono

Kagoshima University
Korimoto, Kagoshima
890-0065, Japan
+81-99-285-7187
simozono@cc.kagoshima-u.ac.jp

ABSTRACT

A Wearable LED matrix sign system which shows a tweet of Twitter is discussed. The wearable LED matrix sign of the system is a mobile sign and it can be located any place any time, if a person wears the sign and goes there at the time. The wearable LED matrix sign can be controlled from a remote place by a manager because its contents can be modified using Twitter. The manager also can know where is the LED matrix sign using the GPS function of the LED matrix sign or calling the person who wears the sign. The LED matrix sign system can be used for special events such as conferences on a campus. It also can be used for emergency evacuation.

Categories and Subject Descriptors

H.4.3 [**Information systems**]: Communications applications

General Terms

Bulletin boards, Internet

Keywords

Signage, Wearable, Twitter, Campus information, Emergency

1. INTRODUCTION

We have many signs on our campus. In order to manage them and keep them up to date, we can use LED matrix signs today. If they are portable and they can be located any place any time, and if they could be controlled from a remote place by a manager, they can be more useful for special events such as conferences on a campus.

SIGUCCS'15, November 09–13, 2015, St. Petersburg, FL., USA
ACM 978-1-4503-3610-9/15/11.
http://dx.doi.org/10.1145/2815546.2815551

Emergencies on a campus are also special events. Public relations in an emergency is very important. Good public relations may save people's lives which might not be saved if there were no public relations. And it is hard to predict the location and the time in an emergency, so an LED matrix sign, which can be located any place any time, is also useful in an emergency.

We can use a flexible color LED matrix[5], an Arduino board[8], and a high-performance battery[10] today. We also can use a smartphone and we can acquire information at any place and any time today using the smartphone. We have developed a wearable LED matrix sign which shows a tweet of Twitter by combining the latest technologies such as the above technologies, and our previous work[2][3]. The wearable LED matrix sign is a mobile sign and it can be located any place any time, if a person wears the sign and goes there at the time. The wearable LED matrix sign can be controlled from a remote place by a manager because its contents can be modified using Twitter. The manager also can know where is the LED matrix sign using the GPS function of the LED matrix sign or calling the person who wears the sign. So the manager can update the message on the wearable LED matrix sign depending on the location of the sign.

2. OUTLINE OF THE LED MATRIX SIGN SYSTEM

Figure 1 shows the outline of the wearable LED matrix sign system. A message, which is submitted to Twitter from a smartphone or PC, is shown on the LED matrix of the LED matrix sign system. The location of the wearable LED matrix sign is shown on the smartphone or PC using Twitter.

The letter which is shown on the matrix is a letter of the message which is tweeted on Twitter with the designated hash tag. All parts of the message are shown by scrolling the message from right to left. The system searches the latest Twitter message with the designated hash tag periodically, and shows the message on the LED matrix sign. The system also acquires the location of the LED matrix sign periodically, and shows the location, as a link to the location on the Google map in a Twitter message, on the smartphone or PC.

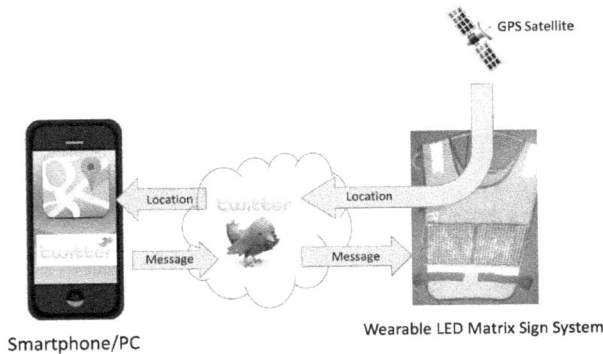

Figure 1. Outline of the wearable LED matrix system.

3. POSSIBLE USAGES

3.1 Signage for conferences

When we have a conference in our campus, we usually prepare many signs for guiding participants to the appropriate conference rooms. Signs for the conference are placed temporarily. They are not placed permanently. Signs for the conference should be noticeable to many people. Some rooms for the conference usually have several sessions. So signs which guide the participants of the conference into their intended rooms should be changed frequently. There also may be unplanned changes.

Our wearable LED matrix sign system meets all of these requirements. When the conference is held, some members of staff wear the LED matrix sign, and go to the places such as the entrance of the university, the buildings of the conference, the entrances of the conference rooms, and intersections or branches to the conference rooms. The manager can know where the sign is, and the manager can send the appropriate content to each sign. The manager can change the contents of each sign just by tweeting messages with appropriate hash tags.

3.2 Signage for emergency evacuation

Providing appropriate information for evacuation to students and staff in a campus in an emergency is one of the most important and difficult work of managers on the campus. The manager should acquire current status of many places, predict the status for the near future and provide appropriate information to people who may suffer from the dangerous status. Sometimes, the information should be provided to selected people in order to avoid panic. In a case of gun man attack, the information should be provided to people excepting the gun man.

Twitter and other social networking services are indispensable as robust communication tools when phone lines are down. We learned this fact when we met the great east Japan earthquake in March 11th, 2011[1].

Our wearable LED matrix sign system also meets all of these requirements. The sign system can be used in an emergency just like the usage of a conference.

4. RELATED WORKS

4.1 tshirtOS

Ballantine's T-shirt OS[9] is also a wearable LED matrix system. If the OS is widely used, this OS will overcome our system. However, this OS has not been widely used yet. So our wearable LED matrix sign system may be useful now.

4.2 CuteCircuit

CuteCircuit[11] is a company which provides shining dresses. The dresses twinkle by LEDs, and the pattern of the twinkle can be controlled by a smartphone. The dresses of the CuteCircuit are made for stages, not for signage of our campus.

5. CONCLUSION

We have developed a wearable LED matrix sign system which can be controlled by Twitter. We also discussed the usage of the system as a temporary campus signage and a public relations tool in an emergency. This wearable sign system can also be used for other purposes than for conferences and emergencies in campus, such as guiding students and staff to the appropriate places and telling them what they should do without a loud voice, when a ceremony is held in a campus.

6. ACKNOWLEDGEMENT

In order to develop the wearable LED matrix sign system, we have used hardware, software and data of [4][6][8][12]. We thank them.

7. REFERENCES

[1] Omori, Yoshio, 2011. Crisis Management in the Aftermath of 3/11: A Comparison with Kobe. In *Nippon.com*. http://www.nippon.com/en/in-depth/a00104/

[2] Yamanoue, Takashi, Oda, Kentaro, and Shimozono, Koichi, 2012. A M2M system using Arduino, Android and Wiki Software. In *Proceedings of the 3rd IIAI International Conference on e-Services and Knowledge Managerment* (Fukuoka, Japan, September 20-22, 2012). IIAI ESKM 2012. IEEE Computer Society Washington, DC, USA 123-128. DOI= http://dx.doi.org/10.1109/IIAI-AAI.2012.33.

[3] Yamanoue, Takashi, Oda, Kentaro, and Shimozono, Koichi, 2013. An Inter-Wiki Page Data Processor for a M2M System, In proceedings of the 4th International Conference on E-Service and Knowledge Management (Matsue, Japan, Augast 31 - September 4. 2013). IIAI ESKM 2013, IEEE Computer Society, Washington, DC, USA. 45-50. DOI= http://dx.doi.org/10.1109/IIAI-AAI.2013.48.

[4] Shinonome bitmap font family, http://openlab.ring.gr.jp/efont/shinonome/

[5] 16x16 NeoPixel WS2812B Digital Flexible LED Panel: http://www.ledlightinghut.com/16x16-ws2812b-digital-flexible-led-panel.html

[6] Accessory Development Kit: http://developer.android.com/tools/adk/index.html

[7] AdaFruit: https://www.adafruit.com

[8] Arduino: http://arduino.cc

[9] Ballantine's tshirtOS: http://www.tshirtos.com

[10] Cheero: http://www.cheero.net

[11] CuteCircuit: http://cutecircuit.com

[12] Twitter4J:http://twitter4j.org/

Are You Prepared for Tomorrow? Developing and Offering Technology Repair Services

Brandon Lindley
Columbus State University
4225 University Avenue
Columbus, GA 31907
+1 706-507-8396
lindley_brandon1@columbusstate.edu

Andrew Turner
Columbus State University
4225 University Avenue
Columbus, GA 31907
+1 706-507-8106
turner_andrew4@columbusstate.edu

ABSTRACT

In order to align with the University's goal of providing best-in-class technology and information-based services, to meet the increased needs for our students, we have developed a repair shop which provides a cost-effective method for repairing students' computers, tablets, and smartphones. By our students' constant need for hardware/software repair and replacement, we were able to utilize the student technology fee in order to provide them with three repairs on personal laptops and desktops per semester free of charge. In addition, tablet and smartphone repairs are available for a flat fee of $50. By choosing the repair shop over local competitors, students have saved over $200,000 over the past 18 months. Due to promotion, successful repairs, and student feedback via social media, we noticed an increase in the demand of repairs over the past few years which has led us to improve our methods and increase efficiency internally. This paper intends to examine our repair shop from the beginning until now and inform other university-based help desks on the benefits of providing this service to their students.

Categories and Subject Descriptors

H.4.1 [**Information Systems Application**]: Office Automation – *equipment, time management, workflow management.*

General Terms

Design, Experimentation, Human Factors, Management, Measurement, Performance, Standardization.

Keywords

SIGUCCS, Help Desk, Repair Shop, Innovation, Service Development, Management.

1. INTRODUCTION

In order to stay aligned with university goals and continue to offer additional services, the Columbus State University (CSU) Help

Desk decided to start examining what students might need to further

SIGUCCS '15, November 09-13, 2015, St. Petersburg, FL, USA
© 2015 ACM. ISBN 978-1-4503-3610-9/15/11...$15.00
DOI: http://dx.doi.org/10.1145/2815546.2815562

their academic achievement. Through polling and multiple surveys, the results showed that many students needed help repairing their broken laptops and other computing equipment.

Like all academic institutions, the next challenge is finding the funds required to develop and implement this type of service. Not only would office space be required, but also personnel, tools and equipment, and training - all of which are very costly.

2. DESIGN AND DEVELOPMENT

The original idea of the Repair Shop was to offer a convenient and low-cost, or no cost, repair service for CSU students. An IT committee, charged with finding the funding to operate this service, proposed a funding model using student fees to the Student Technology Fee Committee. Once the Tech Fee grant was approved, Repair Shop operations were organized under University Information Technology Services Student Services division, with the assistance of the Help Desk.

2.1 Hiring and Training

The original grant application gave the Repair Shop enough money to fund one full-time coordinator and two student assistants at nineteen hours per student per week. In order to promote the mission and goals of CSU, the coordinator was hired internally and moved from another area in the department. At the time, this newly hired coordinator was CompTIA A+ certified with many years of technical experience in repairing computer hardware and software. Further, he would be responsible for providing resources and training the student assistants. Since he had no experience in management, the coordinator was sent to managerial training in order to effectively communicate his ideas and lead his employees. Upon completion of his training, the coordinator also developed selection standards for hiring student employees. Potential candidates would not be required to have extensive technical knowledge, but must have excellent critical thinking and analytical skills. A talent for troubleshooting was more important than programming prowess. Since the students would be working and interacting in a help desk environment, strong interpersonal skills were necessary. These attributes were difficult to find in one person since these are not common traits for individuals working in the information technology field.

The coordinator would be solely responsible for creating the hands-on training that would be required for all student employees. The training included step-by-step instructions on how to replace hardware such as LCD screen, keyboard/trackpad, hard drive, RAM, and optical drive replacements. Also, students were trained on proper procedures for removing malware, software repair and replacement, and other software-related issues.

2.2 Purchasing Equipment

Just as the funding was difficult to acquire for hiring personnel, the funding for equipment was equally challenging. Extensive research had to be completed on which tools and equipment would be necessary to operate a computer repair shop. Like all state-funded institutions, the Repair Shop was not allowed to shop for competitive prices; it was required to purchase equipment through certain approved vendors. In doing so, obtaining the equipment in a timely manner was difficult. Due to our inexperience operating a repair shop, we purchased certain items that were not as critical to the repair process as others. The paradox we encountered was that we needed tools to fix the computers that were checked-in, but we needed computers to repair in order to figure out which tools were necessary.

2.2.1 Tools for Hardware Replacement

The Repair Shop knew that it would need certain "standard" tools of the trade, including basic screwdrivers, USB cables, external hard drives, and network-testing equipment. After opening, we developed a list of other tools that we needed in order to complete the necessary repairs. These parts included an external hard drive docking station, high-speed USB hard drives and PCI card, a specialized screwdriver set, anti-static mats, lighted magnifiers, and an abundance of USB flash drives that would be used for software installation and testing.

2.2.2 Tools for Software Replacement

The Repair Shop knew that it would need "standard" tools of the trade for software troubleshooting and replacement, such as malware removal tools, hard drive testing software, and data recovery software. Some advanced software, including SpinRite and EaseUS Recovery, was purchased after opening. We also found no-cost software such as Malwarebytes and AVG that the Repair Shop could install on students' personal computers.

2.3 Processes and Procedures

Because we repair students' personal computers, there were many processes that we needed to implement to protect our Repair Shop and our students from liability. Before opening, it was necessary to meet with the University's lawyer to discuss all of the legal obligations that pertain to operating a computer repair shop. Some of the legal issues that needed to be addressed were: data integrity, information security, legally/illegally-obtained media, software, and media (mp3/video, Adobe products, and copyrighted images/pornography, respectively), and issues of liability. The university's lawyer suggested that the Repair Shop should have a release form that required a signature from the student that would absolve CSU of any responsibility for damages incurred while in its possession. After the release form was created, the processes and workflow could be established. Since this was an effort between the Help Desk and the Repair Shop, we needed a seamless flow in communication between the two areas.

2.3.1 Check-in, Workflow, and Check-out

To check a device into the Repair Shop, the student first brings his or her device to the Help Desk. From there, either a Help Desk employee or a Repair Shop technician assesses the device and attempt to diagnose the problem. After the analysis takes place, the Help Desk employee completes the release form which contains all pertinent contact information for the student, a description of the problem, any visible damages that might already be on the device, and any other valuable information that might be important during the repair of the machine. After the student signs the waiver, the Help Desk employee brings the device into the Repair Shop area where it is placed in a queue to be assigned to a technician.

Once the equipment is received by the technician, he or she begins the repair process. The process differs based on what kind of repair is taking place. For software troubleshooting, the student does not pay for software needed by the Repair Shop technicians for the repair. Exclusions to this rule include any recovery discs or operating systems needed during a hard drive reformat or replacement. For hardware repairs, however, the student must purchase a replacement for any broken hardware or hardware deemed ineffective by the Repair Shop technicians. Some of the hardware replacement purchases include LCD screens, hard drives, keyboards, and RAM. Once the necessary equipment is received, the technicians complete the repair and submit the device for coordinator approval. The coordinator examines the device, makes any necessary changes, and places the device in a designated pick-up area of the shop.

In order for any of these processes and procedures to work effectively, two things are of vital importance: The ticketing system, which holds all of the pertinent information entered during the entire workflow process, and communication, which comes from both the Repair Shop technicians and the students. Not only does the ticketing system hold all of the information about the work orders, but it also notifies the students of all actions being performed on their devices. The Repair Shop technicians update the tickets during the repair process to keep the students informed of the status of their devices. It will also tell them what tasks have been performed and any additional information or parts that might be required from the student.

3. IMPLEMENTATION, OBSTACLES, AND CHALLENGES

The CSU Repair Shop officially opened in fall of 2010 with the hours of 8:00 a.m. to5:00 p.m. weekdays. The opening semester saw approximately 150 repairs. Some of the original processes and procedures had to be changed in order to improve the workflow process. Lack of specialized training, workflow inefficiencies, shortage of personnel, and space constraints led to a repair shop operating at less than optimal performance. From this, many challenges arose. For example, due to space constraints and a shortage of staff, the Repair Shop could only bring in and hold thirty computers at a time. As a result, during the first year of operation, the Repair Shop never got below its thirty computer capacity--resulting in a slow turnaround time and having to turn students away. This is an image from which the Repair Shop is still attempting to recover.

The Repair Shop also faced hardships with communication between the Repair Shop and students, the marketing of its services, and student employee motivation which hindered efficiency at the Repair Shop.

Communication between students and the Repair Shop technicians has always been a struggle. Because most of the information is transferred through the ticketing system and email, it is difficult to quickly reach the students to receive the parts and exchange information necessary for the repairs. During the early years of the Repair Shop, the average turnover time was approximately two weeks. This resulted in students expressing dissatisfaction with the service.

One of the largest issues that the Repair Shop has faced is an overall lack of knowledge of its services by the student body. Even though the Repair Shop has steadily progressed in repairs since its opening in 2010, many students are still unaware that the Repair Shop exists and what services it offers.

Student employee motivation is another struggle that the Repair Shop faces. Some student employees have no long-term investment with the institution, which can cause them to not perform at optimal levels or take their job seriously. Punctuality is often the leading issue that manifests through student apathy.

4. OPTIMIZATION AND RESULTS

During the first few years after the Repair Shop opened, it averaged approximately 250 computers and laptops per semester. As predicted, the majority of these were virus-related problems. Virus and malware-related computer problems accounted for over 85% of the machines that were checked-in to the Repair Shop. The rest of the problems were hardware and software replacement, and wireless troubleshooting issues. Due to some of the obstacles and challenges previously described, the Repair Shop was still flooded with computers and not enough motivated staff to complete tasks within even a relatively lax timeframe. Even with the relaxed timeframe, the average turnaround time for all computers that come into the Repair Shop is 1-3 business days. However, additional time might be required due to the severity of the machine or the purchasing of new equipment for the repair.

The original Repair Shop coordinator ended up leaving CSU to advance his career elsewhere after 4 years running the shop. This left a hole in the operational capacity of the Repair Shop and in the morale of its students. The coordinator had hand-selected the students, then he left for a new career. Morale and productivity sank to an all-time low for approximately eight months before a new coordinator was hired for the Shop. Because of the lack of a direct coordinator the new coordinator came into a Repair Shop that was in disarray. Tools, screws, computers, and computer parts were scattered all around the shop. There were parts everywhere, and no semblance of structure was to be seen anywhere except in the ticketing system where work orders were updated. This culture had to change.

4.1 Workflow Optimization

After a few weeks of getting settled in, the new coordinator met with his team to figure out where they were getting slowed down in the repair process. Over the course of a few weeks, they developed a workflow strategy that mimicked a triage and categorization type of system for computers. Since the Shop operates on a first-come, first-served system, however, the normal processes for triage did not necessarily apply. The purpose of the new system that the Repair Shop developed was to organize computers into certain categories based on how infected the computer was, and determine how much time would be needed to repair the machine. Before the new coordinator arrived, the technicians would scan the same machine multiple times with multiple virus scanners because they were not communicating well with one another. When the new system was implemented, it changed the way that the Repair Shop ran. Each category of the triage system, tiers, as they are called in the shop, contained different scans based on the amount of time it would take to complete each scan. The tier system is designed for software

troubleshooting and malware issues. Hardware malfunctions do not get placed in the tier system since they only have one resolution: replace the broken hardware with working hardware.

Tier One is the Shop's most all-encompassing category. The majority of virus-related issues that come into the Shop fall into this tier. It is designed for basic malware problems: fake antivirus software, malware, adware, malicious malware extensions, startup issues, and Internet settings (IP proxies). For the past two semesters, 86% of the computers that are checked in to the Repair Shop come in for virus-related problems. Unless there is a serious problem, they all fall into Tier One.

For more threatening virus and malware-related problems, the Shop escalates the machine to its Tier Two category. This category contains computers that are infected beyond reasonable use, machines infected with ransomware like Cryptolocker, or infected with the FBI virus. Tier Two is predominantly for computers that are unable to be controlled daily by their owner. For these machines, the technicians will generally perform all of the scans for Tier One support as needed before attempting the Tier Two troubleshooting and scanning procedures. Unless the problem is a known entity like Cryptolocker, the Repair Shop follows normal operating procedures and attempts Tier One resolution prior to escalation.

The purpose of the Tier Three category is for computers that will require reformatting due to virus and malware-related threats. On rare occasions, viruses and malware infect the computer so badly that the only efficient way to fix the machine is to reformat the hard drive. This is not the best situation for the Repair Shop or for the student. The student will not normally have their original operating system discs on hand, thus requiring the student to purchase them from the manufacturer. If the hard drive does not have a recovery partition, the Repair Shop is not able to reformat their machine until it receives a legitimate copy of Windows or a factory recovery disc.

4.2 Addressing Challenges and Additional Services

The tiered system has allowed the Repair Shop to operate more efficiently and stay well below the maximum computer threshold. In addition to being below its maximum capacity, technicians now have enough time to communicate to the students via text message, phone, and email in addition to the ticketing system. Further, the shop has added additional communication steps in the ticketing system in order to better serve its student-customers.

With the assistance of the Help Desk, the Repair Shop has implemented an extensive marketing campaign to address the marketing inefficiency of the previous Repair Shop services. This marketing campaign includes participating in all student orientation sessions throughout the summer. During these sessions, the Help Desk and Repair Shop set up a booth to talk to parents and students alike. The purpose of the booth is to educate students and parents about the services that the Help Desk and Repair Shop provide. Furthermore, orientation classes are offered for students and parents.

To meet the growing market for mobile devices utilized in the classroom, CSU decided to send the Repair Shop coordinator to mobile device repair training for certification. With this certification, the coordinator is able to repair cracked screens, water damage, power ports, etc. on smartphones and tablets.

4.3 Results

The Repair Shop averages approximately 250-300 repairs during the fall and spring semesters, and roughly 150 repairs during the summer. The table below provides a monetary value of student savings based on statistical data analyzed by the Repair Shop. By choosing the Repair Shop over Best Buy, CSU students can save an average of $225 on virus repairs and $150 on hardware repairs and replacements per repair. These figures were calculated from Best Buy's Geek Squad estimates.

**Table 1. Average Money Saved by Choosing
CSU Repair Shop over Best Buy**

Semester	Amount Saved
Fall 2013	$50,404
Spring 2014	$50,028
Fall 2014	$85,804
Spring 2015	$62,556
TTD	Total: $248,792

5. CONCLUSION

From starting a Repair Shop to where it is today, the Repair Shop has overcome many challenges and obstacles that have allowed the Shop to grow and meet the students' demand for information technology services. By improving the Repair Shop's processes, increasing student motivation, increasing efficiency, and enhancing communication, the Repair Shop is now in a position to better serve the CSU community. Over the past five years, not only has it met the need for those services, but it has also advanced in services to include offering mobile device repair services and an additional Repair Shop on our downtown, River Park campus.

6. ACKNOWLEDGMENTS

Our thanks to ACM SIGCHI for allowing us to modify templates they had developed, Mo Nishiyama, and Dan Herrick for their editing prowess.

Author Index

Appling, Julio G. 91

Ashraf, Muhammed Naazer 43

Bauer, Matthias 3

Beers, Jon 99

Burrows, Cyd 49

Capitulo, Lendyll 79

Chapman, R. Kevin 109

Cornell, Elizabeth 117

Danilov, Dmitri 129

Endo, Shuhei 121

Freudenberg, Travis 147

Fritsche, Gale 75

Fritz, John 39

Fujimura, Naomi 121, 125, 141

Gittens, Mechelle 67

Honken, Robin 17

Hoskins, Carla 137

Ito, Eisuke 141

Janz, Kenneth 17

Johansson, Anders 137

Kasahara, Yoshiaki 141

Kusunoki, Kazuyuki 121

Lawrence, Joshua 33

Lawyer, Raymond Scott 133

Lewis, Stephen G. 23

Lind, Artjom 129

Lindley, Brandon 151

Malchow, Martin 3

Matusky, Randy 113

McCray, Randi R. 55

McRitchie, Karen 27

Meinel, Christoph 3

Mendoza, Sean H. V. 63, 85

Meshkaty, Shahra 49

Mocko, Andrea 39

Morgan, Rob 11

Morgan, Theresa 137

Morger, Jessica 59

Murphy, Trevor M. 113

Noguchi, Shunsuke 125

Obana, Masahiro 141

Oda, Kentaro 149

Palumbo, Timothy 105

Rawlins, James L. 55

Rhone, Patrick O. 1

Rogers, Vicki Leigh Noles 95

Servedio, Jen 99

Shimozono, Koichi 149

Turner, Andrew 151

Vainikko, Eero 129

Vinyaratn, R. Eddie 145

Ward, Shamar 67

Yamanoue, Takashi 149

Yoshimura, Keiichiro 149